LOW-COST
MARKETING

Savvy Strategies for
Maximizing Your Marketing Dollars

MARK LANDSBAUM

Adams Media
Avon, Massachusetts

A Streetwise® Publication.
Streetwise® is a registered trademark of F+W Publications, Inc.

Published by Adams Media, an F+W Publications Company
57 Littlefield Street, Avon, MA 02322 U.S.A
www.adamsmedia.com

ISBN: 1-58062-858-3

Printed in the United States of America.

J I H G F E D C B A

Library of Congress Cataloging-in-Publication Data
Landsbaum, Mark.
Streetwise low-cost marketing / Mark Landsbaum.
p.   cm.
ISBN 1-58062-858-3
1. Marketing. I. Title.
HF5415.L2634   2004
658.8--dc21   2003004468

This publication is designed to provide accurate and authoritative information with regard to the subject matter covered. It is sold with the understanding that the publisher is not engaged in rendering legal, accounting, or other professional advice. If legal advice or other expert assistance is required, the services of a competent professional person should be sought.
— From a *Declaration of Principles* jointly adopted by a Committee of the American Bar Association and a Committee of Publishers and Associations

This publication is intended to provide current and prospective business owners with useful information that may assist them in preparing for and obtaining business capital loans and investment funding. This information is general in nature and is not intended to provide specific advice for any individual or business entity. While the information contained herein should be helpful to the reader, appropriate financial, accounting, tax, or legal advice should always be sought from a competent professional engaged for any specific situation regarding your enterprise.

Many of the designations used by manufacturers and sellers to distinguish their products are claimed as trademarks. Where those designations appear in this book and Adams Media was aware of a trademark claim, the designations have been printed in initial capital letters.

Cover illustration by Eric Mueller.

This book is available at quantity discounts for bulk purchases. For information, call 1-800-872-5627.

Visit our exciting small business Web site: www.businesstown.com

Contents

Contents

Acknowledgments

I want to thank my wife, Jan, who has been my mentor, my conscience, my inspiration, and without whom I certainly never could have written this book. I also must acknowledge the invaluable lessons I learned from a marketer par excellence, Gerry Foster, whose commonsense approaches are invaluable revelations. I'm also indebted to the hustle on my behalf by my agent, Jacky Sach at BookEnds. And finally, I must thank whomever it was that came up with the concept of deadlines, without which I would never finish anything.

Preface

Successful marketing of a small business isn't brain surgery. In good times, it even seems that businesses practically market themselves. But, of course, they don't.

When economic times get tough, when cash flow is crimped and particularly when starting up a new business, it is obvious that marketing on autopilot is a quick path to disaster.

This book provides entrepreneurs with the nuts-and-bolts common sense necessary to steer clear of disaster and to plot a course to profitability. Marketing, just as any other aspect of running a business, should at the very least pay for itself. To put it another way, how you market your business should be a net gain in the cash register, not a net loss. The most expensive marketing is marketing that doesn't work.

Streetwise® Low-Cost Marketing will help small business owners and marketers profitably conceive, target, and execute their marketing efforts.

Customer satisfaction should be at the root of all marketing decisions. The reader will discover how to evaluate and address a target market. Integral to this effort is identifying a market's desires and expectations and crafting a plan to meet them. Once a marketer has a plan, it is simply a matter of delivering an effective and satisfying message and then fulfilling the promise to the customer.

In *Streetwise® Low-Cost Marketing*, entrepreneurs will find a host of proven but often-neglected and innovative but often-overlooked solutions, as well as helpful tips on how to exploit the latest marketer's tool, the Internet.

Needless to say, these "low-cost" solutions and tips won't break the bank. Moreover, if executed properly, they should be profitable, which is the ultimate measure of "low-cost" marketing.

Small business is the backbone of the U.S. economy and the most resilient manifestation of free enterprise and free markets. But producing a good product or service for a fair price is not enough in itself to guarantee success. A small business must deliver a persuasive, effective message to its target market if it has any hope of delivering its product or service at a profit. That's the mission of this book.

The Essential Principle: "What's in It for Me?"

Marketing That Pays for Itself—and More

The most expensive type of marketing is marketing that doesn't work. It may be mistargeted, poorly executed, badly conceived, or just lame-brained. In the worst case, it is marketing that spends more money than it makes. But marketing that breaks even is also expensive, because even though it pays for itself, it generates no profits. It treads water. That means the money spent on marketing could have been spent profitably in other revenue-generating ways like hiring more sales staff, modernizing equipment, or partnering with complementary businesses.

So, in a very real sense, even if your marketing budget breaks even—that is, it brings in as many dollars as its spends—it is still a balance sheet loser because it is money that could have been used in more profitable ways.

If you have money to burn and your bottom line is irrelevant, you can close this book now. For the rest of you, the first and most important way to view your marketing strategy is the way you view production, distribution, management, and every other aspect of your business. It must be profitable.

The Most Inexpensive Type of Marketing

Since expensive marketing is marketing that generates no profits, it follows that inexpensive marketing is marketing that makes more money for the company than it costs.

Conceivably, inexpensive marketing also can be very costly in that it may "cost" a lot of money to do it. In other words, the marketing technique, tactic, or tool requires a lot of money to implement, but it still is inexpensive in the grand scheme because it pays for itself and generates a profit. A $50,000 marketing campaign that generates millions of dollars in sales certainly should be viewed as "inexpensive" in light of its huge return on investment, even though $50,000 is a lot of money.

A third way to view marketing costs might be called "cheap" marketing. But "cheap" does not really capture the essence of this approach. "Cheap" connotes not only inexpensive but something of little value. But that is not the case here. A better way to view this type of marketing is that it not only generates profits, but it costs few dollars to implement. It's the best of both worlds. We call it *low-cost marketing*. Profitable, but not costly.

The Key to Success

For small businesses, entrepreneurs, start-ups, and solo practitioners—indeed, for the 95 percent of American businesses that have fewer than 100 employees—low-cost marketing is often the key to success. It is a profit center that for a relatively modest investment reaps disproportionately high returns. In fact, low-cost marketing will always be better than the inexpensive yet "costly" (that is, of little value) variety. If you could make the same profit by spending $50,000 or $500, which would you prefer? Why tie up more of your capital than necessary when it could be used in other profitable ventures?

Massive multinational corporations can afford to gamble on "costly" marketing, the kind that requires a really fat checkbook. If this big-bucks, very costly marketing also turns out to be expensive (that is, profitless), big corporations can generally absorb the loss or hope to make it up on their next costly campaign.

But the rest of us do not have the luxury of being able to afford big bucks for no profit. For us, low-cost marketing is the reasonable, affordable route to success. The thing to keep in mind is that this approach is "low-cost" but not cheap. That means it not only spends fewer dollars, but it also generates profits. It is not enough to merely keep the marketing budget low—it must be profitable.

> Low-cost marketing will always be better than the inexpensive yet "costly" (that is, of little value) variety.

Get Over Yourself!

The surest way to be unprofitable is to violate basic tenets of marketing.

Allow me to introduce the most common violator of the first basic tenet of marketing: Mr. Obnoxious. You may have met him at a dinner party or at a ball game. He's the fellow whose number one topic is himself. Indeed, he's only interested in himself. When he approaches, you reflexively turn away and pretend not to see him. You may even flee. The reason for your adverse reaction to Mr. Obnoxious is obvious: His overriding interest is something that doesn't interest you at all. Frankly, you'd prefer that he talk about a topic that *you* are interested in. A topic like . . . well, yes, a topic like you.

If you've ever met Mr. Obnoxious, and we all have, you discovered firsthand the indomitable rule that's the basis of all marketing:

Talk about yourself and you end up talking to yourself. Talk about the other person and suddenly you have the undivided attention of an enthralled audience.

As obvious as this should be, it is a lesson lost on all too many. Those who learn the lesson and who behave accordingly are generously rewarded. Those who refuse to learn pay dearly.

Maintaining Your Objectivity

Here is why considering the other person first at all times is such a difficult lesson to learn: Most small business owners and other entrepreneurial folks are closely bound to the things they do. Many absolutely love their work. Many identify closely, and even personally, with their product or service. This single-mindedness is invaluable to the entrepreneur in building the business from within, but it is a double-edged sword. The unintended consequence is that many of these business owners assume that the rest of the world shares their deep affection for what they do, for their products and services, and even for them personally.

Haven't you met entrepreneurs who, when asked to identify their target market, proudly proclaim, "Everyone!" as if everyone wants, needs, or must have what they sell? While this elevated sense of self-importance can be very helpful for the entrepreneur in facing the intimidating obstacles and repeated failures inherent in building and operating successful businesses, it also can result in unrealistic expectations. The danger is that these folks may come to believe that their product or service is every bit as important to the rest of the world as it is to them. In marketing, that's a fatal error.

When it comes to marketing their product or service, many entrepreneurs come to resemble Mr. Obnoxious. They are overbearing, self-important, self-absorbed, and completely oblivious to what their potential buyers—the people who will make or break their business—really want to hear. Instead, all Mr. or Ms. Obnoxious can talk about is themselves, what *they* want, how swell *they* are, how terrific *their* product or *their* service is.

And they assume that potential buyers share their opinion. They are wrong. And the consequences of being wrong can be devastating.

The Two Essential Questions

In reality, a business's target market—the people the business must sell to—has two essential questions:

What's in it for me?

and

Why should I buy it from you?

Everything else flows from properly answering these two basic questions. Fail to address them and it will not matter how well you research the market, or how good your product or service is, or how clever your ads and printed collateral material are. You will only be talking to people who don't want to listen. To them you will be Mr. Obnoxious. Clearly, those who fall into this trap fail to address the most pressing and indeed the most critical threshold issues on the minds of their potential customers.

Worse yet, ignoring these basic issues will be among the most expensive mistakes a business can make. That is because unless you address what your customer wants, nothing else you do will matter. And everything else you do will only be so much wasted time and money.

Fortunately, in terms of low-cost marketing, properly addressing your target market's two essential questions is about the least costly thing you can do to ensure your success. The only price you pay is to sacrifice your ego by putting the customer's ego and self-interest first. Sadly, many strong-willed, self-important entrepreneurial types find this is still too high a price to pay. Those who can make the sacrifice, however, employ the most effective low-cost marketing possible. And they reap the benefits.

> Properly addressing your target market's two essential questions is about the least costly thing you can do to ensure your success.

You may object to this approach. That is a common reaction. A lot of business owners respond simply that, "I can't do that!" Or, "That's not what I got into business to do," or "I am not interested in being in that line of work." Notice, however, that each of these objections has to do with the business owner himself. They have nothing to do with the customers, the people who shell out the money to keep the business alive. Decide whether you are in business to serve yourself, or to serve your customers. You may prefer pleasing yourself. But if you want to be profitable, please your customers. The purpose of marketing is to make your business profitable, not to puff up your ego.

Making Yourself the Customer's First Choice

Once you have removed your ego from the equation, you can address your market's second fundamental question.

Answering the first question—"What's in it for me?"—requires applying common sense. Answering the next question—"Why should I buy it from you?"—requires uncommon skill. It is here that techniques, tools, and tactics separate the successful from the rest.

The ultimate goal is to establish yourself in your target market's mind as the preferred, or better yet, the only, solution. If, for example, your potential buyers want the most convenient delivery of pizzas to their doorstep, your task is to establish yourself as synonymous with fast delivery, or better yet *fastest* delivery. In Chapter 2 we detail how to distinguish yourself from competitors and emerge as the preferred solution in your customers' minds. But generally, the concept can be expressed with three prongs: offer the best quality, the most affordable price, or the most convenience. Few people have found a way to combine all three. Obviously, if you provide the "best quality" it is virtually assured that you cannot also provide the "most affordable price." So pick one or two of the three. Then employ the appropriate techniques, tools, and tactics to establish yourself in your customers' minds as the preferred, if not the only, solution to their desires and needs.

> The ultimate goal is to establish yourself in your target market's mind as the preferred, or better yet, the only, solution.

Never Lose Sight of Your Target

Once you have so identified yourself and positioned yourself as "the" solution, the marketing begins. But it begins with the confidence that you are not only providing what your customer wants, but also with the assurance that you are the customers' preferred provider.

As you progress through this book, consider these two questions as touchstones. Constantly refer back to them. It is easy to become enamored with the latest faddish gimmick or with a clever new technique. But do not lose sight of your target market's two essential questions.

What's in it for me?
Why should I buy from you?

Everything you say to existing and potential customers should answer these questions. All your marketing collateral should address what is uppermost in your target market's mind. If you frame every dialogue in this context, you will not go far wrong. And you will also save a lot of money.

Customers Know Best What Customers Want

One of the difficulties in marketing this way is knowing what your customer really wants. Clearly it is a bad idea to assume that you know. Yet that is another of the common pitfalls for many marketing campaigns—the assumption that we already know what the customer wants. Too often this assumption is rooted in wishful thinking: "There's a room full of rubber widgets in the warehouse, so the customer must want to buy rubber widgets."

Almost always, the best way to know what a customer really wants is simply to ask. Can there be any doubt that customers know best what they want? Who would know better? This is so obvious that it is remarkable how often it is ignored. This issue is addressed in greater depth in Chapter 4, Chapter 7, and Chapter 10. But the basic concept is that you should apply this fundamental truth to every facet of your marketing, and guard against your own know-it-all-ism and complacency.

Keep Tabs on Your Customers' Desires

Unless you continually assess your customers' desires, you are likely to look up someday and find yourself selling vinyl records to a compact disc–buying market. Therefore, it is important to guard against losing touch with your customers, and consequently losing track of what it is they want from you. Be assured, someone out there, perhaps your stiffest competitor, is going to great lengths to avoid losing touch.

Nevertheless, the temptation is to assume that you already know what your customers want, especially if you have been in business a while. However, tastes change. To guard against this tendency to assume, cultivate

Two-Way Marketing Flow

One of the benefits of marketing is that it not only informs your customers about you, it informs you about your customers. Let the market chart your course. When Elaine Floyd began her newsletter business targeting corporate clients, she envisioned providing customers with first-class service, which she did. The business was profitable, but it was not long before Elaine discovered a larger, more lucrative market within the market. She paid attention and began marketing her expertise in a different way, not as a contract service to corporations, but as a consultant and educational business to teach others to perform the services she had been selling. Elaine changed directions by responding to market demand simply because she listened to what customers wanted.

the habit of continually asking your customers what they want. The buying public is notoriously fickle, and what is in demand today will not necessarily (or even likely) be in demand tomorrow. Although keeping tabs on your customers' desires and demands in this way can stress a low-cost marketing budget, in the long-run it is less expensive by far than losing customers because you have lost track of what they really want from you. If you think it is difficult and costly to keep tabs on existing customers' preferences, you should know that it is many times more costly to be forced to learn the preferences of potential new customers and then mount a campaign to attract them.

Keep in Touch

Don't be afraid to ask your target market what it likes best and what new thing it may desire. Incessant sales pitches via telemarketing or direct-mail campaigns run the risk of alienating your customer base. But your customers have a much greater tolerance for questions than they do for sales pitches, particularly if the questions are clearly not sales pitches in disguise. So periodically contact your customers simply to find out what is on their minds. Let them know that, at least in this communication, you are not asking for the sale. Ask if their buying preferences have changed. In the future, do they want red instead of blue? Are they willing to pay a premium for overnight delivery, or would they prefer slower service at lower cost? There are countless questions that can help you to fine-tune your marketing campaign, and even to alter your product line or services if only you take the time to ask. To reduce the cost of such invaluable surveys, include questionnaire forms with all sales. Every time a product is handed across the counter or shipped or mailed, include a questionnaire that's clearly not designed to immediately sell another product but only to find out what your customers would like in the future.

Sell What Customers Want to Buy

Now that you know that you must address these obvious questions—What's in it for your customers? Why should they buy it from you? And what do they want from you?—there is one more threshold issue that you should ingrain into your marketing psyche:

Sell what your customers want to buy, not what you want to sell.

Think back to that warehouse full of rubber widgets. You may sincerely believe rubber widgets are a godsend. You may be absolutely certain that rubber widgets will turn the tide of civilization and save mankind from itself. You may have a personal fondness for and devotion to rubber widgets. But in the end, none of this matters.

What Really Matters

What matters is whether your customers feel the same way about rubber widgets. If your customers prefer aluminum widgets, and particularly if they have told you so, you had better stock up on the metal ones and forget about trying to sell rubber ones.

Any salesman worth his Rolodex will tell you that closing a sale is unimaginably easier when the buyer already wants what you are selling. And salesmen will tell you that trying to force a sale—that is, trying to persuade the buyer that he should want something that in fact he does not want—is one of the surest ways to kill a deal. As a marketer, you too are a salesman. You are selling desire. If your customers don't want rubber widgets, it is going to be a tough sale. And trying to force rubber widgets onto aluminum widget buyers will surely kill the deal. It's a ploy from Mr. Obnoxious's playbook.

Don't Sell What You Want to Sell

By now you have no doubt detected a pattern. The underlying principles of good marketing—and especially of good, low-cost marketing with its inherently smaller margin for error—all have one thing in common. It's all about your customer, not about you.

One of the built-in handicaps for the entrepreneur is that he or she is

Getting from "Me" to "You"

Perform this experiment on your printed marketing material. Circle and count the references to "I," "me," "our," and any other words that refer to you. Now circle and count the references to your targeted customers. The ratio of self-references to references to your customers will reveal at a glance how self-absorbed or customer-oriented your material is. A good rule of thumb is a ratio of one to eight, or greater. That is, you should mention your customer at least eight times for every time you mention yourself. Use this technique to evaluate how well your ads, collateral, and other materials stress what's in it for the customer.

often the creator of the product or originator of the service being sold. It's his or her baby. Entrepreneurs don't like to give up their vision. This is one reason that the type of personality required to launch a new enterprise is often at odds with the type of personality required to manage an enterprise. The creator is personally invested in the product or service. The manager—and his marketing department—are not. Their responsibility is to make the enterprise competitive, successful, and profitable. That means they must shed the egotism of the creator and adopt the flexibility of the marketer.

The Customer Is Always Right—Really

In this era of cutthroat competition, it is fashionable to express contempt for any system that puts another's interest ahead of our own. "The customer is always right" has been reduced to a platitude left over from a less cynical age. But the reality is that absent a monopolistic hold on the market, every business is at the mercy of its customers. In that sense, the customer certainly is "always right." If your customers don't want rubber widgets, you market rubber widgets at your peril.

The irony is that marketing to your customers' desires ultimately serves your own desires. Your success is rooted in how well you address their needs. Remove your ego from the equation and replace it with theirs. Set yourself up as their preferred provider. Tell them what they want to hear. Then count your profits. They should be ample.

> **Chapter 2**

USP and AIDA:
Formulas for Success

PART ONE   PUTTING THE CUSTOMER FIRST

■ CHAPTER 1 The Essential Principle: "What's in It for Me?" ■ CHAPTER 2 USP and AIDA: Formulas for Success
■ CHAPTER 3 Benefits Versus Features ■ CHAPTER 4 Test and Track Continually ■ CHAPTER 5 Repeat Customers

Two Essential Acronyms to Know

In the alphabet soup of marketing jargon, two acronyms float to the top. They are USP and AIDA. One has to do with appealing to your target market, and the other has to do with motivating your target market. Both are borrowed from the advertising world, where they serve a similar purpose in giving focus and effectiveness to a selling campaign. USP and AIDA are inseparably entwined with the ultimate success of your marketing. Consequently, both are necessary components of your marketing strategy, and neither works very well without the other. But it is a good idea to get them in the right order.

Your USP

First up is USP, or your *Unique Selling Proposition*. This is in effect your personality projected into the mind of your buying public. It addresses that essential question in potential customers' minds, "Why should I buy it from you?"

But it is more than mere personality. It is uniquely *your* personality. And most importantly, it distinguishes you from your competitors by offering benefits to the buyer that are unavailable elsewhere.

The One and Only

Not only does your USP tell your customers that they should buy from you, but it also presents you as the only one—or at least the best one—to give them what they want in the way they prefer it. It says that you are *uniquely* situated to meet their desires. No one else does it quite the way or quite as well as you do.

The value of a USP lies in its uniqueness. To convey to widget-buying customers that you have the widgets they desire is one thing. But that merely gets you in the game, along with all the other purveyors of widgets. It is your *Unique* Selling Proposition that sends the signal that you alone can deliver precisely what the customer wants, or at least deliver it better than anyone else. When you have a USP, you clearly are not just in the game. You are the presumed winner. The preferred vendor. Not just *a* product

Avoid "Me-too-ism"

When creating your Unique Selling Proposition, avoid "me too-ism." Do not advertise yourself as a clone of your competitors. Do not assume that because your competitors are selling with a particular spiel that it means you can, too. Do not claim to be "just as good as . . ." If the customers have no reason to switch to you, why should they? And if your customers do choose you, why should they remain if you offer them nothing special? You risk losing customers to competitors who suddenly offer something special. Nip that problem in the bud by stressing the "uniqueness" of your Unique Selling Proposition.

they want, but *the* product they want. Not just another service provider, but an unparalleled service provider.

Narrow Your Focus

Establishing your uniqueness can be risky. To become unique can require narrowing your focus. It is difficult to be regarded as the expert, or the best, or the number one in a field, if that field is only one of several fields in which you dabble. Would Rolls-Royce have attained the same ultra-luxury image if throughout its history the English carmaker had simultaneously offered inexpensive economy models under the same label? Not likely.

It is difficult to remain unique and also appeal to a broad market, which by its nature is made up of a variety of desires. American carmakers realized this early on, and Ford Motor Company and General Motors segmented their markets by segmenting their product lines. They offered high-end, luxury products like Lincolns and Cadillacs, and they also offered affordable products like Fords and Chevrolets for the more economically minded. They marketed each independently of the other, careful not to confuse the USP of one with the USP of the other. No one buying a Cadillac ever mistook the car's benefits for the benefits that attracted Chevy buyers.

How to Establish Your USP

So how do you establish your own USP? The first thing to keep in mind is that you cannot effectively claim to be something that you are not. This is particularly true in today's market, where buyers are savvier and less loyal than ever. You may trick a customer once into buying what you sell, but if you disappoint him, don't expect him back.

With all the competition out there, buyers comparison shop. Needless to say, unless you are selling multimillion-dollar mansions, you need repeat business. The product or service that gives unfulfilled promises will be sold only once, if at all. A disappointed customer is like a megaphone spreading bad news about your business.

Count on the woman who bought a briefcase with a defective zipper to tell all her briefcase-buying friends about her disappointment. So whatever promises you make in your USP, first of all be certain that you can fulfill them. Not incidentally, this is the right thing to do as well as the effective thing to do. It may surprise many people that doing the right thing can be the same thing as doing what works. But almost always this is the case, contrary to the negative spin of antibusiness critics.

The Five Ws and One H

Since you must deal with reality and not hot air or wishful thinking, you need to figure out precisely what it is that sets you apart in a beneficial way from your competitors. Break out the pencil and paper and make a list of the five Ws and one H, that is:

- *Who* buys your product?
- *What* benefits do you sell?
- *Why* do people buy from you—to obtain pleasure or to avoid pain?
- *When* do you sell?
- *Where* do you sell?
- *How* does your product or service solve customers' problems?

When answering these questions, avoid listing exceptions to the rule. List your best customers, the most typical reasons they buy, and the normal time, mode, venue, and method of sales. And when answering the second question, be sure to list only the greatest benefits that you offer.

The idea is to distill the heart of your business, your core appeal to your best customers. Your answers to these six questions are the fodder for thinking through your USP.

Boil Your USP Down to One Paragraph

Incorporate your answers in a single paragraph that sums up the *what, where,* and so on. Now take out your editor's blue pencil and cross out the lesser points. You may find that some questions do not pertain to what makes you unique. For example, perhaps you sell from 9 A.M. to 5 P.M. on Main Street, just like all your competitors. If so, scratch that out.

Finally, craft what's left into a single sentence that says in a straightforward manner what you do to set yourself apart from competitors to the benefit of your customers. That is your USP. It might look something like this:

> *"We manufacture the highest-grade widgets and deliver them anywhere in the world within thirty-six hours with an absolute money-back guarantee if you are not entirely satisfied, no questions asked."*

Or it might look a tad less ambitious. Either way, the USP is your thumbnail description that clearly and quickly answers the question, "Why should I buy from you?" It may be unfortunate that in today's fast-paced, impersonal market we need to boil everything down into sound bites. But it also is reality. If it takes you thirty minutes to explain to prospects why they should buy from you instead of your competitors, you probably have lost the sale.

It's about Them, Not You

Here's the tricky part. Your USP has to match up with an existing gap in the market, or establish a new, untapped market. If competitors already are singing the same song, you have managed only to queue up behind them as just another peddler of the same old stuff. If there is nothing

Using a Famous Face or Name

One very successful genre of USP is akin to the cult of personality. This is a common approach in industries from fast food to casual wear. In such cases, the only distinguishing beneficial characteristic of the product or service may be that it is associated with a personality or a celebrity.

But the perceived benefit is real enough in the mind of the buyer, who takes pride in flaunting designer clothes bearing the name of somebody the wearer will never know, or in dining at a restaurant whose fare may be indistinguishable from the greasy spoon across the street but which carries the famous name of a big shot from the movies or TV.

unique about your USP, get out that paper and pencil and try again. There are already enough "me too" peddlers, and they all compete for the same scraps.

The USP exercise is another way of recognizing your market niche. As we have seen, those who try to be everything to everyone are doomed to be regarded as being not very much to anyone. When you give your customers no particular reason to prefer you to the competition, you are reduced to surviving on the buying public's capricious whims, which are entirely uncontrollable and unpredictable.

Worse yet, you may be forced into competing strictly on price, since no other substantive factors distinguish you from the competition. If you can be certain to always underprice the competition and still make a profit, you can survive by selling "lowest price." But in most industries there will always be someone who can underprice you. Downward spiraling price wars are tough to win. And while you wage them, your profit margin dwindles.

Be First, Best, Quickest, Most— Not Cheapest

A more likely USP to be effective is to be first in your field. Those who arrive first typically gobble market share up and retain it. People remember a winner. But who remembers who finished second? If you can carve out a niche as the "first" in providing what you do, you have the opportunity to become synonymous with the product or service, like Xerox, Coke, and Scotch Tape.

Typically USPs are fashioned around selling points like service, selection, guarantees, and, yes, even price on occasion. But your USP need not be tangible, although it must be real. That is, it must be a real perception held by your customers. Perfume manufacturers have long understood this. They do not sell smelly water. They sell romance, sex, and desirability. Those intangibles are very real in the minds of the buyer.

Broadcast Your USP as Widely as You Can

Now that you have carved your USP into stone, throw it around like pebbles. Use it on all your material—marketing, advertising, and everyday correspondence. Find a way to incorporate it with your logo and on your stationery. Have your staff commit it to memory. Make your one-sentence, easy-to-remember USP synonymous with your company. You can almost never say it enough. Hammer away at it every day until it is indelibly imprinted in your employees' and in your customers' minds. It is, after all, you. Uniquely you.

Your USP should be as commonplace as your logo, as quick to verbalize as your name and as closely identified with what you sell as your product or service itself. Here are a few suggested uses that do not add a dime to what you already are paying in marketing costs.

1. Put your USP on the tagline of your e-mail signature, your business card, your stationery, your invoices, your sale and bid sheets, your catalogs, your Web site, your packaging, and your storefront signage.
2. Incorporate it into your ten-second introduction at business functions, your cold calls, your telephone answering script, and your voice-mail message.
3. Instead of saying "I sell widgets," recite your USP as the answer to "What do you do?"

Now that we know who you are, it is time to turn our attention to the people who make you what you are, the folks who give you sustenance. Your customers. Your clients. The people who pay the bills.

AIDA: Attracting Your Customers

This is where the second acronym comes in. AIDA. It stands for *Attention, Interest, Desire,* and *Action.* These are the ways to attract, lure, and involve your clientele. The four steps are an escalating process that progressively intensifies the level of communication and increases the target's commitment. As you might expect, it also is important to get these steps in the right order.

Get Their Attention

As we have discussed, unless you want your target market bored to distraction, it is best that you talk about their needs and desires. But before you can do that, you must get their *Attention*. It has been estimated that an individual is bombarded with as many as 20,000 messages a day through television, radio, billboards, advertisements, publications, and all forms of media, the vast majority of which are obviously uninvited. A lot of other interests are vying to communicate with these people just as you are. The targets of all this unsolicited attention react as one might expect them to, by ignoring or otherwise blocking out the unwelcome messages. During the late twentieth century the ability of people to tune out the incessant barrage of visual and audible noise developed almost as a subconscious defense mechanism. Eventually people could stare right at an ad and not even see it. They heard, but the sounds were not recorded in their minds.

From your perspective as a marketer, this is not good news. This defense mechanism makes it rather difficult for you to deliver your very important message to your targeted individuals because they mistakenly perceive you as part of the undesirable background noise, rather than what you really are, the bearer of very special products and vital services.

How to overcome this resistance? How can you accomplish the first step in the AIDA formula, getting your target market's attention? Two general approaches have shown relative success, depending on the nature of the message and the nature of the target. A shorthand reference for these methods might be called "shouting" and "pertinence."

Shouting is simply being so loud, so pronounced, so noticeable that the message rises above the din of competing messages. The downside is that the message runs the risk of being tuned out simply because it is so obnoxious. Billboards are an example of this approach. They loom above and dwarf competing signage. But there are a lot of billboards. Can you even recall the last three billboards you saw? What were their messages? Despite their overbearing dimensions, they did not leave much of an impression, did they?

The audio counterpart to billboards is high-intensity, hard-sell radio and television commercials. These are distinguished by the jolt they deliver to the senses because they so greatly exceed the volume level of the programs and other commercials that immediately preceded them. The difficulty with this tact is the commercials run the risk of being more annoying than instructive. As we have seen, people learn to tune out annoyances. Nevertheless, many times loud and obnoxious messages can accomplish the first step in the AIDA formula and get the attention of the target market, albeit sometimes grudgingly.

Pertinence is perhaps better understood as offering a message that connects with the target's value system. This tact relies on pushing the right button—the responsive button. Rather than merely startling the target with a loud or visually imposing message, the pertinence approach communicates by piquing curiosity, interest, concern, apprehension, or some other deeper emotional response than simply an eye-popping, ear-splitting shock to the nervous system. This is clearly a more subtle, more refined approach. Moreover, it offers the additional benefit of moving the target closer to the second step in the AIDA formula: Interest.

Create an Interest

Once you have the target's attention, the next challenge is to keep it. At this point it is imperative to appeal with something of *Interest*. A shout or a tease or even a threat may momentarily grab attention, but if there is nothing of interest, the targets' attention will quickly drift away, bombarded as they are with dozens of other messages competing for their time.

Whereas Attention might be the "Whoa! What was that?" phase of AIDA, you might consider Interest the "Hmmm . . ." phase. In other words, it is here that the target begins to ponder that there may indeed be something important, relevant, or meaningful in the message.

Create a Desire

It is no small feat to establish a message of interest. But people are interested in a lot of things that they do not buy.

Push Hot Buttons

To get your target market's attention, connect to your target market's hot buttons. If you sell clothing to teenage girls and young women, promote a "Kiss-athon." Invite the gals to bring their guys to the big event and lip-lock for the duration. The longest kissers win a shopping spree, the length or scope of which you can limit to make sure you can afford it. Or simply give the winners a bundle of gift certificates. Get the word out by passing out and posting fliers at local schools and colleges and stuffing them in the already scheduled mailings to your customer database. Partner with one of the local radio stations by offering your storefront on Kiss-athon day as the remote site for their broadcast and running commentary. Simply announcing this promotion will grab the attention of your young market.

USP = Desire

To create Desire in your target market, you need to focus on your Unique Selling Proposition. This is your best sales pitch to your best customers, the niche that you have carved out as yours and yours alone. Once you have their attention and they are interested, build their desire by stressing your best benefits. Let the potential customers know the answer to their overriding question, "What's in it for me?" An example might be when selling to homeowners in crime-ridden neighborhoods: "When you need a home security system right away and cannot afford for it to fail, you can rely on us. We manufacture the most reliable security systems available and deliver and install them anywhere in the United States within thirty-six hours with an absolute money-back guarantee if you are not completely satisfied, no questions asked."

There is still a long way to go to win over the targets.

The next hurdle is to establish a *Desire* for what you have managed to create interest in. Each successive step in the AIDA process brings you closer to communication. At this stage you begin to more fully impart the benefits that your prospective customer stands to gain from what you're offering. It is no longer enough just to be obnoxiously loud or an odd curiosity. Here you must deliver. This is the sales pitch, as it were.

Here you must convey your best reasons for your targets to part with their money. It is here that "What's in it for me?" becomes the operative question of your potential customers.

Be mindful, of course, that at any instant the listener can opt out. Ours is an age of limited attention spans. Every target is armed with a virtual remote control clicker. That means every marketing communication is but one uninteresting, undesirable moment from being turned off. At this stage, where you need more of the target's time and attention, it is imperative to keep the message tuned to their interests and desires. They want to know, "What's in it for me?" Don't muddle the message with what's in it for you.

Finally, if you have overcome the thousands of competing messages and won the attention and then piqued the interest of your target markets, if you managed to arouse a burning (or at least a smoldering) desire for what you offer, it is time to close the deal.

Oddly enough, many effective marketing messages, indeed entire campaigns, bring the target right to this point, teetering on the precipice of decision, then fail to close the sale. Perhaps it is shyness, the reluctance to presume that they should ask. Perhaps it is arrogance, the assumption that there is no need to ask. But whatever it is, it is wrong.

Prompt Their Action

Having worked so hard and so effectively to get the Attention and develop an Interest and build a Desire, it is imperative now to prompt *Action*. Countless product brochures manage the first three steps of the AIDA process flawlessly but leave off instructions on how to order. Too many advertisements hook and motivate but fail to tell the reader what to do next to get the product. All too often sales letters sweet talk and persuade but do not deliver clear and emphatic instructions on how recipients can spend their money on the product they have fallen in love with.

To prompt your target market's Action, always ask for the sale. It is not low-cost marketing to invest your valuable time and your hard-earned money getting the attention, interest, and desire of your customers, only to fail to finish the job. Always close the deal and do it with an enthusiasm that reinforces in the buyers' minds that they have made the right choice. Do not let doubt cloud their decision at the last moment and risk them backing out. For example, if your Web site offers widgets for sale, do not simply provide a link to your shopping cart. Take the opportunity to remind buyers in no uncertain terms that they are making a great decision: "Click here and in twenty-four hours you will be enjoying our peerless widgets, the best widgets in the West."

This fourth and final stage of the escalating AIDA progression needs to be as clearly stated, as urgently expressed, and as persuasively declared as were the first three steps. This is arguably the most important step in the journey. Nothing else done up to now matters a whit if the prospective buyer does not sign on the dotted line. Here is where the instructions for how to do that are laid out with motivating vigor. Little things mean a lot. "Call now" and "Send your check today . . ." are the types of command instructions necessary to move the attentive, interested, desirous customer to purchase. Do not be shy or arrogant. Use them.

The Lure of Free Samples

If you manufacture and sell widgets and need to get them on the shelves of retail outlets, to get your target market's interest, try offering free samples. Since you already have succeeded in getting your targets' attention, what could possibly be of more interest to them than seeing for themselves how well your goods or services benefit them? Make the offer, and retailers will realize that at very little risk other than giving up some temporary shelf space they gain an opportunity to gauge public demand for the product at no cost. For you, the relatively low cost of providing a few dozen widgets is a great savings compared to the almost always higher costs of trying to persuade retailers through direct-mail campaigns, advertisements in trade publications, in-person sales calls, or paying "slotting" fees for shelf space.

> **Chapter 3**

Benefits Versus Features

What Customers Are Really Buying

One of the greatest misconceptions in marketing is that people buy soap. No one buys soap. Not really. Not even the shopping-averse husband whose wife dispatches him to the supermarket with written instructions to buy "s-o-a-p." Even he is not buying soap. He just does not realize it. His wife may have told him to get "soap," but only to simplify his chore. If she had told her husband what he really was being sent to buy, he would have scratched his head and looked at her agog, unable to comprehend.

In fact, he is buying cleanliness and hygiene. He is buying health and freedom from infectious disease. He is buying comfort and pleasantness. Even more so, he may be buying social acceptability. Depending on the brand, he may also be buying sex appeal, or even a sense of environmental responsibility. But he is definitely not buying soap. No one buys soap.

People buy benefits, not soap. Soap is a water-soluble concoction of fatty acids made from animal or plant fats, treated chemically with a strong alkali-soluble salt like sodium or potassium with a base rather than acid chemistry that reacts with and neutralizes acid, all lumped into a solid bar, then wrapped in paper. No one sets his heart on having such a thing. No one longs for stuff like that. No one even imagines needing anything of that sort. Nevertheless, that is what soap is. But what people set their hearts on having, what they really long for, and what they need are benefits.

Features and Benefits: What's the Difference?

Recognize the difference between features and benefits. This is a feature: A vacuum cleaner has ten amps of power. This is its benefit: Your carpets will be so clean they will be perfectly safe for your toddling children to romp and play. This is a feature: A car has four wheels and an engine. This is its benefit: Everyone will gawk with envy when you tool up to the class reunion, obviously behind the wheel of a symbol of success. This is a feature: A consulting firm will create a twenty-page report with observations and recommendations. This is its benefit: Your profits will soar when you learn the secrets about your business unveiled in this report. This is a feature approach: "Send us your donation and we will send you a receipt."

This is its benefit: "For the equivalent of less than the cost of a cup of coffee a day, you can feed a hungry child living in poverty and humiliation, and get a deduction on your income tax."

"What's in It for Me?"

The key is to think as your customers think. How is that? They want to know "What's in it for me?" It would be a mistake to think that Mitsubishi and Mercedes-Benz customers simply want automobiles. Mitsubishi's sporty Eclipse ads tout the fun to be had behind the wheel. Mercedes-Benz's ads ooze with prestige. Fun and prestige. That is how their customers think. That is what their customers want. The marketer of a successful line of women's makeup products used to explain that, "I don't sell cosmetics, I sell hope." It is the rule, not the exception, that cosmetic sellers stress youth, not face paint.

Neither our hypothetical wife nor her shopping husband would think to list soap's obscure characteristics if they were asked to name indispensable products they need or want. Likewise, no one is dying to get their hands on aluminum cans of inedible, thick, goopy, brown liquid. But everyone who owns an automobile knows that oil is indispensable if they want motoring freedom, or the comfort of mechanized transport, or the prestige of backing the luxury car out of the garage. But it is freedom, comfort, and prestige, not thick, goopy liquid that they buy.

Clearly, buyers are not so much concerned with what a product or a service actually is in concrete terms as they are with what it can do for them, how it benefits them. And even more so, they are attracted by their perception of that benefit, which can far exceed reality.

One problem for marketers is that the difference between benefits and features can be blurred. Therefore, it is important to keep the distinctions in mind. Features have

Which Benefits?

For some products, such as luxury items, benefits are portrayed to deliver good things to the buyer, such as health, wealth, happiness, or comfort. But many, if not a majority, of purchases are based on avoiding pain, or other negative consequences. Consider two marketing themes promoting a product that can either promise "good health" or promise "no heart attack." Clearly the two promises may go hand-in-hand. But it is the marketer's decision which to emphasize. The "good health" promise is a "pleasure-seeking" approach that may appeal to a twenty-year-old woman. But a fifty-five-year-old man in a high-stress occupation is likely to be more concerned about avoiding a potentially fatal heart attack than simply achieving something as nebulous as "good health." To know which approach—pleasure or pain-avoidance—that you should take requires knowing your target market and its preferences.

their place in marketing, and a valuable place it is. But when features nudge ahead of benefits, they become counterproductive.

The Banana Rule

To remember how to distinguish a benefit from a feature, remember the banana.

Here are some of a banana's features:

- A banana is very yellow.
- It is a plump member of the herb family.
- It is grown on stalks twenty-five feet high.
- It is the largest plant on earth without a woody stem.
- It contains potassium and vitamins A, B, and C.
- It originated in Malaysia and spread throughout Asia, India, and Africa hundreds of years ago.
- Bananas begin green.
- Then they turn yellow.
- Then they turn brown.
- Then they turn black.

In other words, a banana's features are a list of its physical traits, its origin, its contents, and its stages of development. All of these things are neutral and, in and of themselves, unappealing to potential buyers.

Here are some of a banana's benefits:

- A banana is delicious.
- It is easy to eat and can be peeled by hand, requiring no utensils.
- It can be eaten raw, baked, fried, broiled, or boiled.
- It is a healthy food, believed to reduce the risk of death from strokes by up to 40 percent.
- The yellow ones are good cooked, eaten raw or mixed in waffles, puddings, cakes, and pies.
- Even the brown ones are good to eat and cook if their flesh is firm.
- It is an all-purpose food wonderful in sauces, spreads, jellies, jams, or for frosting, candies, pie fillings, cakes, tarts, doughnuts,

turnovers, custards, and in soups, stews, casseroles, soufflés, or even made into flour for bread.

In other words, a banana's benefits include how delicious it tastes, how easy it is to use, how healthy it will make you, and how many wonderful uses it has. There is certainly nothing neutral or unappealing in this list of benefits to potential buyers.

It is a feature of a banana that it can be brown. But it is a benefit of a banana that it can be eaten even if it is brown, and that is because many foods cannot be eaten safely when they turn colors. Very often features imply that benefits exist, but they do not clearly spell out what the benefits are. Among a banana's features is the fact that it contains vitamins. But the benefit of vitamins is that they make eating bananas a healthy thing to do.

Simply listing features requires your target market to decipher or deduce the not-always-obvious benefits associated with those features. Do not make buyers work hard to figure out how a feature can benefit them. Do not put an unnecessary and sometimes difficult additional step between getting your target's attention and asking for the sale. This approach sells a banana's features: "Brown bananas for sale." Instead, spell it out and sell the benefits: "Brown bananas are delicious and entirely edible."

Sell Benefits First

When charting your marketing strategy, make two lists. Make list number one your product's features and the other list its benefits. The obvious benefits should occur to you quickly. But you may have many hidden benefits disguised among the list of your product's features, such as itemizing features like "vitamins" instead of identifying the benefit of "health."

If your product has ten prominent features to it, take each one in turn and closely examine how that feature

Transform Features to Benefits

Here is how to transform your feature-laden marketing collateral into benefit-rich language. First, list all the features of your product or service. If you sell stereo equipment, include everything from size and weight to function and purpose. If you provide office services, include everything from telephone answering and mail sorting to typing and filing. Next, take each feature one at a time and describe in as few words as possible what actual function the feature provides for your customer. For example, "telephone answering" might be expressed as "routing customers to the representatives who can help them best." Finally, translate that actual function into benefit language that describes clearly and concisely the ways your customer stands to gain, such as, "Captures callers you are losing with your recorded message phone routing."

Costly Wrong Words

In your marketing budget it costs you just as much to say the wrong word as it does the right word, but the wrong word will return much less on your investment. That means the right word is ultimately the low-cost alternative. Couch your benefits in terms that either promise pleasure or the avoidance of pain. If your cellular telephone weighs only 3.4 ounces, listing "3.4 ounces" in your ad may mean little to buyers, unless they are compiling a chart of the comparative weights of competing cell phone models. But identifying that "3.4 ounce" feature as "lightweight" conveys the benefit immediately, as anyone can attest whose pocket, purse, or belt has sagged with the weight of a heavy cellular phone. Size and weight matter. Do not portray these vital statistics as dry, lifeless features. They are vigorous, desirable benefits.

benefits the buyer. Most likely it does. If it does not, there is really no reason to even mention it. Not many products are laden with features that serve no beneficial purpose. The marketing sin is in labeling these features solely as features, and not connecting them with the benefits they deliver. This exercise may help you to mine unrecognized benefits from your product or service, and give you a clearer vision of how you can appeal to your customers. More than one entrepreneur has discovered that the benefits he thought he was selling were only part of the customer appeal. Ferret out those hidden benefits by closely examining the features of your products and services. You probably have more to offer than you realize.

Emphasize What You Deliver, Not How

A common trap in the feature-versus-benefit struggle is the tendency to emphasize how something is done, rather than what is done. You have heard the old saw, "I asked him what time it is, and he told me how to build a watch." Well, there is a lot of watch-building explanation going on in the marketplace, and for the most part, customers just want to know what time it is.

When stressing a benefit it is imperative that the people hearing your message clearly understand that it is a benefit. It may very be very true that your widget manufacturing process includes sorting, inspecting, weighing, testing, and measuring that ultimately benefit the customer. But from the customer's standpoint, all those processes amount to is watch building.

The important benefit is that those procedures ensure that the customer will buy a uniform widget that is:

- guaranteed for dependability
- interchangeable with other widgets
- sure to function properly

Those are the benefits. And those should be the points stressed in your marketing rather than the process that brings them about.

The Importance of Features

Even though features are secondary to benefits, they also can have an important place in your marketing. Once having clearly and emphatically stressed the benefits, features can be cited—and should be cited—to reinforce the message and to give rational evidence to the emotional claims that you have made when citing benefits.

As we have seen, benefits are laden with emotion. They push hot buttons. They appeal to desires. They sometimes are entirely irrational, such as the idea that a bar of soap may make the person who bathes with it sexier.

Features exist in the cold hard realm of reality. People, despite their persistent attempts to prove otherwise, are rational by nature. They like to believe that they have good, practical reasons for buying the things they buy, even if they have none. It is much easier to sleep at night after spending $800 on a chartreuse chaise lounge for the patio deck if you can rationalize to yourself that it really was a practical purchase because it is made of nearly indestructible recycled plastic that will last for years and helped to conserve natural resources.

Features Can Add Punch

In short, features are the excuses buyers can use to justify their decisions, good or bad. We would be remiss if we did not offer up our best excuses for buying our products and services, particularly since our products and services are excellent and worthwhile in the first place. By listing the features at this stage, we make the buying decision easier for the customer, and consequently move him that much closer to the purchase.

However, in some purchases, features are more than just

Listen to Your Customers

To sell benefits may mean just a slight change in emphasis. Consider the case of a computer repair service that advertises "twenty-four-hour service." Good, but it could be better. Instead, stress the benefit: "We are here to help you any time, day or night." In some cases selling benefits may mean just listening a little better to your customers. For the health club that is selling memberships, when a prospective member inquires about losing weight, stop shoving the cardiovascular benefits at her; instead, tell her about the opportunities for weight loss. If you are selling employee handbooks, it is probably not simply to add another unopened tome to your customers' shelves. What most of your customers probably desire is peace of mind, the kind that comes from knowing they are legally protected from employee lawsuits. Tell them that *that* is what you are really selling.

Lowest-Cost Tips EVER

Here are the lowest-cost marketing tips you will find anywhere. The following are among the most powerful marketing words in the English language:

save time, save money, easy, convenient, perfect, automatic, no charge, lifetime guarantee, unconditional guarantee, full warranty, no questions asked, the real thing, the original, the first and best, the one and only, greatest, unmatched, friendly, comfortable, convenient, one-stop, best, fastest, toughest, most reliable, most durable, user-friendly, exciting, professional, fabulous, clean, amazing, fresh, fun, honest, better than ever, cutting edge, new, indispensable, educational, innovative, luxury, elegant, ornate, plush, beautiful, gorgeous, excellent, profitable, bargain, value, famous, all-time best, enjoy, hot, cool, power, solid, romantic, safest, helpful, prestigious, stylish, superior, traditional, on time, under budget, useful, unique, ideal, equality, parity, workable, and (fill in the blank) *is worth a thousand words.*

excuses and more than the icing on the cake. Sometimes, they are necessary to close the deal. As consumerism has flourished in recent decades, comparison-shopping has become almost the rule, rather than the exception. And with advances in technology, such as Internet shopping services that automatically return prices for a particular item from multiple vendors, features are playing an increasingly important role in buying decisions.

Use Features to Close the Sale

When all else is equal—that is, when price, quality, delivery, and so forth are virtually identical from several vendors—the distinguishing characteristics may boil down to the extra "bells and whistles" associated with a product or service. Those are very often features, rather than benefits. Even when a buyer is not particularly interested in an additional feature, the mere fact that one product comes with more features than the other at no additional price can be perceived as an advantage. After all, a $5 widget with three knobs must be a better bargain than a $5 widget with only two knobs. You get a whole extra knob for no extra money.

The thrust of this chapter is that marketing offers buyers two things, features and benefits. In order to more directly answer the customers' overriding question—"What's in it for me?"—it is critical to stress the benefits of what is sold, rather than the features. But features can and do play a vital role in closing many sales. They serve as the rational excuse that buyers give themselves for choosing to satisfy their emotional desires. Features also can be the tie-breaking factors when competing with other products or services that offer fewer bells and whistles for the same price.

If you take anything from this chapter, let it be this: "Sell benefits first, and use features to close the sale."

> **Chapter 4**

Test and Track Continually

Finding Out What Works Best

There probably is no more significant question in marketing than, "What works?"

All the esoteric theory, all the painstaking execution, all the elaborate planning, all the precision targeting, all of everything that marketers do to achieve their goals is virtually meaningless if there is no way to know what works. Unless marketers know what works, they are like quail hunters in the dark, shooting into a pitch-black sky then wondering if they hit any birds. How do they decide where to aim next? How do they know whether they are wasting ammunition?

Always Follow Up

Unlike some endeavors in which feelings are enough to gauge success, in marketing what works is determined by the results. It is not enough to simply feel good about what you have done. Yet there is a lot of marketing going on out there in which entrepreneurs and their marketers rest on what they presume are their laurels, basking in the afterglow of what they assume to have been a success—without any real way of knowing one way or the other.

Moreover, what works best can be determined only by comparing results. Therefore, it is imperative that marketers track their tactics and their campaigns and compare them one to another. Only in this way is it possible to know the relative effectiveness of one scheme in comparison to another. Certainly it is preferable to basking in the afterglow and assuming that you are doing as well as you can.

A fatal flaw of the underachieving marketer is to try a tactic, be generally pleased with its results, then become complacent and stick with it (sometimes for years) without trying variations or other options that might improve the bottom line. If a mailing campaign featuring a two-for-one sale with a one-week expiration date returned 100 leads and resulted in twenty-five sales netting a $10,000 profit, how is the marketer to know whether a mailing campaign featuring the same sale terms, but with a two-day expiration date, won't result in a $12,000 profit? The only way to know for certain is to try them both, then compare the results.

Test for Effectiveness

There are a few basic rules of thumb to keep in mind when testing. Generally, they are:

- Always follow up to gauge results
- Test for effectiveness
- Test only one variable at a time
- Measure effectiveness (costs per sale, per lead, per contact)
- Be patient for trends to develop

An Unexamined Campaign Is Not Worth Doing

Any marketing campaign that is carried out but not examined after its completion is a lost opportunity. And opportunity is the least that may have been lost. Some small business operators bounce from one marketing scheme to another, flying as it were by the seat of their pants, navigating by feel rather than reason, operating on hunches rather than facts. One month they may decide newspaper advertisements are the way to go, then the next month switch to a direct-mail campaign.

When asked why they switched, the only answer is often merely a vague feeling that they may do better with a different approach. Ask them to quantify their hunch, and chances are they cannot. Chances are they cannot even identify all the costs involved in any of their campaigns, let alone the direct revenues resulting from them. This is because they have never followed up, let alone tested one method against another.

Following up is implicit in the concept of testing, but surprisingly even some marketing schemes that are designed to be tested never are, simply because no one followed up. Typically marketers who fall into this trap regard follow-ups

Just Ask

The direct approach is the most effective way to follow up on a marketing campaign. In other words, just ask. If your business has a sales force, ask them to inquire what brought a customer into the store. If a receptionist is the first to greet anyone who telephones or walks in to your office, have her standard greeting include, "How did you hear of us?" When one of your service repair personnel makes a call, make sure that one fact collected is the reason that the customer chose your company. Have a clipboard or handy form for salespeople, receptionists, service providers, and anyone else to jot down how customers were brought to your doorstep, or you to theirs. Then tally the results and compare them to your ongoing marketing tactics to get a feel for what is working and what is not.

Build in Tallies

To follow up on the effectiveness of a marketing strategy, build in a way to tally results. For example, always place a code on coupons to correlate them with a campaign. Some coupons—especially those with no expiration dates—have long lives and can turn up weeks, months, even years later. An identical offer of 10 percent off on children's summerwear may have a greater or lesser appeal in the summer than it has in the spring. But if you do not code your coupons, you may not be able to distinguish one from the other.

as unnecessary, or as not the best use of their time. They would much rather rush into a new project, or come up with a variation of what they already have done.

Following up is not as exciting as creating new stuff. But the admirable eagerness to press on with new efforts can be tragically shortsighted. These folks are quail shooters in the dark, reloading and firing into the blackness without a clue of whether they were successful the last time, or will be successful the next time.

Make a Thorough Review

To avoid the seat-of-the-pants approach, marketers should resolve to follow up on all marketing efforts. But a casual review will not do. It gives a misleading picture. It is necessary to have standards to apply in measuring a campaign or a tactic. That means identifying all pertinent costs, which include staff time, not just accounts payable, and identifying all revenue that can be attributed to the campaign.

For example, if you have an in-house staff for creating newspaper ads, factor in the time and the prorated cost of the staff person when calculating the cost of the advertising campaign. Then later, when you want to compare the total costs and respective bottom lines of something like a newspaper ad campaign created in-house versus a newspaper ad campaign created by an outside agency or even by the newspaper's own advertising department, you will get a realistic comparison.

One of the most frequent hidden costs of marketing programs is buried in staff payroll. It may appear on casual inspection that the in-house campaign is lower cost and therefore more profitable than contracting out because of the relatively high fees charged by outside advertising agencies. But if you are paying a full-time staff person to spend eighteen hours a month, twelve months a year to create your ads, you may be paying a comparable price or even more than if you contracted out for the work, especially after factoring in your employee's insurance, health care, and other benefits. The only way to know for certain is to set up a system to follow up by tracking all pertinent costs.

Likewise, it is important to be able to identify the revenue generated by a marketing campaign. But this can be more difficult than identifying costs because not every sale can be attributed to a particular marketing effort. For example, a video rental business reasonably can expect to rent movies every day to repeat customers who return on their own volition without prodding, and to new customers who may wander in for any number of reasons. Certainly, it is fairly easy to measure the increase, if any, in rentals during the period directly after a local newspaper ad campaign, or after mailing discount coupons to your database of customers and prospects.

But other variables may make such a measurement imprecise, misleading, or even dead wrong. First, seasonal fluctuations in business can account for increases or decreases entirely apart from the effects of marketing or advertising campaigns. Rainy weekends can produce spurts in video rentals. Unexpectedly warm weather can lure people out of the house and away from their VCRs, depressing rentals.

Second, when do the effects of the ad campaign begin, and even more difficult to determine, when do they end? You may reasonably conclude that an increase in rentals two days after your ad runs may be directly attributable to the ad. But can you also attribute an increase in rentals the following week to the week-old ad? When does the ad stop getting credit for rentals?

Always Test for Effectiveness

Low-cost marketers' may complain that they cannot afford to test innumerable variations of every marketing tactic. That may be true enough. But by the same token, can they afford not to test?

Imagine a marketing campaign that mails out fliers that return 20 percent above the cost of the campaign in profits. What if improving the offer could increase the return to 50 percent? The 30 percent profit difference between the two campaigns is revenue that will never be realized if the second campaign is never tried. Testing to determine which of the two offers is more profitable is the only way to know if you can improve effectiveness. It is shortsighted to believe that not going to the expense of a second test mailing somehow can save money when the second mailing may be a more profitable campaign.

But what if the second campaign turns out to be a dud? Would the reluctant marketer be right to have opposed it? Have we wasted money by testing? Only if you do not learn from the experience. What you have learned for certain is that one of the campaigns is more effective—meaning more profitable and consequently lower cost—than the other. Even if the first of the two campaigns turns out to be the better one, you now have the reassurance that is so valuable to low-cost marketers. You know that you have identified the more efficient and more effective expenditure of your marketing dollar. And you would never have known unless you had followed up. That is how to identify which of the two campaigns constitutes low-cost marketing.

> Even if the first of the two campaigns turns out to be the better one, you now have the reassurance that is so valuable to low-cost marketers.

Always Test One Variable at a Time

Testing requires patience. The impatient want to do several things at once. Multitasking, they believe, is more efficient. The only problem is that when testing the effectiveness of marketing tactics, unless you test only one thing at a time, you cannot know which thing is responsible for the effect that you see.

For example, perhaps a box of widgets will sell better if shoppers can more easily find it on the shelf. But what is the best way to make the box more visible to a hurried shopper? Perhaps if the box were larger, it would be more noticeable. Perhaps if the box were more colorful, it would be more noticeable. Imagine that widget shelf sales increased after you make the widget box 50 percent larger, and change the color of the box from dull brown to bright red.

But which change was responsible for the increase in sales? Assuming that each change (box size and box color) had a comparable cost associated with it, this marketing tactic may have been twice as costly as needed to accomplish the desired increase in sales. Since the changes were implemented simultaneously on the same package, there is no way to know whether increasing the size of the box alone may have been enough to increase sales, or if it was the brighter color packaging alone that attracted more buyers.

To eliminate the confusion, introduce one variable at a time to isolate its effect. In the case of the hypothetical widget box you may find that changing the box's size increases sales 5 percent, but that changing the box's color from brown to red increases sales 40 percent. Profits from increasing box size may barely pay for the added costs required to make the box larger. Making the box red rather than brown, however, not only pays for the cost of the color change, but generates substantial profits as well. The low-cost marketing solution therefore is to change the color, but not the size. Again, there is no other way to determine these results other than following up on the changes, testing them, and, in particular, testing one variable at a time.

Make Sure Results Are Useful

It is not enough, however, to simply follow up, test, and isolate variables. It is critical that the testing results are relevant, and that means that the results need to be expressed appropriately.

Consider the case of a woman's clothing boutique that embarks on a new incentive plan to reward customers with a $10 credit on future purchases for every friend they send in who buys something.

Of course, it is necessary to follow up to determine whether any friends are being referred. To do this, the boutique may institute a tracking system that requires the referred friends to either mention who referred them, or to turn in some type of a referral card. Identifying the referrers and who they referred allows the store to credit the original customer with her $10, and to track how many people the marketing tactic brings in the door.

But the store may also want to note how much, if any, the referred friend spends in the store. That requires a more sophisticated tracking system that links the original referring customer and the new referred customer's purchases. In this way, the store can measure how much in sales each original customer generated through her referrals. This information not only helps track the cost versus revenue of the referral marketing tactic, but it also identifies which original customers may be worth cultivating further such as by offering them larger incentives, perhaps a $20 credit. The friends that Ms. Jones refers each may average $250 in purchases per visit, compared to the friends of Mrs. Smith, who spend only $7 on average. It certainly makes more sense to offer $20 credit incentives to Ms. Jones, whose referrals amount to a $240 profitable return on average, rather than to Mrs. Smith, because the store suffers an average $3 net loss on each friend she refers.

Of course, adhering to the principle that we should track only one variable at a time, the incentive offers for Ms. Jones and Mrs. Smith and all other customers must be identical. It would be impossible to make meaningful comparisons if Ms. Jones was offered a $20 incentive and simultaneously Mrs. Smith was being offered only a $10 incentive.

Always Measure Effectiveness

In measuring marketing tactics such as these, it also is important to know what to track, what to measure, and what to compare. For example, to name just a few measurements, should you evaluate a marketing campaign on its effectiveness in generating traffic, or in creating leads, or in sales? Be cautious when evaluating such results.

> In measuring marketing tactics such as these, it also is important to know what to track, what to measure, and what to compare.

How to Test Two Variables

Although you should never test two variables together at once, it is possible to test two or more variables simultaneously but apart. Keep in mind, however, that you need to test segments of your market, and that each segment must closely resemble the others. For example, to test the respective results of a 10 percent, 25 percent, and 35 percent discount offer on book sales, divide your test group into three equal segments. But make sure that, as far as possible, each segment is similar in demographics, in buying habits, and in other important variables that might influence their response. The only factor that should vary from one group of your targeted market to another is the discount offer. Now you can feel comfortable in simultaneously testing three different offers, each to a third of your target market. If you have done a good job in ensuring that each third of the sample is similar to the others, this is an even better approach than testing 100 percent of the market with one offer at a time. Results could be skewed if you offered the entire market first a 10 percent discount, and then a 25 percent discount, and later a 35 percent discount. This is not the best way to compare the offers against each other for a number of reasons, not the least of which is that you may not receive purchases for the 25 percent discount because they already took advantage of the 10 percent discount and do not need two of what you are selling. Each successive offer can be tainted because the test subject may have been influenced in some way by the previous offer.

If a radio advertising campaign is designed to bring additional traffic to your shoe store, be wary in measuring its success by how many shoes are sold. You might be able to get a good handle on how many customers were brought in by the radio ad. The easiest way to find out is simply to ask them as they enter the store. But whether the radio ad is responsible for sales made once the customer has entered the store is more problematic.

Make No Snap Judgments

Perhaps people visiting your shoe store on Monday after hearing the ad bought $750 in shoes and accessories. But on Tuesday people who heard the ad and visited your store spent $1,250. Remember the principle of measuring one variable at a time. The ad was the same on Monday and Tuesday, but the results were dramatically different. Are there other factors involved? Perhaps on Tuesday your best salespeople returned to work after taking Monday off. Perhaps on Tuesday your clerks had stocked the shelves with hot new stylish sandals that were in boxes in the storeroom on Monday. Perhaps Monday's store hours were from 10 A.M. to 5 P.M., but on Tuesday a late surge in customers persuaded you to stay open until 7 P.M.

The point is, do not be anxious to attribute everything to a single marketing tactic. If all things are equal—in this case personnel in the store, stock on the shelf, and hours of operation—it may be meaningful to judge the effectiveness of the radio ads by measuring sales at the cash register. But if other factors vary from day to day, it may be risky to put too much emphasis on sales when evaluating the effectiveness of the radio ads.

What do you know for certain about the radio ads? You know how many customers told you they came to the store because they heard the ad. Once inside the store a variety of other factors may influence whether they purchase, or not, and how much they spend.

The lesson: Don't jump to conclusions. As in the case of this hypothetical shoe store, it may not be reasonable to attribute shoe sales directly to the radio ad campaign, but it may be entirely reasonable to measure how much added traffic the ads generated.

Be conservative in attributing results. Measure one variable at a time. Do not attempt to measure how many sales are generated by a campaign designed simply to increase foot traffic. In a campaign designed to generate leads, it is unfair to measure how many sales the campaign generates. All the marketing tactic was designed to do was to bring in qualified leads—that is, potential buyers. From that point on, the leads are the responsibility of the sales force, and at the mercy of the product's appeal, and influenced by price and a variety of other factors that the campaign to generate leads has nothing to do with.

The lesson is to know what you are measuring when you evaluate a marketing tactic. You can evaluate the marketing cost per sale, per lead, per contact, and any number of other outcomes, but be sure that the tactic can reasonably be deemed responsible for the effect you are measuring.

Be Patient for Trends to Develop

Finally, when tracking, testing, and measuring, allow enough time for trends to develop. Every test has its optimal size and duration. Unfortunately, it is difficult to estimate those optimal numbers in advance. The tendency is to pull the plug too soon. Better to have too much or wait too long than to not have enough or not wait long enough.

Obviously, a questionnaire that samples ten of your 1,000 customers is not going to give you a definitive view of everyone's buying preferences. But it also is not necessary to quiz all 1,000 to feel confident with the results. The adequacy of your sample will be influenced by many factors, not the least of which is how diverse your 1,000 customers are. The more narrowly focused your business, and the more uniform your customer base and potential market, the more confident you can be with smaller

Consider the Big Picture

When identifying the costs of a marketing tactic and the revenue it may generate, always consider the big picture. A postcard mailer, for example, involves costs other than printing, paper, and postage. Other costs to consider include:

- Creative costs to create the piece
- Indirect costs in time required to create and execute the mailing plan
- Staff costs not only in hours and wages but also in lost productivity
- Wear and tear on equipment
- Utility expenses for using computers, lights, printers, and other equipment
- Additional toner or ink if you are printing the postcards yourself

It is necessary for all of these in-house costs to be fully identified before you can compare the true cost with the cost to contract out for the same service. You may find that the not-so-obvious in-house costs make it more profitable to contract out your mailing.

samplings. Unfortunately, there are not many rules of thumb to apply here, since so much depends on the nature of your business and your market.

Worse yet, when testing to determine what works, time is not on your side. It would be wonderful to know in one day how well a promotional campaign will work. But the fact is that it can take days or months for a campaign to run its course, and even longer to gauge its results. The buying public operates on its own schedule, not on yours. Make sure to give your tests ample time to run their course. If you are keeping periodic track of continuous results, such as counting coupons returned every day, you can deduce that the test has concluded its usefulness when redeemed coupons begin to drop off significantly.

Of course, the best way to keep tests from droning on endlessly is to arbitrarily set a deadline. Coupons can be an excellent example of this technique. Rarely, if ever, should you issue coupons that do not carry an expiration date. Not only does the expiration date bring an end to your test, but it also dramatically increases the coupons' effectiveness, something that we will take up in more depth in Chapter 14.

> **Chapter 5**

Repeat Customers

The Easiest and Cheapest to Market To

There may not be a more universally accepted truth in all of marketing: It is considerably more expensive to sell to a new customer than to a repeat customer.

Different marketing gurus have their own estimates of exactly how much more expensive it is. Some say it cost three times as much. Others insist it is more like ten times. There are "experts" who will tell you it really costs much more than that. But on the basic point, they all agree. It is much more expensive.

Many of the reasons for this marketing fact of life should be self-evident to any seasoned businessperson. Some of the reasons may be less obvious, but no less important.

Recall the fundamentals that we have covered up to this point. First of all, the customer wants to know "What's in it for me?" and "Why should I buy from you?"

Now recall the fundamental formulas for success. Before you can make a sale you need to get customers' attention, create an interest, then build a desire for what you are selling, and finally prompt them into action. All the while you have walk the tightrope that stresses on the one hand what is unique about your product or your service while simultaneously appearing to be customer-centric, rather than self-absorbed. That's all. Gee, what a snap.

The Advantages of Familiarity

Imagine traveling that road with a brand-new customer. Daunting is the word that comes to mind. Each step in the process is an arduous battle to win customers who do not know you from all your competitors, and do not much care to. You are a complete stranger to them, and vice versa. At any stage in the long process of winning first-time customers these strangers can opt out, which means that all the time, effort, and money you have invested will go for naught.

By contrast, imagine the difference when dealing with a return, or repeat, customer. First of all, getting their attention ought to be considerably easier, particularly if doing business with you was a pleasurable or rewarding experience the first time around. Second, previous buyers clearly already have discovered "What's in it for me?" Your product or service is no longer an abstraction in their mind because they have experienced firsthand how it benefited them.

We should note here that if your product or service failed that test—that is, if the buyer found what they bought from you to be lacking or flawed or worthless—luring back these repeat customers will be even more difficult and expensive than attracting new customers. But for our purposes, you assume that you sell a product or a service of value that is going to win customers' loyalty, not sour them on you.

Remember, you cannot effectively claim to be something that you are not. You may trick customers once, but if you disappoint them, don't expect them to return.

Getting Repeat Customers to Act

When returning customers recall that their previous experience was satisfying or, even better, their second question, "Why should I buy from you?" is already answered. So it is not only easier to get the attention of these repeat customers because you did such a good job for them the first time around, but they also should desire more of what you have. All these steps that are so daunting with first-time customers should be substantially easier with repeat customers, which means that you can concentrate more on the final stage of the process—prompting them to act.

A Different Approach

The distinction between appealing to first-time buyers and repeat buyers is a subtle difference in approach. The online bookseller Amazon.com is a good example. If you buy books from Amazon you may not even recall what the Amazon Web site looked like the first time you visited it. That

Back Up Promises

It is critical to back up the promise your marketing spiel makes, but how can you know if your customers think you have? One low-cost way to find out is to include in every sale an evaluation form that asks that precise question: "Did you get everything you expected in this purchase?" And include a checklist of common benefits that you know your customers desire. Slap a postage stamp on a self-addressed envelope and include it with the evaluation form to make it easy for the customer to reply. One last note on this tactic: Do not forget to tally and evaluate the response when it shows up. And if there was any dissatisfaction at all, pick up the telephone and call to find out how you can make it right or prevent it from happening again.

Personalize for Appeal

When appealing to repeat customers, personalize it. At the time of purchase, collect some tidbit of innocuous personal information—nothing too private, but something that you can mention in your next communiqué. For example, if you are a wholesaler and your customer, a restaurant, orders a carton of shrimp, establish a personal relationship with the buyer. In your next letter, handwrite in the margin a comment such as, "John, did you get to sample any of that shrimp? They tell me it was among the best we've had lately." Personal notes are ingratiating. First names assume personal relationships. And questions about the person rather than the business create bonds beyond common financial interests. The cost? Pretty low. The time it takes to make a mental note at the time of sale, and the time it takes to scrawl your personal message on the sales letter or invoice.

is because if you have bought any books at all from Amazon you probably have enabled or triggered some of the features the bookseller uses to tailor its site to return customers.

Based on your previous purchases, Amazon automatically recommends other books on similar topics. It also encourages you to create "wish lists" of books that you can recall later for future purchase. It offers periodic reminders by e-mail when new books are published by authors whose works you have previously enjoyed. In other words, the Amazon experience for repeat customers is geared to prompting action rather than attracting your attention or creating an interest, all because of what the bookseller already has learned about your preferences. Contrast that to first-time Amazon visitors, who see a generic Web site, no doubt featuring a lot of titles and other products of no interest to them. The generic approach is necessary for first-time buyers because Amazon is trying hard to stress the fundamentals by answering "What's in it for me?" and "Why should I buy from you?" while also getting the visitors' attention, arousing their interest, creating desire, and only then prompting action.

From Shotgun to Pinpoint

Since Amazon has no clue what first-time visitors are interested in, the appeal to them must necessarily be broad, a shotgun approach that hopes one of a great variety of offers will touch a hot button.

But Amazon has learned something about returning customers and therefore can offer them more targeted titles, and emphasize other things like ease of purchase, convenient one-button buying, and a handy shopping cart instead of spending a lot of time and words on off-point attention grabbing.

For the low-cost marketer, return or repeat customers represent a shortcut to the checkout line. It is the difference between asking, "What would you like to see, apples, oranges, or bottled beverages?" and asking, "How many of these oranges shall I put in your shopping cart?"

Clearly, the return or repeat customer is the easier customer for marketers to persuade. Consequently, they also are the lowest-cost customers to market to. This is another area where marketing gurus have a range of opinion, but they differ only in degree, not in substance. Some say it takes a minimum of seven contacts or impressions before a new customer is ready to purchase. Others estimate considerably more, dozens or even scores of contacts, citing as evidence the subtle reinforcement techniques employed in mass marketing and mass media advertising.

But whatever figure is accurate, almost no customers can be expected to purchase nonimpulse items the first time they are exposed to them. So unless you are selling bottled water to desert hikers, the chances are you will have to expose your product or service several times to prospective customers before you have moved them from paying attention to taking an interest. And even then, you are only part of the way home, still having to create a desire and prompt action.

Every contact, every impression, has a cost associated with it. If it is an advertisement, it has to be run a second, third, fourth time, or more to break through and make an impression. If it is a telephone call, a direct-mail letter, a billboard, or a radio commercial, it is a pretty good bet that your targeted prospects are not likely to act on their first exposure. Clearly, new customers are difficult terrain for low-cost marketers.

Pleasing Versus Disappointing

What is the low-cost approach to cultivating these critically important repeat customers? One surefire way to bring them back is to back up the promise you made when they purchased the first time. Some people do not regard product (or service) reliability and customer satisfaction as marketing tactics. They are wrong.

Not only are they marketing tactics, they are among the lowest cost and most effective. Hardly a dime need be spent from your marketing budget to achieve this marketing coup. If disappointing customers emotionally alienates them, pleasing customers has the same kind of dramatic effect in the opposite direction. The very best low-cost marketing tactic to bring back the

Turning Problems into Opportunities

If you are an author and a new edition of your book has just been published, you may be stuck with hundreds of copies of the first edition that you bought to sell yourself. Rather than writing off the old inventory as a total loss, mark them down to a ridiculously low price and include with each a certificate offering an equal amount of credit toward the purchase of the latest edition. Buyers who may have been reluctant to plop down $25 for the new edition may be willing to pay $5 for the older one, especially if they can get a $5 credit toward the purchase of the new book. Be sure to list in the certificate all the new features that are included in the new edition, so the buyer understands why he needs the newer book after sampling the older one.

lowest-cost customers (repeat buyers) is to knock their socks off with service, satisfaction, or reliability on their very first purchase.

The next time you review your product line or your service offerings, look at them with a marketer's eye. Are there defects, shortcomings, or potential disappointments buried in what you offer for sale?

If your business cultivates repeat customers by offering superior service, it can be tempting to water down that service simply to attract more volume and new customers. But if your appeal has been the quality of your service, your return customers have been coming back because that is what they like. New customers who can be attracted by fast service or inexpensive service may temporarily boost traffic, but once you return to your core offering, those who were lured by "cheap" and "quick" will not return, and you may well have alienated your best customers—the repeat customers—by watering down the very feature that brought them back, your high quality.

The bottom line is there is no lower-cost marketing tactic than delivering what you promise and making customers happy. And all it requires is that you concentrate on doing what you do best.

Keeping your customers happy affects more than the customer at the checkout counter. For whatever reason, people tend to complain more than they tend to compliment. Satisfied customers are potentially walking marketing tools for your business, and every person with whom they speak can be infected with the contagion of their happiness. Unfortunately, unhappy customers are potentially walking marketing tools that you would be better off without. That is because every person with whom they speak can be infected with the contagion of their dissatisfaction.

Happy Customers Bring in New Buyers

Think back to the costly nature of trying to lure first-time buyers. Recall how much more costly it is to try to lure back unhappy buyers. Every potential first-time buyer that an unhappy customer infects becomes even more costly to attract, which makes him or her the most expensive people to market to. Since they have never done business with you, they are very difficult (and expensive) to attract in the first place, and now they are even more so because they have heard bad things about you.

Want more bad news? Consider that every unhappy customer complains about you to many people. If you thought it was expensive and difficult to appeal to a first-time buyer who knows nothing about your business, imagine how expensive and difficult it is to appeal to a lot of first-time buyers who have heard bad things about you.

While happy customers are not as likely to tell as many people about you, they are likely to help you reduce your marketing costs. That is because they help you achieve some of the fundamental goals that you must achieve to lure in new buyers. When they boast about your service or your product, they effectively are answering the questions of potential new customers, "What's in it for me?" and "Why I should buy from you?" Moreover, they have their friends' attention, which is another step in the process you do not have to pay for.

So for the potential first-time buyers infected with your good news, the marketing cycle is shortened much as it is with happy repeat customers. Obviously, to keep your marketing costs low, you want as many of these as you can get, and as few of the disgruntled and unhappy as possible. The best way to do that is to deliver what you promise and make customers happy.

Apart from the quality of what you sell, there are other low-cost marketing methods to create happy customers. One way is to make it easy for them to do business with you.

Who has not complained these days about endless telephone message labyrinths or clueless sales clerks or unresponsive waiters? Even if what you sell is the best around, if it is difficult to buy, you may be creating those expensive unhappy customers who spread the high-cost virus of bad reputation.

Make It Easy to Buy

Another approach—and another one that does not necessarily drain your marketing budget—is to make it easy for customers to buy from you. On the Internet this concept is illustrated by the one-click purchase options. Once having filled out shipping and credit card information, all buyers have to do the next time they return to a Web site is click on the "one-click" purchase option and all the forms are automatically filled in. No more page after page of name, address, credit card number, expiration date, etc. The purchase has become almost transparent.

Close Sales Quickly

Early on in the World Wide Web's evolution, many marketing examinations found that customers would back out or decide against (or their Web browser crashed) midway through the purchase routine. As any salesperson will attest, once buyers have decided to buy, you do not want to give them a lot of opportunity to change their minds. Anything can happen. Doubts can creep in. Second thoughts may percolate. Browsers may crash. *Close that sale fast.*

The same principle applies to any venue, not just Web sites. The easier you make it for a customer to buy, the more likely you are to make the sale. And the easier it is to make the sale, the fewer frustrations the customer experiences. And of course, a customer who is not frustrated is a happy camper. And marketing to happy customers means low-cost marketing.

Go the Extra Mile

One way of making it easy for buyers to buy is to find a way to say "yes," even when the inclination is to say "no." Here we enter the realm of diplomacy. It might also be called "going the extra mile." And once again, this is a tactic that can be employed without necessarily putting a dent in the marketing budget, because it is a function carried out by sales personnel.

Consider two scenarios played out in otherwise identical women's clothing stores. In store A, the customer requests the dress that was in this morning's newspaper advertisement. Alas, the clerk says, the last dress was just sold, sorry. Meanwhile, in store B, the clerk says the last dress was just sold, but we have some other dresses very much like it at an even better price, plus if you have your heart set on it, I can telephone around to our other outlets and see if any are left there, and if you would rather not drive all the way across town, I can have it delivered here tomorrow if they have one.

The difference between the clerk in store A and the clerk in store B is that the first one is a cash register attendant. The second one is a savvy marketer.

Now guess the difference between the customer in store A and the customer in store B. Yep, one is infected with dissatisfaction—a costly marketing expense—and the other is infected with happiness and satisfaction—definitely a low-cost marketing "virus."

The marketing cost to transform clerks like the one in store A into clerks like the one in store B is negligible, and probably a function of the sales department anyway, not the marketing department. But whichever department pays for the training, it promises to pay for itself many times over in satisfied customers, who become repeat customers and who spread their satisfaction to others who have yet to discover your business, but nevertheless have become easier—and less expensive—to market to.

Turning an Uncertain "No" into a Definite "Yes"

Shoppers, particularly first-time customers, have a lot of "No's" to spend before they spend their money. That is to say, most people will say "No" when they mean "Not yet," or "Tell me more," or even "Persuade me." Top salespeople know how to read these subtleties. But most marketing tactics and techniques do not have the luxury of being able to read subtleties in a potential buyer's voice or demeanor.

So in the case of your marketing collateral, for example,

Thoughtful Reminders

Retailers strain valiantly for excuses to lure back their customers with special sales pegged to faux events from Groundhog Day to Bastille Day. Why not capitalize on what customers think is important, instead of obscure calendar entries? Every customer has a birthday. Many have spouses or girlfriends or boyfriends. And each of those has birthdays. When recording customer information, do not forget date of birth. And why not ask customers if they have a special person in their life whose birthday that they would like to be reminded about in advance? What husband would not jump at the opportunity to get a mailer or a phone call reminding him of the opportunity for getting his loved one a birthday present? Couple the reminder with recommendations, and you not only have cultivated a happy repeat customer, but you have made the sale easy, too.

build in options that permit those who really mean "Not yet" or "Tell me more" to keep the dialogue open, rather than slamming it closed with an absolute "No."

One way to do that is never to ask a question that can be answered "No," but to offer other noncommittal responses such as, "Please send me more information on . . ." or "I'm not ready to buy yet, but I would like to be on your mailing list." Persistence in marketing means never ceasing to make offers such as those that keep the dialogue open. And of course, the only added cost is the extra ink. If you want to save on ink, have a box for the customer to check off that says, "No." But if you can afford a few more letters, try something like, "Please put me on your mailing list." Both are low-cost marketing since you are going to print up your marketing collateral anyway. In this case, splurge. Buy a few more vowels and consonants.

Market Every Day

It follows that if you are consistent and persistent that there probably is value in being constant, as well. All marketers would love to have their message in front of their target market 24/7. Alas, low-cost marketing that is not. But as an entrepreneur or small business operator, you are somewhere doing something 24/7.

Creative Business Cards Work

Take a tip from Carl Karcher. Don't pass out vanilla business cards. Give the recipient some reason to keep, cherish, or use them. He founded the Carl's Jr. fast-food chain more than sixty years ago, and to this day Carl carries free coupons for hamburgers that are good at any of the company's hundreds of outlets coast to coast. Whenever he meets someone new, Carl hands them a coupon, which is nothing more than a business card with his own signature and the notation that it is good for a free meal. Any business that lends itself to free samples is a good candidate for this approach. The service station owner's business card can be good for one free gallon of gas. The video rental operator's card can serve as a free rental coupon. The opportunities are endless.

There is no need to obsess about it, but if you believe in what you sell, if you know that what you have is good for the people who buy it, you should have no reluctance to let others know. That means that you have no reason not to market in some way, every day.

Market Equally in Good Times and Bad

Finally, marketing budgets often are slashed precisely at the time they are needed most. There is nothing low-cost about cutting back on your marketing when it is most crucial.

Some businesses market feverishly when business is booming because they have cash to spend, and all but eliminate their efforts when business slumps. Others do not market when business goes well because they do not see the need, then panic-spend when business slumps to desperately drum up customers.

The low-cost lesson here is to market equally in good times and bad. Have a budget, and stick to it. If your budget is based on sound marketing principles, it will work in good times and bad. In Part Two, we delve deeper into the foundation of sound marketing planning.

> **Chapter 6**

Planning Your Marketing: As Easy as 1, 2, 3

Set Reasonable, Measurable Goals

Think big, but realistically. Do not seek impossible results (like cornering the market on rubber widgets within your first year) or set impossible-to-measure goals (like becoming "successful"). Here is an example of a clear, achievable goal: "We want to increase measurable sales to our catalog sales by 15 percent after twelve months and for the increase in sales to offset any increase in marketing expense by 50 percent." Certainly a 15 percent increase in sales is worth seeking, but it is equally important to know whether any increased marketing expenses gobble up that increased profit. The second part of the goal—"offset any increase in marketing expense by 50 percent"—demands that if you add $100 to the marketing budget, it must generate at least $150 in new income. This accountability requires that any new expenditures not merely generate more revenue, but also must pay for themselves, plus some.

An Unplanned Journey Costs More

Planning for the successful marketing of your business is something like planning for a vacation trip. Imagine that you and the spouse and kids pack up the car and drive all day, then spend the night in a hotel only to wake up the next morning, tumble out of bed, and stare blankly at one another because not one of you has a clue where you are supposed to go next or what you are supposed to do next. The kids finally decide they would like to go swimming in the hotel pool but realize they did not bring their bathing suits. The husband yearns to drive to the scenic local lake to fish but discovers that fishing is not allowed in the summer. The wife wants to travel inland to quaint shopping boutiques but finds out that the shops are much too pricey. Because none of you had thought through the trip beforehand, you spend most of your two weeks complaining, blaming each other, and being faced with a host of unpleasant surprises. Not much of a vacation.

If such lack of planning can ruin your family's two-week summer vacation, imagine what it can do to your business where there is even more at stake than fourteen days in the sun. So it is a good idea to take at least as much care in planning your marketing strategy as you do in planning the trip you and the family will take on your summer vacation.

As the old saw goes, if you do not know where you are going, any road will take you there. The converse, of course, is preferable in vacations and in business.

In business, to know where you are going before you embark, the destination must be defined. It can be defined in any number of ways. One way may be to describe it as the amount of profit you want to make. Another may be the market share you want to capture. Another could be simply to be recognized as a bona fide provider of your type of service. Or more ambitiously, to become respected as a leader in your field. On the other hand, you may simply seek to become competitive. But whatever it is that you strive to accomplish, in the final analysis, your marketing plan, its strategies, tactics, and tools all must be measured against how effectively they help you to reach your goals. To do that, you must know before you begin where you want to end up. Otherwise, you will never know whether you are on schedule, within budget, or even whether you have arrived.

Therefore, your first challenge before you even place an ad or hand out a business card is to clearly and succinctly define your goals. Certainly make them meaningful. But absolutely make them measurable. Anything less is high-cost marketing.

Your marketing plan should contain not only a clearly defined set of goals, but also the methodic means that you plan to employ to achieve those goals. It serves as your road map to success. It is the autopilot that enables you to advance daily without reinventing the wheel every morning. Your marketing plan is your insurance against waking up one day with no clue where you are supposed to be or where you should go next.

To the extent possible, the tactics, tools, and techniques that you employ also must be measurable in terms of their effectiveness. That does not mean you simply count up the number of promotional postcards mailed this year and compare the total to last year. It means measuring the results of the postcard mailings, and comparing them one to another.

Who, What, Where, Why, When, and How

In planning your marketing journey, use the five Ws and H—who, what, where, why, when, and how. If you can specifically answer these questions, you can equip yourself with a road map that will keep you on course. These need not be your final answers, and each may change during your journey. But they let you at least set your course:

- "Who"—the customer that you want to cultivate, more precisely the customer profile
- "What"—the product or service that your customer wants to buy
- "Where"—the locale or venue of the sale, such as online, a street corner shop, in your office, in the client's office, in the mail

- "Why"—the benefit that the customer perceives that your product or service provides—the reason for buying
- "When"—the timing of the transaction, such as a store open from 9 A.M. to 5 P.M. or a Web site that does e-commerce around the clock
- "How"—the means that you communicate the benefit to the customer, such as newspaper ads, direct-mail campaigns, e-mail promotions, business cards, free samples

If you embark on your marketing journey without having taken the five Ws and H into consideration in your planning, you are setting out without a road map.

Rule #1: Know Your Target Market

Having your destination in mind is only part of the journey. You still have to get from here to there.

The absolutely, most essential, and without a doubt first rule for achieving your marketing goals is that you must know your target market. You have to know who you want to sell to, and you must know as much about what they want to buy as possible. This is actually every bit as important as knowing what you sell, which presumably you already know. If you get this step wrong, you may inadvertently end up singing the praises of air conditioners to Eskimos. That is not low-cost marketing either. It is very expensive marketing, and ultimately disastrous.

Everything in your marketing plan and your marketing efforts must be determined by the nature and the desires of the people to whom you sell. This is foundational. It also is one of the easiest steps to ignore, and one of most frequently ignored as well. Too often entrepreneurs in love with their product believe that the market should love it too, and for the same reasons that they do. As we have seen, assumptions like this are dangerous. And costly.

Consequently, it pays to do your homework before you do your marketing. That is, if you already do not know your target market, invest some time and, yes, dollars to learn about these existing and potential customers. Markets are not all that mysterious. They practically shout what they want. And they are virtually mum about what they do not want. Here is a no-brainer tip: If your market is not asking for it, it is unwise to try to sell it.

What to Measure?

Once you have decided to identify your target market, what should you measure? What do you count? Be selective, or you can be overwhelmed by mountains of data that serve no purpose. Guard against the tendency to merely collect information for the sake of collecting it. Collect data that is useful in first identifying your target market and its desires and, second, that can help you find more customers like those in the general population. Beyond customers' feelings about you, there are two other general types of data. One is demographic makeup, such as age, sex, marital status, number of children at home, race, income level, education, occupation, etc. Another is the psychographic profile, such as lifestyle traits, for example, whether they buy books, go out to eat, vacation out of state, and so forth. Not even the government needs to know everything about everyone (at least not yet, thank goodness). Your job is to whittle down the potentially endless list of demographic and psychographic identifiers to what is germane. Keep in mind that what you want is information that will first help you to understand who your current customers are, and then to find more people like them. Extraneous data only makes the collecting more difficult—and expensive—and only detracts from the clear picture that you want of these people.

> Your job is to whittle down the potentially endless list of demographic and psychographic identifiers to what is germane.

Rely on a Variety of Formats and Sources

Market research is available in a variety of forms, broken down by industries, product preferences, demographics, buying habits, and so forth. And it is available from a variety of sources, industry groups, government agencies, and private researchers, among others. But the best and most reliable market to research is the one you already know best and have easiest access to—your current customers. After all, who would know better what they want from you than the people who already buy it? You will not go too far wrong by beginning your market research with this audience. Then, based on what these proven buyers tell you, you can more intelligently and more economically expand your research to the market in general.

We deal in greater depth with this in Chapter 7, but for our purposes here suffice it to say that it is crucial to understand the nature of your target market and its desires. You should be able to draw a portrait in words describing your best and your typical customers (they most likely will not be the same), and to clearly identify what they want from you.

Survey Yourself First

Here is a low-cost wake-up call. Before you conduct any surveys of your current customers, take the survey yourself. You can do this regardless of how you survey customers—by e-mail, snail mail, telephone interviews, or focus group. Have your staff join you in answering the same questions that you will submit to your customers. Minimally, the questions should determine what customers believe the benefits are that you sell, in what areas they think you are not adequately delivering what they want, and what types of offers prompt their purchases. Add at least one more item; that is, describe your best and typical customers. (Your customers also should be asked in the surveys to provide this information in the form of demographic and psychographic traits.) Tally up your in-house results, then survey your customers and compare their answers to your own. This can be an eye-opener. You may discover, for example, that the customer service you brag about in all your marketing collateral is regarded by customers as a glaring weakness. This low-cost, in-house survey can be very instructive for identifying the areas within your organization that fail to match up with the perceptions of your market. By measuring your staff's perceptions first, you add value to the survey of your customers' perceptions.

By measuring your staff's perceptions first, you add value to the survey of your customers' perceptions.

Do Not Assume

Do not assume that what sold yesterday will sell tomorrow. Customers are fickle. Do not wait until sales drop before you act. By then, it is too late. The customers have fled. Be proactive. Constantly gauge your market's appetite, or you will not know when to change the menu. Here is one way that essentially costs you the price of lunch times six times (or twelve times, or twenty-four times) every quarter—perhaps as little as a dollar or two a day when spread over three months. Randomly select a half dozen (or a dozen or two dozen) customers, depending on your budget. Once every quarter treat them to lunch, either all in one group or in smaller groups if that is more manageable. It is important to make sure that your guests are chosen randomly each quarter to ensure that over time you are getting a true cross sample of your entire customer base. The only condition of their attendance should be a willingness to answer two questions. First, "What do they like about your product or service?" and second, "What do they want that you don't provide?" Beyond that, let them do the talking. You just take notes. Over the course of a year you will get a pretty clear idea of what your customers perceive as benefits, and what they perceive you to lack. Over several years, you probably will be surprised to see how these opinions change. Use their comments to guide your marketing, and to spot changes before they manifest in customers abandoning you. Be out in front touting the benefits customers say they want as soon as you sense a substantive shift in sentiment.

Rule #2: Give Them What They Want

Now that you know your target market, the second rule to apply is to be certain to give these people what they want, and not try instead to force upon them what you want to sell. It is convenient if what you sell already meshes perfectly with what your target market desires. But too frequently small businesses discover that what they thought they were selling was not at all what their customers thought they were buying.

Take the case of a seaside motel that may view itself as a romantic getaway for couples in love, but in reality it is viewed by its best customers as a family retreat for parents with kids in tow. Romantically themed ads and specials for "Lovers' Getaways" will fall on deaf ears, or at least not maximize the motel's marketing dollar.

Often bringing what you sell into agreement with what your target market wants to buy is simply a matter of couching it in the proper terminology, or emphasizing something that you had been downplaying.

Our seaside motel, for instance, might make the adjustment without changing the benefits that it touts, but instead simply selling them in family-friendly terms rather than the language of an adult love nest. The "romantic sea view" might be flaunted instead as "close to the beach." The "room service for lovers' breakfast in bed" can be advertised instead as "pajama breakfasts for the whole family." Other benefits, like "free cable TV movies in your room," may need no revision in their wording.

Sometimes, however, you may discover that target markets want something drastically different than what you thought you were selling. In these cases, the real entrepreneurs step forward. They are the ones willing to sell what the buyer wants to buy, rather than insisting on selling what the seller wants to sell.

The motel operator might discover through market research that his ample dining facility and oversized meeting room perfectly fit the demand for corporate retreats, particularly with the enhanced amenities of a seaside locale. Rather than concentrating on the lovebird or the family markets, the motel operator may find that he can book business meetings and conventions year-round—and probably at steeper and more profitable rates.

Rule #3: Always Follow Rule #1 First

This is a very important rule. If you understand the importance of knowing your target market and of selling what your target market wants to buy, this third rule should be obvious. It is simply that you should always do Rule Number One before Rule Number Two.

In other words, do not try to sell what you "think" your target market wants from you until you first learn what it is your target market actually does want. Clearly, this means no guessing. You must know, not presume.

Do You Need a Marketing Consultant?

Acquiring the knowledge of your target market and its desires may require hiring marketing consultants. Or it may not.

Two factors will help you decide whether this is a task that you can do in-house, or if you must contract out to have it done.

Can Your Staff Do It?

The first factor is whether you have the expertise or available staff in-house to do the job. As valuable as research is in charting your marketing course, incomplete, flawed, or erroneous data is of no value, and indeed can end up doing more damage than good. That kind of research results in high-cost, not low-cost marketing.

The second factor in determining whether to conduct your market research in-house involves time and expense. Can you afford to assign internal staff? Interestingly, this factor is not necessarily contingent upon the size of your business. A lot of large businesses find it more economical to contract out for market research because their in-house staff may require long (and expensive) learning curves, or because in-house staff can be more productively assigned to other tasks. So even if you have the expertise in-house to do the job, you may find it more economical (that is, low-cost) to contract out for the work.

Considering Contracting Out

If you clearly do not have the in-house expertise to conduct elementary market research, the low-cost solution is to contract out for the service, preferably to a competent agency or an expert. Naturally, you will want to evaluate quotes based in part on the greatest expertise and lowest bid. However, it is always a good idea to look askance at the absolute lowest bidder, who may have to cut corners to come in that low, and it is probably prudent not to select that one.

But even if you have the expertise in-house to conduct your own market research, it still may not be the most economical (low-cost) use of your personnel. This is not always an easy determination to make. The short-term costs of diverting employees from their normal, presumably productive jobs to conduct your market research are fairly easy to calculate: The first step is to figure the number of hours they will spend multiplied by the number of dollars per hour those employees cost, including their prorated fringe benefits. But do not forget to also factor in the productivity that will be lost in the short term while those employees' normal jobs are not getting done. Moreover, if someone else on staff must be paid overtime to fill in while your advertising manager is reassigned to market research, that also is part of your actual market research cost.

The long-term costs of diverting in-house staff are even more problematic to calculate. Obviously, the idea behind market research is to end up with more effective marketing of your product or service, which increases the profitability of your bottom line. The gains in sales, the increases or decreases in your marketing costs, the increased productivity

> Even if you have the expertise in-house to conduct your own market research, it still may not be the most economical (low-cost) use of your personnel.

of marketing campaigns, and a variety of other long-term effects are diffi-cult to project.

One thing is fairly certain, however. If the short-term costs of using in-house personnel for market research result in greater marketing produc-tivity and increased profit, it is a pretty good bet that the long-term costs will too.

Benefits of Contracting Out

Contracting out has other inherent benefits. An outside contractor is less wedded to the institutional prejudices of your company. Consider the problems that may arise in assigning the head of your own advertising department to conduct market research. Will an advertising executive be influenced by his own self-interest? Will he tend to shape questions and interpret data, even unconsciously, according to his self-interested perspec-tive? How likely is it that an advertising executive will come back with con-clusions that call for reduction in the advertising budget?

These kinds of built-in conflict are not absolute bars to using in-house staff. But they are cautionary red flags that you should be aware of when weighing whether to contract out for the service.

On the flip side of the issue there are a number of points in favor of drawing on in-house staff, not the least of which is their familiarity with what has worked and has not worked to date, and their accumulated knowledge, which can be immensely helpful in determining what kinds of questions to ask, and whom to ask. Contracting out, by the very nature of the act, involves bringing strangers up to speed on numerous fronts. And that takes time, and consultants charge for their time.

The best low-cost route may be a middle ground in which you seek the counsel of market research experts to help you decide whether to con-tract out for your market research. Be mindful, of course, of the conflict when experts stand to gain by recommending that not only should you con-tract out for research, but that you should hire them to conduct it. One way to avoid this inherent conflict is to make it clear up front that as a condition of being paid for their advice, they must understand that you will not hire them to do the actual research if they ultimately recommend contracting out for that service.

Do You Need Outside Research Data?

Finally, at some point your in-house researcher—or the outside expert you hire—must determine whether you need outside research data, and if so, how much, what kind, and where to get it. Chances are you will need some. Few companies are comprehensive in collecting meaningful data even from their existing customers, let alone on their industry or market niche per se.

In your research you will collect essentially two kinds of data. The first kind is your customer profile, which is detailed information about existing customers—who they are, what they want, where they live, how they make buying decisions, and so forth. If you have no customers yet, you will want to make the same kind of assessment of the segment of the market that already purchases the type of product or service that you want to sell.

For that information, you probably will have to go outside your own company to government agencies or private firms that have already compiled such data, or will compile it for you.

Refining the Data

But even if you have compiled your own data from your existing customers, eventually you need to obtain the second kind of data, which is the number of people who match your customer profile in the general public

Low-Cost Research Sources

For outside market research data, there are a number of low-cost possibilities. Many industry trade organizations provide information to nonmembers, but even if membership is required, the cost of your annual dues is probably much less than paying for another company to compile such information. The government also collects vast amounts of data on every industry and on buyers' habits. The Economic Census of the U.S. Census Bureau, the Federal Trade Commission, and the Department of Commerce are good places to start; numerous local, state, and federal agencies can also be helpful.

and where you can find them. Unless you are a multinational, billion-dollar corporation, this kind of information almost always must be obtained from others. Otherwise, you would be marketing to the entire world, most of which has no interest in what you sell.

This is an area in which that low-cost middle ground option can be hugely helpful. A consultant well versed in market research can recommend not only the type of data that your business should collect, but is likely to also know where and how you can get it at the most reasonable prices. Such a market research consultant may be your best low-cost investment in the preliminary steps of equipping yourself for that journey that gets you from here to your destination, however you define it.

► **Chapter 7**

Research Sharpens Focus

Part One

Part Two

Part Three

Part Four

Part Five

PART TWO   PLANNING FOR SUCCESS

Spying, the Proper and Polite Way

Research can be costly. Businesspeople know that generally we get what we pay for. Of course, paying a lot does not guarantee that we get something of value. And by the same token, just because the price may be low it does not necessarily mean what is bought is worthless.

Indeed, there are many ways to keep your market research costs down and still glean extremely valuable data that can help formulate and execute an effective marketing strategy.

One way is to spy on your competitors and on your customers. Spy, but spy politely, and legally, of course. Let us be clear here that what we mean is not some nefarious skulking around like a secret agent, or an industrial snoop snatching trade secrets.

No, this kind of spying for research is more like paying close attention to what is already in front of your face. It is what you do when you buy something from a competitor or observe the buying patterns of a customer. The point here is to do it systematically, and to track your observations.

Research That Creates Loyal Customers

Consider the case of a mail-order catalog company that is experiencing a rash of complaints from customers who are trying to return purchases. For this case, the reason that items are being returned is a separate problem. Nearly every company can expect to have returned purchases. The key here is to turn a negative experience into a positive experience for purchasers so they will come back and buy more, rather than scratch you off their list of preferred providers. Research has found that when you solve problems for complaining customers, they not only will do business with you again, but will be even more loyal than a noncomplaining customer. Why? Because you proved that you are good to your word and back up your promises.

Analyze Complaints

For now, let us deal with the return process that seems to be generating complaints. A logical question may be, "How do our competitors handle returns?"

There are two "spying" techniques that can help you find out. The first one is simply to ask. It does not cost anything to pick up the telephone and call your competitors to ask what their return policy is, and what the procedure is if a customer has a complaint. They may even be willing to mail or fax you their written policy. This ultra low-cost approach will probably reveal your competitors' official procedures. Take careful notes. But do not rely too much on what you have gathered.

The next technique will probably be more revealing. Test your competitors' real-life procedures against their written policies. Order an item from each competitor, then return each for refunds, according to their procedures. If your business has three major competitors, three telephone calls, three orders, and three returned packages should give you a pretty good idea of how easy or difficult it is to return purchases to them, how long the process takes in each case, how closely they adhere to their written policies, and, finally, how they compare to your own company's policy and procedure. Test as many times as you feel necessary to get a handle on what is typical for each of your competitors. This should not cost you much, other than perhaps postage, since you are returning the merchandise for a refund.

The benefits of this research go beyond simply knowing how you stack up in comparison to your competitors. First, use the findings to improve your own policy and procedure, borrowing from what seems to work well for competitors to iron out the bumps in your own customer service relations. Next, turn the negative experience that began with returned merchandise into a marketing advantage.

Improve, Then Compare

Once you have implemented the improvements to your return policy and complaint handling, you can speak with

Spying Made Easy

If you are tracking sales with a database, you can learn a lot about your customers' buying habits. Note patterns in purchases. If you sell office supplies and Customer Jones ordered a big supply of folders and copy paper in April, June, and August, you may be safe in assuming that he buys two months' worth each time. So you may want to prod Mr. Jones in September to remind him that he may be running out of folders and copy paper. A postcard works fine, and costs only pennies. Remember, though, that there is a fine line between doing something on your customers' behalf and invading their privacy. If your reminder is too explicit ("You spent $421.35 in June"), Mr. Jones may recoil with visions of Big Brother looking over his checkbook.

some authority on how you favorably compare with your major competitors. You might then:

1. Create a comparison chart that shows step-by-step how your return policy and complaint handling is superior to that of your competitors.
2. Publish the comparison in a prominent position in your catalog, on your Web site, and in all your marketing collateral.
3. Include that chart along with every invoice and every order.

Through this low-cost and relatively easy-to-conduct research, you have not only eliminated a problem, but also improved your service and generated another benefit in the minds of your customers, a benefit they are reminded of everywhere they look even if they never return a purchase.

Researching the Market

What works with competitors can also work with customers. Consider the hypothetical case of the Widget Toy Company, which is weighing whether to introduce a new product. Rather than overt questioning such as often occurs in focus groups and in written surveys in which the bias of the surveyor may be apparent, the company chooses to spy instead to get a more frank and honest response.

With the permission of a retail outlet's store management, the toy company stations a survey taker next to the shelf where its new toy is displayed alongside competitors' products. The next step is a matter of finesse. We do not recommend ever misrepresenting yourself in research, or in any other business endeavor. But not offering your affiliation upfront is different. With that in mind, the surveyor can stand with clipboard in hand and wait for customers who are perusing the toy shelf until they take an interest in the Widget Toy Company's new product.

The questioning might follow this tact, "I noticed that you were looking at the new Widget toy. Do you think the price is too high? Too low? What do you think of the company? How do you think the new toy could be improved?"

The benefit of this "apparently" independent approach is that it probably tends to elicit a more sincere response. By comparison, if the surveyor were to first identify himself as the Widget Toy Company representative, the shopper may not be as willing to offer an honest critique. The difference in responses may be subtle, but subtleties can make or break a new product. One last caveat: if the shopper asks the surveyor whether he is affiliated with the Widget Toy Company, the surveyor should always answer truthfully.

But the surveyor also should note on the form that the shopper was aware of the affiliation when answering the questions. A comparison of answers from shoppers who were both aware and unaware of the surveyor's affiliation may reveal the subtle differences between shoppers who believed they were talking to independent third parties and those who believed they were talking to Widget Toy Company representatives.

By spying in this way, the Widget Toy Company ought to be able to glean the degree of customer acceptance, and even flag potential problems before committing 100 percent to manufacturing the product line. The responses also may provide fodder for new marketing approaches if shoppers express pleasure with features the manufacturer previously had not even thought to stress, such as, "I really like the fact that the toy is too large for small children to put in their mouths."

Collect Industrywide and Niche Data

Add focus to your research with another low-cost technique by collecting data on your industry or market segment that is available free or for reasonable fees. As mentioned in the previous chapter, many trade organizations compile market research data for use by their members.

One of the drawbacks of doing your own research is that you must make the threshold decisions of what you are seeking and where to ferret it out. A common and costly mistake is to consider broad industry data as somehow reflective of your narrow industry niche. When analyzing industry or consumer data, the low-cost approach is to always seek the most specific details pertaining to your product.

If you are a wholesale flower grower specializing in pansies, petunias, and wallflowers, it is one thing to know what the demand is for flowers in your distribution area, but quite another to know the trend for annuals (the kind of flowers you sell) rather than for perennials (the kind you do not sell).

One of the drawbacks of doing your own research is that you must make the threshold decisions of what you are seeking and where to ferret it out.

Database Goldmines

Customer databases are worth their weight in marketing gold. Not only can you evaluate the buying patterns of customers, which can help you tailor low-cost and high-profit sales offers to them at strategic times, but you also can evaluate your market in segments. If you are a wholesale woman's apparel company selling to boutiques and chain stores, it is worth your while to analyze your market niches. As population distributions change, your market may too. Keep tabs on the trends that you can read with your customer database. Although you may not want to discontinue a line of young woman's dresses simply because sales have slumped, it is worth noting that demand for more matronly garments has increased, while orders for young misses dresses are waning. The women of your label-conscious market may be aging, and with age shedding the more risqué attire they were comfortable wearing in their twenties. By researching the data of your sales trends, you may be able to adjust your marketing—and product line—to compensate for the change in your market's taste.

> As population distributions change, your market may too.

Low-Cost Resources

One low-cost research resource is the U.S. Census, which can help you segment your market. If you are a restaurateur catering to a hip dinner club crowd, you may want to closely eye the demographic trends of your geographic drawing area. It is not always easy to do that from inside your restaurant. After all, you see only the ones that come in. If the demographic characteristics of the neighborhood surrounding your restaurant have rapidly changed, you may want to reposition your marketing and your customer appeal sooner rather than later. Census data is available in most large public libraries and online at the U.S. Census Web site (✍ *www.census.gov*) as well as on CDs for nominal fees. Some companies like SRC LLC in Orange, California, that sell custom census analysis also provide a good amount of searchable census data online for free (✍ *www.freedemographics.com*). For your purposes as a restaurant owner, the significance of census data is in the way it has charted the changes in your neighborhood. When your restaurant opened fifteen years ago, the neighborhood may have been a higher socioeconomic level featuring a lot of young, childless married couples buying their first houses, and a host of single adults in condominiums and apartments. The census may show that as the community has aged, the neighborhood has gradually morphed into second- or third-owner homes and apartments that are now crowded with large families and young children. Ethnic changes also are reflected in the census data, which can be equally helpful. It is not easy to pick up your restaurant and move it to another community that looks more like the one where you began. But what began as a trendy dinner club may have a future as a family restaurant with "kiddy menus" to attract your new neighbors, if you find out in time with this low-cost research.

Do not be sidetracked by data that is skewed by a factor that at first may appear to be related, such as the general category of "flowers," but on closer examination is immaterial to your marketing, such as "perennials."

Segment Markets

The lesson is to keep your research on target. It is important to identify as specifically as you can your market segment when describing your target market profile.

The grower who specializes in flowering annuals needs to know who buys them and why, whether they are buying more or less than previously, and a variety of other facts. But those buyers may or may not be the same customers who buy perennial flowers. General information on flowers may not help much.

In order to find the kind of meaningful, specific market research information that is needed, first get a firm grip on your target market's demographic and psychographic profile. Here is a list of demographic and psychographic traits. Not every characteristic will be important to your business.

- Age
- Sex
- Own or rent home
- Address (city and state)
- Occupation
- Marital status
- Education

- Children (number, ages, living at home)
- Income level
- Hobbies
- How long at current address
- What magazines they read
- What television programs they watch
- When they last went on vacation
- Where they vacation
- The number of people in their household
- How often they attend movies
- Where they buy groceries (or any other pertinent products or services)

The information above will help you understand the "who" of your target market. The information below will help you understand the "why" by identifying your target market's behavior.

Some Profile Questions

- Why do existing customers buy from you?
- How did your customers first hear of you?
- Why do they stop buying from you?
- How does your target market find out about your competitors?
- What is it they like about your competitors?
- What is it they dislike about your competitors?
- What would it take for your buyers to buy more, or more often?
- Do they find your sales staff helpful, product quality sufficient, service satisfactory?
- What reputation does your business have?
- How about the reputation of your product (or service)?
- Do your customers feel that what you sell is priced right?

Finding the Top Buyers

A timeless sales axiom is that 20 percent of your customers account for 80 percent of your sales. While not true for every industry, particularly retailers, this estimate often is a good rule of thumb. Obviously, this top 20 percent are your best customers. Call them Top Buyers. On average, each Top Buyer accounts for sixteen times the sales of each customer not in this top-level group. Imagine a customer base comprised entirely of Top Buyers. Mouth-watering, no?

Is it possible to transform the 80 percent who account for only 20 percent of your sales into such super customers? Perhaps. But keep in mind that they already are getting the same information that Top Buyers are getting—the same offers and the same level of service—and for whatever reason they still have not stepped up to that level. It may be more likely that you can clone the top 20 percent than it is that you can convert the bottom 80 percent of your customers.

To clone more Top Buyers from the general public, you must know what it is that sets the top 20 percent apart from the rest of your customers. In what ways are they different? What demographic, psychographic, and other traits differ from the 80 percent segment of your existing customer base?

Once you can identify the differences, then you can market to new customers who match the profile of your top 20 percent, rather than to those who match the profile of the bottom 80 percent.

But until you can entirely replace average buyers with Top Buyers, it is still cheaper to market to existing customers than new customers. What is it that you need to learn to transform these average buyers into Top Buyers? It is worth finding out whether you can transform some of those average buyers into Top Buyers. The low-cost approach is to ask them how to do that.

Since you already do business with these people, that conversation can occur in a number of ways. You may include a questionnaire with every product you deliver, or have salespeople orally ask the questions. The survey can be a follow-up mailer, sweetened with an offer for a rebate, or a discount on a future purchase to encourage the customers to fill out the form and return it. The questions can be included in your routine follow-up telephone call to evaluate the buyer's satisfaction. (You do make those, right?) Focus groups consisting only of these average buyers are another low-cost method of conducting such surveys.

> To clone more Top Buyers from the general public, you must know what it is that sets the top 20 percent apart from the rest of your customers.

Do a Competitive Self-Evaluation

Another low-cost, yet invaluable approach to market research is the self-evaluation. While this can be helpful in identifying strengths and weaknesses, recognize the bias. Your bias. Chances are you are blind to some of your own faults and you inflate some of your strengths. To conduct such a self-evaluation, you might rate a number of qualities on a scale of one to five. For instance, candidly assess factors such as:

- Products
- Price
- Quality
- Selection
- Service
- Reliability
- Reputation

- Availability
- Appearance
- Advertising
- Public relations
- Credit policy
- Return rates
- Customer complaints

This list is not exhaustive, and depending on your industry you may be able to add to it, or delete some of the factors. For the evaluation to be meaningful, however, you should have something to compare it to. Ask yourself the same questions of your competitors. Watch that bias. You cannot pass this test by cheating. In fact, unless you are willing to be entirely honest, you can do more harm than good.

The results of the self-evaluation are good on a number of levels. They help you identify at a glance where your strengths and weaknesses are, and how you stack up against your competition. Often times entrepreneurs simply assume they hold an edge over competitors, say in reliability or in quality, because they have never actually taken the time to compare such traits head-to-head. Forcing yourself to sincerely do so can be very useful. For example, you may identify areas in which you hold a clear advantage over the competition that had not previously occurred to you. If those areas also jibe with what your target market wants, you have just identified a brand new marketing strategy, an area where you can lure customers away from your competitors because of your advantage.

The self-evaluation also can be helpful in identifying areas where you are performing poorly, either in absolute terms or in relation to your competition. Identifying such weaknesses, perhaps in product selection, serves a couple of purposes. It can alert you to an area where you may choose to improve, or it can warn you away from touting a benefit that you cannot deliver. Either way it is useful research data to help focus your marketing strategy.

Identify Your Gatekeepers

One of the most valuable marketing tools for a small business is the gatekeeper. These are the people who send customers your way. They may be direct referrals, like an accountant who recommends your accounting software to customers. They may be simply links in a natural chain of progression, like a commercial printing company that maintains a list of qualified graphic artists for its clients. They may be reciprocal arrangements like networking clubs that typically limit membership to one person from each industry; when any members have associates, clients, or friends in need of a service or product, the members refer them to the appropriate members of the networking club.

Gatekeepers can operate on a variety of levels, informal to formal, or gratis to expensive. They may operate horizontally (from one organization to another) or vertically (from one level of a company to another). Some companies have a rotating list of vendors they recommend to customers, while others keep less formally organized directories. Some gatekeepers may expect the equivalent of a finder's fee, while others are simply glad to pass on potential customers even without expectation of you returning the favor.

A horizontal arrangement might include a commercial printer that specializes in four-color printing, but also serves as a gatekeeper for another noncompetitive printing establishment that handles only quick one- or two-color printing jobs. The four-color printer would rather not disappoint a customer by turning away his one-color brochure job, and instead

Negotiate Joint Ventures

High-cost marketing is paying for floor space in a retail establishment in order to introduce your latest impulse purchase item, for example chocolate bubble gum, before you even know if the public wants to buy it. Here's a low-cost method to research a product's marketability. Offer a retailer a free rack display full of your chocolate bubble gum on the following conditions: You pay no floor or shelf fee for the trial period and the store gets to keep the proceeds of all sales. If the gum bombs, the store pockets whatever proceeds from the sales that were made, and you save the expense of gearing up to stock dozens of stores, and paying dozens of shelf fees. But if the gum sells out, the store and you have found a winner, while it cost the store nothing and cost you only the wholesale price of whatever product you can afford to give away.

Don't Just Collect, Analyze

Market research is not worth the ink and paper it takes to print it out if no one takes the time to analyze it. There is nothing low-cost about doing a lot of work, collecting a lot of data, paying for reams of research, and then letting it sit on a shelf gathering dust. Unless you are willing to commit the time and effort necessary to evaluate what you have collected, you may as well have burned dollar bills to watch them smolder. As with all business endeavors, halfway generally means failure. A salesman halfway through a sale means no sale. Market research that is merely collected but not analyzed is not market research. It is recyclable paper. Take the time to make your investment, however low-cost it may be, worth every penny. Commit upfront to analyzing what it is you gather.

please him with a referral to the noncompetitive printer he knows and trusts. Obviously, such mutually beneficial arrangements can work in both directions.

A vertical arrangement would be the printer and graphic artist. But like the horizontal gatekeeping relationship between two printers, the vertical relationship of a graphic artist and a printer also can work in both directions. And because the flow through gatekeepers can be in either direction, you need to cultivate these key conduits not only for what they can do for you, but also for what you can do for them.

Identify Potential Gatekeepers

From a research standpoint, it is worth your while to identify all the gatekeepers you already have, some of whom you may not even regard as gatekeepers. Then, your further research should be concerned with identifying potential gatekeepers that you have not yet cultivated. Who are the people and businesses that can serve as free (or even for a fee) gatekeepers? Sometimes they are not obvious.

A salesman who needs to communicate with corporate executives will probably tell you that vital gatekeepers for his business are executive secretaries. If your sales staff requests only marketing collateral for the business executives they are trying to buttonhole, it very well may be worthwhile to build into the budget a little ingratiating collateral like flowers or theater passes to brighten secretaries' days. Here is a tip so your ingratiating efforts are not mistaken for bribes: Clear any substantive gifts with the secretary's boss beforehand.

What Does It Cost to Get One Customer?

Market research is generally considered to be all the stuff that you want to know in order to get and to keep customers. But another low-cost in-house bit of market research can give fuller meaning to all that stuff. It requires a comprehensive view of everything you do to attract customers.

To know whether your marketing is efficient, you must know what it costs to get one customer. A rough calculation may simply be to divide your total marketing budget by your customer base.

It is more difficult to calculate what it costs to keep a customer. One way to look at the ongoing costs of keeping customers is to look at the ongoing value of a customer. Some questions to ask:

- How long do you keep a customer?
- Is your customer list this year different than last year? Than five years ago? Than ten years ago?

As part of your low-cost market research, you may want to institute a system that not only tracks customer purchases, but that can give you an idea of a customer's lifetime value to your company.

A truer evaluation of your marketing budget is its effectiveness over time in keeping customers happy, and bringing them back repeatedly. If your research shows that customers are short-lived, that they stop buying and move on after a year or two, it may indicate that your marketing is working to attract new customers but not retaining the old ones.

> **Chapter 8**

Creating a
Marketing Plan

Part One

Part Two

Part Three

Part Four

Part Five

A Map to Success

A marketing plan will not put your business on autopilot. But it sure beats starting from scratch every morning. Consider it your map to success.

Your marketing plan is where you pull together all the elements of your research, detail your strategy, make sure that it dovetails with your business plan, and finally set forth a clear and methodical means of putting it in action. Implementing your marketing plan brings it to life by systematically stepping you through the marketing jungle's thicket—but let's not get ahead of the game. You need a plan before you can implement it.

There are those who will endlessly belabor the possible color choices for a trifold brochure, but not give a second thought to the marketing plan that the brochure is expected to bring to life. Details deserve your attention, but it is important to get the big picture right first.

Define Your Target Market

The biggest element of that big picture is your target market. These are the people (or if you are a business-to-businesses enterprise, the businesses) to whom you sell now and to whom you hope to sell in the future. Obviously, the better you know these people, the easier it is going to be to market to them. Your marketing plan is where you describe them as your target market profile. If they change, and they very well may over the lifetime of your business, it is necessary for you to change your description of them. Take care not to have an outdated target market profile. There is nothing as potentially counterproductive than trying to sell today to yesterday's customers. Everything else in your marketing plan is derived from or built upon your understanding of who these people are, and what they want. Make sure that your picture of them is up to date.

To paint the picture of your target market, draw on the elements that we have previously discussed. Describe their demographic and psychographic traits as well and as detailed as you can. List every germane characteristic like age, income level, sex, occupation, hobbies, location, what reading material they like, how they spend their vacations, and any other traits that will help you facilitate the conversation once you start talking to

> Take care not to have an outdated target market profile. There is nothing as potentially counterproductive than trying to sell today to yesterday's customers.

them, or narrow the field once you start seeking them among the general public. Add to their profile any buying preferences they have expressed. State in a simple declarative sentence what it is they want from you.

Answer "What's in It for Me?"

This is the answer to your customers' number one question, "What's in it for me?" The answer is probably more important than any other knowledge of your target market. It also will be indispensable when you write your mission statement.

If there are only two portions of your marketing plan that you commit to memory, they should be your target market's profile and your mission statement. Everything else exists simply to make the latter serve the former.

Consider this your low-cost marketing plan workbook. You can start by filling in your target market profile here (you probably should use pencil, until you are more certain):

_____

_____

_____

Distinguish "A," "B," and "C" Clients

Next, your marketing plan should distinguish the segments within your target market. Most small businesses and particularly most start-up businesses can rarely afford to discard customers—at least until they have found replacements.

With that in mind, realize that your existing customer base is likely to contain "A," "B," and "C" customers. "A" customers cannot get enough of you and vice versa, "B" customers are good but could be better, and "C" customers are profitable but barely so and hardly worth the time and expense it costs to maintain them. (Here's a minitip for the low-cost conscious: If you have any "D" or "F" customers, jettison them. They are costing you more money than you make from them.)

The idea is to identify the traits common to each class of customer, and

Unexpected Benefits

Identifying "A," "B," and "C" customers can have many beneficial effects. If you sell consumer electronics like CD players and portable radios, you may stock a variety of styles and price ranges. By identifying your "A" (best) customers and your "C" (lukewarm) customers, you may find a correlation between their status and buying preferences. Perhaps it turns out that the "C" customers tend to buy lower-priced products, are more likely to return them with complaints, and take more of your sales staff's time. The "A" customers may buy higher-priced products, rarely return purchases because the higher-priced products are more reliable, and do most of their homework before they walk in your showroom. It is pretty clear which customers you want more of. As a result, you may choose to discontinue the low-end models altogether and position yourself as a high-end shopper's boutique.

therefore understand how you might appeal to more "A" customers and waste less time and money trying to attract low-profit, high-cost "C" customers. As a rule of thumb, a "B" customer may be capable of moving up the ladder to become an "A." But "C" customers probably never will. Your long-term goal should be to whittle away at those more costly, low-profit "C" customers while attracting more low-cost, high-profit "A" customers, and meanwhile converting as many "Bs" to "As" as possible.

Why Identify Your A, B, Cs?

Why is it important to divide your market base into "A," "B," and "C" customers? The answer is that "A" customers cost you less to attract and maintain, generate more profit, and love doing business with you. "C" customers are more expensive to attract, cost nearly as much as they generate in revenue, and on top of that often require costly extra, unprofitable attention because of their frequent complaints. By dividing your target market into these categories, you are likely to find traits common to "As" that are less likely to appear among "Cs" and vice versa. By identifying the subcategories within your target market, you can focus your marketing efforts on the best customers and downplay or eliminate the marketing that appeals predominantly to the worst customers. Also, by being able to distinguish them by their traits, it makes it easier for you to realistically measure your progress in determining over time whether you are attracting more "As" or more "Cs" as new customers.

Rank Them

It may be a tad premature, but just to get the ball rolling, give a try at identifying only the traits that you think may distinguish your "A," "B," and "C" customers from each other. Below write the traits that you think are unique to, or disproportionately found in, each type of customer (for now, hold off using an ink pen and continue using that pencil):

"A" Customers _____

_____

"B" Customers _____

_____

"C" Customers _____

_____

Formulate Your USP and Market Positioning

The next segment of your marketing plan is where you spell out your Unique Sales Proposition (USP) and identify your relative marketing position among competitors.

Your USP, as we have discussed, is effectively the image of you in the mind of your buying public. It also addresses the question, "Why should I buy it from you?" The key to a successful USP is its uniqueness, which carves out a particular market niche for you in relation to your competitors.

Back in Chapter 2, we addressed six key questions (To whom do you sell? What benefits do you sell? Why do people buy from you, to obtain pleasure or to avoid pain? When do you sell? Where do you sell? How does your product or service solve customers' problems?). You then constructed a one-sentence description of your USP, which summarized your market advantage over your competitors.

Enter your one-sentence Unique Sales Proposition here (still in pencil, please):

_____

_____

_____

Be Concise

Your marketing plan should already be as few words as possible, but it needs to be distilled even one step further. Boil down the essence of your marketing plan to a one-page synopsis and label it "Executive Summary." This will increase efficiency, and therefore productivity, and in the long haul it should save you time, and time is money. A one-page executive summary helps you to refine even further the core of your marketing strategy. Learn to say it aloud. It is a handy litmus test to apply when new marketing schemes are suggested.

Here is a quick reminder: It is critically important that your concise USP statement meshes with your target market's desires. It does you no good to be unique if you are so unique that you fit no market niche.

Define Opportunities Based on Benefits

Now, based on your USP and what you know about your target market, identify your market niche, that is, describe only the "A" and "B" customers, who already constitute a market for what you sell and how you are uniquely positioned to provide it to them.

Enter your market niche description here:

_____

_____

_____

Depending on the maturity of your business, this market niche may be more of a long-term target than a current reality. Today you may be overloaded with "C" customers and cannot afford to wean your business from them. That is okay. Keep in mind that your marketing plan is a road map, not a static picture. Your best marketing niche may take some time to achieve even with your best marketing efforts. That is one of the values of having a marketing plan, to help you see how to make that happen tomorrow even if it is not happening today.

Weighing Your Options

To reach your targeted market, your options at first seem endless. If anything, you have more opportunities than marketing dollars. Every form of communications from print to hot media to mail to personal relationships to the Internet and many more choices is at your disposal—theoretically.

Some, like national television ads, probably are cost prohibitive. Others may be entirely inappropriate for your market. But even local television ads, including cable channels, can accommodate the low-cost marketer's budget. And the creative use of what may seem inappropriate options may make them successful. As they say, think out of the box. The ultimate question is, which of these options and how many of them should you indulge in.

In Parts Three, Four, and Five of this book, you will be given many suggestions for specific tools, techniques, and tactics that you may find suitable for delivering your Unique Selling Proposition to your target market.

But for now, consider the following broad marketing categories as your general options. Not all of them are likely to end up in every small business marketing plan. Not all of them are likely to be compatible with your business, or with your target market.

We will suggest some general tips for how to view these categories in relation to your business so you can weigh their suitability. But you can put down your pencil for now. Do not try to guess quite yet which of these you should employ, or how much you should budget in a particular category.

Certainly, those decisions must be included in your marketing plan, but the time to make those choices will come later. For now, you need only be aware that these are general categories, and that you should begin thinking about how appropriate each may or may not be for your business, your target market, and your budget constraints.

Marketing Categories

Here are some general marketing categories:

1. Marketing collateral
2. Advertising
3. Database marketing

Can't Get Lower Cost Than This

Here's an extremely low-cost (actually, no-cost) exercise for getting yourself to think in terms of benefits, rather than features, when shaping your marketing plan. Stack your favorite magazines and newspapers on the table and grab a marker. Go through the advertisements in each publication, one at a time, and look for two things: either what appeals to you or what is missing. Write on the ads with your marker either that a benefit is missing or present and, if so, what it is. Hone your ability to spot what is beneficial, rather than what is a bell and whistle, and you will be in a better position to identify your own benefits.

4. Hot media (radio and television)
5. Cool media (print publications)
6. Direct (mail-based) response
7. People-to-people marketing
8. The Internet

One of the keys to knowing how well suited these marketing categories are for your business is to evaluate the opportunities that they provide to successfully communicate what customers perceive to be your benefits.

Some categories simply may be unsuited to putting forth your benefits in their best light. For example, if you sell high-tech computer gaming software, the real-time visual representations of its benefits—realistic special effects and lightning quick transformations that exhilarate the player and give the illusion of adventure—are particularly well suited to television and Internet promotions. But those benefits that are the driving factor for your target market do not come across nearly as effectively in radio or print advertising.

Similarly, if you are a catalog sales merchant, direct response (also known as direct mail) is customary for distribution of your main sales tool, the catalog, but may not be as well-suited as a Web site, where countless more products can be displayed, searched, and updated in availability and price for greater customer convenience and at less cost to you. Of course, a Web site will not do you much good if most of your target market is computer illiterate. Everyone, on the other hand, has a street address for mailed catalogs.

Define Features as Secondary Selling Points

Another factor to weigh when considering the eight major marketing categories is whether it is necessary for you to stress features as well as benefits to close your sale. Of course, you should always stress benefits first.

But if marketing your product or service also requires enumerating its features to close the sale, the marketing category you select must accommodate the extra verbiage or extra time it takes to list everything. In many cases, direct mailings, such as catalogs, must close the sale in one contact. That is, all the information necessary to persuade the buyer to buy must be included in that one contact. A catalog is rarely intended to generate leads for future sales, although it can do so. Normally a catalog asks for the sale now. Therefore, if the features of the product are necessary to close the sale, they also must be included in the mailing.

Some Categories Have More Features

Some marketing categories are better at including long lists of features than others. Radio advertisements tend to drone on when the announcer ticks off lists of features. But marketing collateral like brochures and fliers typically can list features of a product beneath the headlines that trumpet benefits: "Be the most elegant woman in the room (the benefit). Our strapless and high-collared gowns are available in petite, small, medium, large, extra large, blue, red, pink, green, or lavender (the features)."

At this stage, a good preliminary exercise is to go through the eight major marketing categories and brainstorm to see how many of them may be appropriate for reaching your customers while staying within your budget constraints. Make notes. (But use the pencil again. Chances are, you will need the eraser later.)

Your market research begins to pay off here. Not only should you know by now from your research to whom you are marketing and what they want, but you should have some idea of what messages they rely on to make their buying decisions, and which media are most appropriate for reaching them.

Those psychographic questions, like which magazines they read and what hobbies they enjoy, are helpful in zeroing in on the venues and message types that appeal to your target market. For example, if you choose print magazine advertising as one of your marketing tools, you had better be aware of which magazines your targeted customers read.

Incorporating Your Market Research

Your marketing plan also should summarize the findings of your market research, which breaks down into two areas: one, a detailed profile of your existing customers, and two, a finding of how many people like them exist in the general population within your marketing area. Research can be a pain to conduct and even more bothersome to analyze. But if you do not know who buys what you sell, you cannot very well know how to find more of them. Imagine such a condition:

"I'm looking for someone."

"What does he look like?"

"I don't know."

And if you do not know how many more like them there are out there, and where to find them, you cannot market to them even if you know what they look like. You cannot be everywhere. Where would you start?

From a low-cost marketer's perspective, it is definitely high-cost to shoot in the dark by guessing the nature of your market, and by taking a shotgun approach to finding new customers.

> From a low-cost marketer's perspective, it is definitely high-cost to shoot in the dark by guessing the nature of your market.

Draft Clear, Attainable Goals with Timetables

After filling in the blanks—to whom you sell, what they want, how you distinguish yourself from competitors, the marketing categories appropriate for your company and for your customers, and a summary of your research—it is time to draft clear, attainable goals with firm deadlines for meeting them.

Obviously, these details cannot be completed until you have chosen the categories of marketing that you will employ (marketing collateral, advertising, database marketing, etc.) and chosen the specific techniques, tools, and tactics to use (magazine advertisements, door hanging brochures, direct-mail fliers, networking organizations, etc.).

Fold Here . . .

The remainder of this book addresses those specifics. So for now, fold down the corner of this page to mark it, and plan to return to this spot later.

Once you have armed yourself with techniques, tools, and tactics to employ in your chosen marketing categories, then you can return here and begin making the exciting decisions for your marketing plan about how much to spend, and on which options to spend it, and the order in which you will implement the techniques, tools, and tactics that you have chosen.

For a mail-order catalog company, an entry in this section—your marketing goals and deadlines for meeting them—might look something like this:

"We will test 10 percent off and 25 percent off coupons in our mail order sales to see if they increase profits from repeat customers."

The actual detail of the marketing strategy, which does not necessarily belong in your marketing plan, is the instruction for how to go about attaining that goal. It may resemble something like this:

"In every even-numbered mail order sale from January 1 to June 30 we will include 10 percent off coupons with all shipped products. Odd-numbered mail order sales will include 25 percent off coupons. Both types of coupons will clearly state that they expire on June 30. For the six-month period of January through June we will track the resulting sales made with redeemed coupons and compare the 25 percent off and 10 percent off coupon purchases to each other and to purchases made by repeat customers who did not include coupons when they ordered. We will evaluate the three options to determine which generated the greatest net sales. We will renew the best option for another six months, but only if the option increased net profits by at least 10 percent over sales without coupons."

This kind of accountability ensures that not only the best option is used, but that discounts will continue only if they reach a certain level of profitability. Accountability should be built in to every marketing technique, tool, and tactic whenever possible. It is not enough to simply offer 25 percent off and expect it to increase sales. Even if the 25 percent discount generates more gross sales, it may represent fewer net dollars in profit than the 10 percent discount. And there is always the possibility that neither discount offer will net more profit than normal sales that include no discount in which the buyer pays full price. The point is, you will not know which

Focus

It is easy to miss the details when getting the big picture. Your company marketing plan is likely to be fairly general since it applies to your entire business. But what works generally to promote your business may not be what you need to promote segments of it If you have a bookkeeping service you may also have a seasonal tax service. Although there may be much overlap in the clientele of your general bookkeeping business and your specialty niche of tax preparation, they also can each stand alone and may each appeal to different buyers. Consider the value of working up a separate marketing plan for those tax preparation customers, who simply are not as likely to be attracted to the benefits of Widget Bookkeeping Company's payroll and accounts receivable services as they are likely to be interested in meeting their dreaded annual April 15 deadline.

option works best until you test them. So when you place a strategy in your marketing plan, be sure to stipulate that it must be tested to determine if it is profitable. Then be sure to specify how the test will be measured in its implementation.

Calculate Your Marketing Budget

You are human, so chances are good that your appetite exceeds your budget. By the time you finish this book, you probably will have accumulated dozens of new ideas for marketing to your clientele. If you have been in business for some time, you probably have already quantified your marketing budget. You know how much you have to spend. That is a good starting point. For those who have never tallied what you spend on marketing, it is time to pore over the books and get a handle on it. And for those who are launching new start-up businesses, your task is even more challenging. A tendency for start-ups is to allocate to marketing whatever is left after paying expenses and business expansion.

There are no hard and fast rules. But do not fret. After all, this marketing stuff is supposed to make you money, not just cost you money. Nevertheless, as a low-cost marketer, you should begin conservatively, at least until you can tell whether your marketing is bringing in more money than it is spending. Say you decide that 10 percent of your company's gross budget can be allocated to marketing. The next step is to rank what you believe to be your most promising (that is, potentially most profitable) marketing strategies. Then it becomes simply a matter of going as far down your ranked list of strategies as your budget permits. The techniques, tools, and tactics that you do not have money for go on your waiting list, ranked from the best to least profitable. If the third item on your marketing budget turns out to be a bust, delete it. With your priorities already established in your marketing plan, you can simply push the strategy at the top of the waiting list up to fill the void.

Write Your Mission Statement

With your marketing plan established, the final step is to write your mission statement. We have saved this to the end because of the hazards of prejudging. But now that you have filled in all the blanks in your marketing plan, you have a realistic overview of what you intend to achieve and how.

Your mission statement is the concise one-paragraph (better yet, one-sentence) summary of how you serve your customers, your company, and your employees. Since marketing to your customers is an integral part of serving them, it needs to be reflected in the company's mission statement. Too often mission statements simply adorn a plaque on the wall or letterhead stationery. They are rarely ingrained in employees' or customers' image of a company. That is a sadly missed opportunity. When viewed by customers, your mission statement is essentially a marketing tool. It should communicate with sincerity and passion to whomever reads it how you benefit them. It is a low-cost reminder to customers and potential customers of the reason that you should be in their lives.

> **Chapter 9**

Implementing Your Marketing Plan

Part One

Part Two

Part Three

Part Four

Part Five

PART TWO   PLANNING FOR SUCCESS

■ CHAPTER 6 Planning Your Marketing: As Easy as 1, 2, 3 ■ CHAPTER 7 Research Sharpens Focus ■ CHAPTER 8
Creating a Marketing Plan ■ CHAPTER 9 **Implementing Your Marketing Plan** ■ CHAPTER 10 Ask and Listen

Incorporating Your Plan into Your Business

A lot of business folks are great at planning. They can draw up wonderful schemes that look like sure-fire winners on paper. But a marketing plan that never goes beyond the plan is like an operatic singer with laryngitis—just a lot of unrealized potential.

It should go without saying that unless you implement your marketing plan, you have wasted the time and money that you invested to create it. But we will say it anyway: do not waste all that valuable research, analysis, and planning. Your marketing department should wear out the pages of your marketing plan by referring to it frequently. In fact, it would be ideal if your marketers refer back to your marketing plan so often that eventually they no longer need to look at it because they have memorized it.

Low-cost marketers make full use of valuable resources, and a well-conceived, thorough marketing plan is as valuable a resource as you can provide them. See that they use it by implementing it.

Integrate Marketing and Business Plans

Your marketing plan does not exist in a vacuum. It is but one of the vital organs that keep your business plan alive. When your marketing plan is humming along as it should, your business plan stands a much better chance of humming along as it should. So take care to integrate your marketing and business plans. Strive to hum in sync, as it were.

To be in sync means to integrate your marketing plan by making its visions and goals coincide with the business plan's visions and goals. (Lest we assume too much, you do have a business plan, don't you?) Much of your business plan—the financial statements, credit histories, balance sheets—is intended to satisfy the questions that will be raised by creditors, lenders, or potential investors.

Credible Proof

Likewise, your marketing plan serves as credible proof that you can deliver on your promise. Your marketing plan should show potential financial backers that you have some logical basis for believing you are likely to achieve the profit that you project. The clarity and reasonableness of your marketing plan serves to persuade investors or venture capitalists that it is prudent for them to believe you can reach and motivate the people to whom you want to sell, that those people in fact exist, and that you will generate sufficient profit from that target market in order to repay investments or loans.

Lenders and investors also evaluate your company's long-term viability based partly on your marketing plan's projections, and on the basis on which the projections are made in order to gauge how reliable your estimates are of increased market share over time.

Investors and lenders watch for red flags such as a lack of an established (or an unlikely-to-be-established) proprietary marketing position. This is rooted directly in your competitive advantage, and the Unique Selling Proposition that you have defined for your business. If you cannot demonstrate why anyone should expect buyers to buy from you rather than from competitors, it is going to be difficult to negotiate favorable loans or to obtain substantive investments. After all, why would anyone invest in or lend money to an enterprise that merely hopes to attract customers?

Update, Update, Update

You also should continually update and sharpen the focus of your business plan as you do your marketing plan. If through marketing analysis you have discovered a new niche for your product, not only must you revise your marketing plan to reflect the change, but you must also make corresponding changes in your overall business plan. The same thing applies if you have responded to market conditions by altering your existing product or service. Make sure to reflect any changes that originate in your marketing department in the appropriate sections of your business plan. And do so in a timely fashion.

A Working Document

Make your marketing plan a working document, not just a reference book. Each of your marketers or you, if you alone are responsible for your marketing, should have a loose-leaf edition of the plan on the desk within arm's reach. No campaigns should be launched without first referring to the "book." No evaluation of a campaign should be complete until it is checked against the "book" to see if new information has been gleaned, or old assumptions disproved. The "book" is loose-leaf for a reason. Every time new data, new findings, or new insights are obtained, the appropriate page or pages should be revised and inserted to replace the old version. Make your marketing plan live and breathe and you will always be up to date on who your customers are and the best ways to market to them.

Eagle-eyed potential creditors and investors are on the lookout for inconsistencies between what you plan to do in marketing your business and what you plan to do in running your business. The two should work in lockstep with no inconsistencies. Logic should tell you that if outside financial backers need to know that your marketing plan and business plan are consistent, you should too. In fact, internal consistency should be even more important to you than to them. After all, it is your business.

Of course, your business plan does not exist solely for the purpose of raising investor funds for start-up or expansion, or for persuading banks to loan you money. It also is the blueprint of your business, providing you the tools for running and analyzing it. So even if you have no need for outside investors, and even if you never need to knock on a bank's door to borrow money, it is still vitally important that your business plan and marketing plan be in synch.

Market to Targeted Segments

In implementing your marketing plan, be sure to market appropriately to targeted segments of your market. It makes little sense to go to the trouble of segmenting your customers in your marketing plan if you fall back on the shotgun approach when you implement it and end up treating everyone the same. For example, if you sell summer sandals and hiking boots and have determined through market research or testing that the sandal buyers respond to low-price incentives while the hiking boot buyers respond to assurances of rugged quality, you may be tempted to include both offers in a postcard mailer to be sent to repeat customers.

The problem with such a mailer is that it carries a divided message, one stressing low price and the other promising long-wearing quality. If neither market segment is interested in the hot-button issue of the other, you probably are wasting valuable space on your limited-size postcard by including messages that the recipients find to be irrelevant.

Worse yet, every valuable square inch of that small postcard that carries the wrong message for a reader is a square inch that cannot carry the proper message. By combining these disparate messages in the same marketing vehicle, you have diluted the effect for both segments of your market by sacrificing some of the benefits of low cost in order to tout quality, and vice versa.

Do not muddle the message. Say one thing to one market segment and say it as powerfully as you can, which means do not dilute the message with what the recipient will regard as ancillary, off-point trivia.

At first blush, it may seem more costly to have two marketing campaigns running simultaneously when one campaign clearly costs less to set up and to implement. But if you have identified two different segments of your market and learned that each responds differently, and that each responds to different appeals, it actually is a low-cost approach to appeal to them separately, even though it requires two marketing campaigns instead of one.

Conduct Market Audits

If you have done adequate research and accurately identified the two market segments, two distinct marketing campaigns should be more profitable on a cost-to-profit basis individually and combined than one vague campaign that appeals to only one segment, or that is so watered down it does not appeal much to either.

Implementing your marketing plan also means keeping a close eye on it. Sure, it is great to be confident that all your hard work, research, analysis, and creative implementation is well-founded, but you still need to make it accountable. To do that, you should conduct regular market audits. That is, you should track and evaluate your marketing efforts. As we discussed in Chapter 4, it is imperative to know whether what you have set in motion actually works. To answer that question requires following up, testing, and measuring.

> Implementing your marketing plan also means keeping a close eye on it.

Resist Temptation

Once again, for the start-up and small business operator the temptation is to do too little rather than too much. It is time-consuming to be constantly evaluating the marketing tactics and techniques that you have implemented, and time is money. But one way to remind your marketers (and yourself) that it pays to build a market audit into your marketing campaigns is to calculate the total savings (or profits) that result from the effort.

When measuring the effectiveness of two appeals, compare the results as you normally would. When your test period has elapsed and Plan B clearly outperforms Plan A, switch over to Plan B entirely. The test period may have shown Plan B to generate 30 percent greater profit than Plan A, and perhaps $7,000 more in net revenue. But the real difference is what Plan B will generate over the lifetime of the campaign, not just for the test period.

If the test period was one month and the balance of the campaign (after switching over entirely to Plan B) lasts nine more months, the actual increase in profits is going to be more like $70,000 (ten months times $7,000 a month). Auditing your ongoing marketing campaigns takes on even more significance when the campaign's lifetime difference is calculated to determine its value, rather than merely the difference during the test period.

For motivation, these extrapolated figures are even more powerful than the shorter-term test comparisons. What marketer does not want to feel $70,000 smarter instead of $7,000 smarter? For that matter, what business owner doesn't? The lesson is to make the measurement of a campaign's effectiveness integral to the campaign itself. In that way, you can give your marketers incentive to track and measure when implementing your marketing plan, and tracking and measuring will become second nature to your marketing efforts.

Implement Continuously

Regard the implementation of your marketing plan as an ongoing process, not the end of the process. As we have seen, you should always be willing to respond to changes in your market, changes in demand, changes in response. The implementation of your marketing plan is a dynamic process. You prod the market and it responds, then you respond to it and the cycle continues. With each interaction you learn more about how to reach and how to motivate your target market.

In this same dynamic ebb and flow there exists another enormous opportunity. Take advantage of the opportunity by testing new products or new services before you decide whether to launch them.

Evaluate New Products and Services

Your marketing plan not only is the means for implementing marketing campaigns that you have conceived, but it also provides this type of opportunity for you to gather fresh new marketing research while simultaneously conducting a campaign. The implementation of your marketing plan also is a chance to evaluate new products and new services, rather than launching them on a hope and a prayer, or initiating a more costly, stand-alone market research survey.

> The implementation of your marketing plan also is a chance to evaluate new products and new services.

Get Feedback

Take the case of Widget Secretarial Service, which provides typing and proofreading on an outsource basis for other small business clients. Every month Widget sends invoices to these regular clients, along with an evaluation form asking for a critique of its services. In this way Widget's owner gets meaningful feedback on the areas in which her service is pleasing or displeasing her clients.

Combining the evaluation form with the invoice increases the chances that it will be noticed, as opposed to mailing it separately when the recipient would have no compelling reason to open the envelope, let alone fill out the form. And because the evaluation form shows up at the same time as the invoice, Widget Secretarial Service can be reasonably assured of learning about bona fide complaints or compliments because her clients are more likely to be candid since they also are simultaneously being asked to make their monthly payments. If they have a complaint, they are more likely to recall it when writing a check.

Add Even Greater Value

This low-cost, low-profile marketing campaign can help Widget Secretarial Service fine-tune its services and keep its customers happy by correcting problems as soon as they are noticed, rather than discovering them only after they blow up following months of neglect.

But Widget Secretarial Service can add even greater value to this already effective marketing campaign by simultaneously testing new products or

The "Dead and Gone"

Your marketing plan is a compendium of what works. It should be kept in a loose-leaf notebook because what works today may not work tomorrow, or to-morrow may reveal something better. When you substitute a new, improved tactic, tool, data, goal, or timetable, don't just toss the old page into the trash. Keep a loose-leaf folder of "dead and gone" marketing plan elements so any bright new ideas can be checked against the graveyard of what once was con-ventional wisdom but has since been replaced. This safeguard only works, of course, if your marketing people check the "dead and gone" folder prior to im-plementing new ideas.

new services. If Widget management is contemplating adding a third service to its existing typing and proofreading services, such as typing transcripts from recorded dictation, the evaluation form can be modified to include questions to gauge potential demand. Widget's clients can be asked if they are interested in having transcripts typed from their dictated tape recordings, and if so, how much they would be willing to pay for such a service.

The piggybacking of this market research survey for a new service onto an already established successful customer satisfaction questionnaire has at least two low-cost benefits. First, it is likely to be noticed because it is accompanying an invoice and an existing marketing piece that already have proven to get recipients' attention. Second, the new service survey is likely to elicit honest answers for the same reason the original questionnaire does—because it arrives with an invoice. Anyone asked to write a check to pay a bill can be expected to be more cognizant of cost-benefit relation-ships of the proposed service.

Update and Refine Continuously

Finally, implementing your marketing plan also requires continuously updating and refining the plan. To ensure this, build in a system to make this automatic, the same way you ensure that every campaign is tracked and measured. Such a system can be as elementary as a form. Your form may provide all the specifics of the campaign, such as media, duration, cost, target market, etc., and a place at the end of the form for evaluation, such as measurements of response, profit, cost, etc.

Add to your form an area to be filled in after the campaign is concluded. Ask questions such as:

"Did the campaign identify a new market segment?"

"Did the campaign reveal new psychographic information about the target market, and if so, what?"

"If a test was involved, which options fared best and which should be downplayed in the future?"

The types of questions that are asked will vary according to your marketing campaign. In some cases all you may need to know is whether the campaign was profitable or not.

But generally it will behoove you to evaluate the outcome more closely in order to fine-tune that all-valuable road map known as your marketing plan so the same mistakes are not repeated and so your marketing decisions can be based on the most current assessment of your target market and what those customers want from you.

➤ **Chapter 10**

Ask and Listen

Avoid a Fatal Flaw

One of the surest ways to make your marketing high-cost instead of low-cost is to be shortsighted. Clever wordsmiths and unscrupulous marketers can fashion deviously misleading advertisements, marketing collateral, and other communications. And even though there are state and federal laws that prohibit false advertising, it is still possible to word offers and enticements and promises in such a way as to be technically legal, but deceptively misleading. Other than the obvious reason not to engage in this kind of marketing (it's wrong, which should be reason enough), even from a purely pragmatic point of view it ultimately is costly, not low-cost. The reason? It takes rare fools to continue coming back to do business with a company that has taken advantage of them. So you may fool most people one time, but you are not likely to fool them twice.

Don't Just Talk—Listen

In implementing your marketing plan you applied everything that you had assembled—your research, your analysis, your campaigns. You executed your plan. You took it public. You engaged your market. You were active, rather than passive.

But as you plan for success, the flip side of the coin needs to be considered, too. Certainly you must be proactive. You must reach out and initiate contact and communicate with your target market to make your marketing plan come alive. You cannot very well wait for your target market to come to you.

But when they come, you must listen. Though you may be revved up with enthusiasm, equipped with keen insight and loaded with exciting tactics, you also should be advised that you must guard against being so full of exuberance and hubris that you forget to shut up and listen.

To be successful, you not only must be proactive, but also reactive. Do not just accumulate customers. Take care of them. You not only must talk, but you also must hear. Listen to customers, competitors, noncompetitors, employees, and, yes, even listen to yourself. All these disparate factions have something worthwhile to tell you that you need to know to capitalize on opportunities when they present themselves and to snuff out troublesome flare-ups before they spread into wildfires.

Marketing boiled down to its essence is communication. Like all communication it has a purpose. Marketing's purpose is to persuade. Like all communication, marketing is a two-way street. You talk, and you listen.

Before You Listen, Facilitate

But before you can listen, someone must be willing to talk to you. That is why to facilitate communication, one of the primary goals of your marketing plan must be to take care of your customers. Certainly complaints from unhappy customers pose genuine opportunities for you to turn negative situations into positive experiences, as we saw in Chapter 5. But the more common reaction of an unhappy customer is simply to abandon you without comment. Customers who are disgruntled, angry, or disappointed are much more likely to simply never return, rather than take the time to lodge a complaint. Even if they may have something to say about how you have disappointed them, they probably are not particularly interested in taking the time to explain it to you. Why should they? You have already disappointed them at least once. In a fast-paced world, it is not uncommon to get only one chance.

If you are getting a lot of customer complaints, the chances are that there are many more customers who have similar grievances but who have simply decided it was not worth their time to complain. They just left. It is much more difficult to turn the negative experiences of customers who have quietly abandoned you into a positive outcome than it is with the customers who go to the trouble to tell you their complaints before they leave. At least in those cases you have a basis for dialogue. Those who abandon you without comment take with them their secret reasons.

This (among other even more obvious reasons) is an excellent motivation to take care of your customers. Disappointed customers who feel that you have genuinely been trying to serve them are more likely to lodge a complaint rather than just disappear. That means you still have a chance to win them over, and bring them back into your family of happy repeat customers.

Tell the Truth

So how can you take care of your customers to keep the lines of communication open? There are probably as many ways as there are types of customers. But generally, there are two principles to keep in mind.

Principle #1: Sincerely try hard to give them what they want.
Principle #2: Always apologize when you fall short.

Even in today's cynical age, people respond to sincerity. Perhaps even more so today. When they think you are lying, they do not care how friendly you are while you lie to them. But if they feel that you are telling the truth, it is much easier for them to accept your friendliness as the genuine article. Think of the stereotypical image of the used-car salesman. Being an honest and sincere used-car salesman must be one of life's most frustrating vocations. Those poor folks have such tremendous stumbling blocks to overcome in dealing with their customers. For them it is not enough to simply make a friendly, honest effort to please a customer. Many of their customers automatically assume that used-car salesmen are lying and therefore that any friendliness is an act and any sincerity a ruse.

Unless your product or service suffers from a similar stereotypical prejudice, you have a great advantage over used-car salesmen. Most people respond warmly to sincerity. Most people—well, many people, anyway— are willing to give you the benefit of the doubt and believe that you are being honest with them. That is, until they catch you being dishonest.

Clearly then, to reiterate, when taking care of your customers, the first ground rules are to be honest and sincere.

For a marketer, being honest and sincere can take many forms. It certainly means not misleading customers with bait-and-switch type ads, and not deceiving them with vague promises that you legalistically weasel out of later. Remember the importance of repeat customers and how low-cost it is to market to them? What do you think the odds are of winning repeat customers when they discover that the offer they thought they were responding

Old Standbys Work

Everyone knows about the "suggestion box." It is one of the oldest and most common means of "listening" to customers and employees. In this fast-paced Internet age, it is tempting to look for new, cutting-edge means of accomplishing the same old tasks. But the "suggestion box" has worked for decades for good reasons. It's easy to use, requires no instructions, allows for anonymity, and results in spontaneous as well as thoughtful responses. And it is delightfully low-cost. If you want to hear your customers and employees, invest in a "suggestion box."

to turns out not to be what it was cracked up to be? Even if they are pressured or conned into buying the first time, do you really expect them to return? And do you think customers are very likely to come back a second time when you nit-pick, such as denying them a discount because their coupon expired yesterday? Reasonability and flexibility are traits that buy a lot more good will—and consequently win repeat customers—certainly more so than does alienating customers by holding hard and fast to such technicalities.

Ask and Listen to Customers

Taking care of customers really means treating them the way you would like to be treated, with consideration, flexibility, understanding, and—above all—sincerity and honesty. Have you noticed something about all these traits? Hardly a one of them cost you a dime. That is low-cost marketing.

If your customers feel you have been forthright and fair with them, when the inevitable mistakes are made (and we all make them), customers are going to be much easier to placate. Do not hesitate. Do not pass the buck. Accept the blame, apologize (sincerely, of course), and either make right whatever went wrong, or in some other way make amends. Of course, there will be those who take advantage of you like the woman who seems to always buy a dress before the weekend, then returns it Monday after having worn it to Saturday night's gala. But nothing prevents you from weeding out repeat offenders. Just make sure weeding out is the exception, not the rule, in your customer service.

Interestingly, in marketing as in politics, social settings, family relations, and nearly every other walk of life, an apology almost always douses the fires of anger. "I'm sorry," may be the most disarming two words in the English language. Sometimes, "I'm sorry" is all it takes, particularly if the customer believes you are sincere in your apology. Of course, you do not want to be in a position in which you have to frequently say, "I'm sorry." That is a sign you are doing something habitually wrong. But you should not hesitate to apologize when it is warranted.

Now that you have incorporated the low-cost secrets of sincerity and honesty into your friendly marketing demeanor, it is time to examine how to listen to your new friends, a.k.a. your customers. To be a good listener in a noisy world, it helps to be aware of what you are listening for. Your customers for the most part have two things to say to you.

Customers Say Two Things . . .

"I want to complain."
and
"I want (fill in the blank)"

In other words, your customers will either complain, or they will ask for something. Being attentive to their complaints, you can forestall disasters by catching and correcting problems early before they have a chance to snowball to disastrous proportions. By listening closely to what customers ask for, you can pick up early on changing market trends and adjust accordingly, beating your competition to meet emerging new demands.

Learn to listen for these messages. They may not always be delivered clearly or forthrightly. They may even be hidden. For example, the Widget Bookstore customer who stands at the counter and requests a dozen copies of the latest bestseller, *How to Milk a Cow and other Handy Farm Hints*, appears to be disappointed when he learns that the $20 book will cost him $240 if he buys twelve of them. His frown and his decision not to buy any books are two indications that he in essence has told the clerk, without actually mouthing the words, "I have a complaint" and "I wanted a discount."

If your counter clerk is marketing savvy, he will have done at least two things in response. He will have genuinely apologized to the customer for not being able to make the sale, and he will have engaged the customer in a conversation that would have ultimately come around to the question, "How much of a discount would you require to purchase twenty books?"

It does not cost anything to engage in that conversation. Yet too many bookstore clerks never get that far. They simply shrug at the no sale and go on to the next customer.

Do Not Wait—Solicit

The bookstore clerk is but one manifestation of how to listen to customers. The same result can be achieved by soliciting what the customer has to say. It may not be practical to orally ask every book buyer whether he or she would be interested in discounts for multiple copies. It might clog up the checkout line. But the question can be asked on a perforated questionnaire, half of which doubles as a promotional bookmarker (also carrying the bookstore name and location), and half with multiple choice answers on how much of a discount buyers would want in order to make multiple book purchases.

The customer can separate the questionnaire from the bookmarker, fill it in, drop it in the suggestion box near the exit or near the checkout counter, and stick the bookmarker in the purchased book. This bit of market research to determine whether your clientele at the Widget Bookstore is interested in discounted bulk purchases is merely another form of "listening" to your customers.

Another tactic for listening to what bookstore customers have to say is to post such a survey on a podium at the entrance to the checkout line. Not only is this an effective way to solicit customer opinions on a variety of subjects, but it can make the wait in line less tedious and even more meaningful for the customer. Of course, the technique can be used to ask any questions, such as, "Was there a book you could not find on our shelves today?" or simply, "Tell us how we can serve you better."

Ask and Listen to Competitors and Noncompetitors

Customers are not the only folks you should be listening to. Listen to competitors and noncompetitors, who each have unique perspectives on your business, one of them more disinterested and the other very interested.

Take, for example, competitors. There are a lot of reasons that your competitors are not interested in talking to you, but if you listen intently, you can hear them anyway. How? Try getting on their mailing lists. Visit their stores. Buy samples of their products. Talk to their customers. Read their ads. Nearly everything they do to market to their customers should be accessible to you. What you want to know is how they position themselves. What is their Unique Selling Proposition? How do they talk to their customers? "Listening" in such a way is not no-cost, but it is relatively low-cost. And after factoring in the cost-savings, or profit-generating, benefits of what

> Listen to competitors and noncompetitors, who each have unique perspectives on your business.

you can learn by listening to your competitors, it can make the low-cost expense more than worth its price.

Learn from Competitors

If your competitors are profitable, by "listening" closely to what they do, how they market, what they say, and how and to whom they say it, you can to some degree benefit from their market research. Unless they are a fly-by-the-seat-of-the-pants operation (and those kinds of operations are rarely very successful), they probably have some basis for their marketing campaigns.

Resist the temptation to draw sweeping conclusions from what you "hear." For example, the mere fact that your competitor is offering free home delivery for purchases of $50 or more does not mean that the tactic is effective, or even profitable. But if your competitor continues the free delivery offer for any length of time, it is probably worth testing yourself. Since there are innumerable tactics and techniques that you have to choose from, you can narrow the field considerably by listening to your competitors and "hearing" what works for them.

Joining and Belonging Boost Results

Yet another low-cost method of listening to competitors involves the camaraderie of industry associations, or even more generic business groups like chambers of commerce. Many times associations serve as your eyes and ears on not just a few selected competitors, but on the entire spectrum of businesses that are in your field. More often than not, industry associations provide periodic reports on the state of their industry, often detailing the successes and failures of particular efforts and member companies. In this spirit of sharing, you will find that many of your direct competitors freely offer up information about themselves that they would be reluctant or unwilling to hand out to a casual inquirer. The cost of membership in groups such as these is normally nominal, and often geared to a sliding scale according to members' gross revenue or their number of employees. Knowing what your competitors know and do can help you improve how you compete with them. On a dollar-for-value basis, membership fees are almost always low-cost.

> Associations serve as your eyes and ears on the entire spectrum of businesses that are in your field.

Not only does information flow freely amongst what in most other settings would be cutthroat competitors, but also so do employees and jobs. Contacts made through trade group associations often serve as job applicants' entrees, and can do more to advance careers than the glossiest resumes. And needless to say, new employees who have worked for your competitors are particularly valuable for what they know. (A cautionary word: This is not to recommend that you cross the line that separates hiring competitor's employees who want to improve themselves and enter that more nefarious practice of stealing away employees only for their debriefing value. That kind of pirating is borderline unethical and has been known to start reciprocating hiring wars that do little good for any of the warring parties.)

Although industry and trade organization membership can be beneficial for your company, what is good for you also is good for your competitors. So understand that information about your own company is bound to make its way to competitors. And there is always the possibility that your delegate to the National Widget Producers Association may be enticed into going to work for a competitor. The best way to safeguard against these two downsides to organization membership is to treat your employees well. Happy employees, like happy customers, keep coming back and do not tend to bolt with the appearance of an enticing new alternative.

Ask and Listen to Employees

Speaking of your employees, listen to them, too. There are a couple of reasons that what your employees have to say is worth hearing. First, they are the people who are in direct contact with your customers. The best information about what your customers want certainly comes directly from your customers, but it is somewhat more difficult to obtain, and that means somewhat more costly. The next best information about what your customers want comes secondhand from your customers through your employees. This information should be less costly and much easier to get, since the people who have it are already on your payroll.

Certainly your marketing staff is already charged with gathering and passing on customer data. But many other departments of your company—

everything from sales, customer service, and shipping to delivery drivers—also have ongoing contact with customers. Typically, the job descriptions for these kinds of employees do not include market research. That is the first low-cost marketing improvement you can make with your staff. Change those job descriptions. Make it second nature for your employees to seek and then pass on the insights, comments, complaints, recommendations, and other words of wisdom that emanate from customers with whom they have contact. If you have three marketers on your staff gleaning your customer's inclinations, you may have thirty other employees who each in his or her way come into contact with customers.

Formalize the flow of customer information through your many employee conduits. Incorporate into all employees' routine tasks the requirement that they ask standard questions of customers when they make contact. It costs nothing for a delivery person to hand a box of widgets to a customer and then ask, "Did you receive your package within the time you expected to receive it?" There is no added cost for a sales clerk to ask a customer, "You bought our blue widgets, would you be interested in red widgets if we stocked them?" These multiple opportunities to learn about your customers provide countless opportunities—low-cost opportunities to be sure—to accumulate valuable market research data that can help you keep on top of changes in demand and keep tabs on new trouble areas within your operation.

> Formalize the flow of customer information through your many employee conduits.

Ask and Listen to Yourself

Finally, after listening to customers, competitors, noncompetitors, and your own employees, do not forget to listen to yourself. No, this is not some exotic form of Zen navel gazing. To listen to yourself means simply to take the time to organize your own observations based on your own experiences and factor them in with all the others gathered inside and outside your organization. As a marketer or as a small business entrepreneur you should not give short shrift to your own perspective. Every manager, whether in marketing or at the pinnacle of the corporate ladder, knows the value of delegating and of relying on capable people to gather information, analyze data, and propose action. But do not forget that there is a reason you are in charge. You have a unique perspective and perhaps even intuitive perceptions, and you deserve to rely on them—not to the exclusion of everyone else's information, but in conjunction with theirs.

To get in the habit of "listening" to yourself, make it a formal practice. Monthly, quarterly, or however frequently it is practical, sit down with a copy of the latest edition of your marketing plan and go item by item, making notations based on what you have observed, or on what has occurred to you since you last reviewed the plan. Better yet, keep an ongoing journal and compare its entries to the marketing plan to see if what you have noted might call for revising or fine-tuning the plan. Also, evaluate what you have noted in relation to how it compares to what your company has gleaned from listening to customers, competitors, noncompetitors, and employees.

The bottom line is that by asking and listening—including asking and listening to yourself—you can sharpen your perception of how to better market to a dynamically changing marketplace. To do less is to risk singing the praises of ice cubes to Eskimos.

▶ **Chapter 11**

Soft Stuff: People-Oriented Marketing

It's Your Baby

One of the most rewarding things about being an entrepreneur and a small business owner is how you personally identify with your company, the excitement of its promising beginning and the thrill of its successful growth. It is your baby. For women, it must be very much like giving birth and raising a child, with less kissing and hugging. For men, it must be like raising a child, and probably the closest that they can come to giving birth.

Sadly, entrepreneurial types too often insist on treating their babies like distant relatives or even like utter strangers, less warm and cuddly, more officious and overformal. They insist on treating their small businesses like multinational corporations, stuffy and stilted, rather than like the personal and friendly creatures that they have nursed from infancy. In doing so, they waste away one of their best low-cost marketing advantages.

As we noted in Chapter 2, you should always keep in mind that you cannot effectively claim to be something that you are not. Phonies do not fool many people for very long.

> Take advantage of the warm and fuzzy personality of your small business.

The other side of the same coin is that being true to your nature almost always pays off in profits. Take advantage of the warm and fuzzy personality of your small business. It has an endearing appeal that multinational corporations would die to acquire, if they only could, and in fact an appeal that they spend millions of dollars feigning. So instead of putting on airs and pretending to be what you are not, put on a smile and get down-home friendly, figuratively speaking of course.

Once you have nursed along your baby and ultimately achieve multinational corporate status, then you can have the best of both worlds: big bucks in your vault and homey familiarity in your customers' minds. (Like everyone's good friends, Ben and Jerry.) But all the money in the world cannot buy what you start out with, that friendly demeanor that comes with a new, small-scale entrepreneurial enterprise. Call it the corner store identity, or the "mom and pop" atmosphere.

Call it anything you like, but take advantage of it while you have it. If you are like a lot of those who have gone before you, you may very well wake up someday and wonder what happened to that homey feeling, which regrettably is often shed with success.

The Personal Touch

To begin capitalizing on your company's small, friendly nature, you personally can—and should—develop personal marketing habits, and make sure that you live by them, which also has the pleasant side effect of setting an example for the rest of your staff to follow suit.

"Hello, I Am . . ."

Begin with the most personal of your marketing tools, the "Hello, I am . . ." introductory greeting. The importance of developing a compelling greeting and then using it as a conversation opener cannot be overstated. Why?

First of all, if you do not already, you should consider everyone that you meet to be a potential customer, or at least to be a potential lead to a potential customer. And as your mother always told you, you will not get a second chance to make that all-important first impression. So these very first words out of your mouth when you meet someone new are likely to create an image that will linger perhaps as long as the new acquaintance knows you. Therefore, make your greeting potent. But sincere.

Your "Hello, I am . . ." introduction should incorporate your Unique Selling Proposition, always mindful of your potential customer's underlying question, "What's in it for me?"

Also be mindful, however, that you cannot spout your marketing slogan like a wind-up doll or carnival barker. You do not want to come off like one of those used-car salesmen that rush to the curb to greet prospective buyers, yammering platitudes and compliments they obviously do not mean.

In fact, your greeting might best be broken into two parts. First, introduce yourself generally by name and, if appropriate for the venue, by your company affiliation. Use your first name alone or your first and last name, depending on how informal the setting. Next solicit information about the person you are greeting, but make sure it too is something appropriate to the setting.

For example, at a business function like a chamber of commerce mixer, you might say, "Hi, I don't think we've met. I'm Joe Smith, glad to meet you. Are you in widgets, too?" Your invitation for others to talk about themselves serves two purposes.

First, it permits you to judge whether they may be interested in what you do and if there are appropriate avenues for you to turn the conversation to how you can serve the person to whom you are speaking. If the response is sketchy, you may want to elicit more information. Your interest in others should put your new acquaintances at ease, perhaps even flatter them.

Express a Sincere Interest

As any good interviewer can attest, people find other people interesting when the other people are genuinely interested in them. The high-pressure used-car salesman gets the inverse response. People detest the guy because they intuit immediately that he is not interested in them. He is clearly only interested in himself and in closing his sale.

Once you have learned about your new acquaintances it should be clear whether they are potential customers or perhaps potential leads to customers. If so, then you can segue into your refined personal greeting that incorporates your USP-laden introduction, in a friendly, nonthreatening manner, and if called for, ever so subtly stated.

Of course, how well you refine the personal greeting part of this conversation is the payoff. You may choose to be clever or flippant, such as the owner of a housecleaning service who, sensing a potential customer, offers, "We love it when you talk dirty to us. We clean houses."

Or you may find that flippancy is inappropriate, like the sales trainer who senses a potential customer and responds, "Oh, you are in sales? I know a lot of successful salespeople. My company trains them. In fact, our trainees improve their sales an average of 50 percent in the first year."

The Thirty-Second Elevator Speech

Your "Hello, I am . . ." introduction is the first cousin to another similar and equally low-cost, people-oriented marketing tactic: the thirty-second elevator speech.

The principle difference between the two is that the first is used to initiate a longer conversation while simultaneously communicating what you can do to benefit a new acquaintance. But the thirty-second elevator speech is a truncated, often higher energy version of this same message. It is so named because it is the type of information that you might have occasion to deliver when meeting someone while sharing an elevator between the fifth floor and the lobby.

The keys to the thirty-second elevator speech are that it must be memorable, it must be short, and it must summarize how you benefit your customers. Another difference between the thirty-second elevator speech and the more laid-back "Hello, I am . . ." introduction is that the latter has the luxury of first learning something about the person to whom you are speaking before you reveal much about yourself. When delivering your thirty-second elevator speech you will probably be lucky to get the other person's name before offering your own information.

Think of the "Hello, I am . . ." introduction as the trifold brochure of oral marketing, and your thirty-second elevator speech as a business card approach. (By the way, in practice it is a good idea to punctuate both of these conversations by offering your business card before you leave.)

Nevertheless, to take advantage when opportunities present themselves, you want to leave your oral business card lingering in the mind of the other person before the elevator arrives at the lobby. Clearly, a thirty-second elevator speech need not be delivered only in elevators. It works anywhere and anytime that you have only a few moments to make an impression.

The idea behind it, and for that matter behind the "Hello, I am . . ." introductions, is simply to condense your Unique Selling Proposition into an oral presentation that can be delivered casually, memorably, and in a nonthreatening manner, tailored to the setting.

You will be hard-pressed to spend any money developing either of these oral marketing tactics, since all they require is for you to practice talking. And that is about as low-cost as you can get. But if two oral marketing tactics for zero dollars is good, three is better.

> The thirty-second elevator speech must be memorable, it must be short, and it must summarize how you benefit your customers.

Develop a Friendly Persona

The third no-cost spoken marketing tactic is to develop a friendly telephone and face-to-face persona, or put another way, the manner in which you are perceived on the phone and across the counter.

This tactic is different from your "Hello, I am . . ." introduction and your thirty-second elevator speech in that it is more about demeanor than about content. Is it not odd that a company that will hire only golden-throated, smiley-faced receptionists and telephone answerers occasionally has grumps and grouches in the upper echelons of management?

If it is important to have gracious and pleasant greeters at the entry points for customers, is it not even more important to have the same customer-friendly attitude at the close-the-sale stage of the process?

None of these tactics in and of themselves is likely to turn a losing proposition into a profitable enterprise. But they all have a cumulative effect. And the effect is very real on your bottom line.

Avoid Customer Rejection Threshold

Presumably, you sell something your target market can benefit from buying. But every obstacle, every negative experience, every patently self-serving, customer-unfriendly barrier that you erect on the route from initial solicitation to closing the sale is an invitation for the customer to say goodbye. Some customers have high thresholds for rude and indifferent behavior.

Some have lower thresholds. But every curt conversation moves any customer closer to his or her threshold. Every affront is an invitation for the customer to abandon you for friendlier pastures. Every indifferent attitude adds another weight to the customer's load.

Everyone Should Adopt the Attitude

Anyone in your chain of customer serving personnel who lacks a friendly, helpful attitude moves your customers that much closer to their respective tolerance threshold and the exit door. The damage done by the rude telephone demeanor of anyone in the chain of employees may be the last straw, no matter how friendly and helpful everyone else has been.

Everyone you employ who deals directly with your customers—on the phone or in person—represents an opportunity to reinforce the image you have worked so hard to cultivate in your customers' minds, and an equal opportunity to sabotage the entire effort. Unfortunately, it is easier to do damage to your marketing image than to do something positive to advance it.

The good news is that by consciously developing a pleasant, customer-first telephone and face-to-face persona, you can avert the damage and reinforce the positive image.

So far in this chapter you have learned how to equip yourself, your upper management, and everyone else in your organization with lower than low-cost effective marketing skills simply by refining the way you relate to customers with spoken words. Next we will discuss two areas in which those oral skills can be used effectively in the outside world: networking and joining trade, association, and civic groups.

People Do Business with People They Like

One of the oldest adages in business is that people do business with people they know. All else being equal, people also tend to do more business with people they like. Clearly then, your job as the primary marketer in your organization is to get your people known. And liked.

Entire tomes have been penned on the mystical skills and sophisticated tactics required for networking. Let us dispense with the myths. Networking is not as mysterious a skill or as haughty a tactic as some make it out to be. Normal people—even abnormal people—network just fine every day. Networking might be likened to becoming someone's friend.

If you do not have any friends, you may not be a great networker, but then again, you may anyway. A lot of painfully shy people have found that personal networking is a great compensation for their shyness. In fact, networking can give introverts the legitimate excuse they need to force themselves to engage others.

Make Your Policies Known

The best way to avoid complaints is to clearly communicate upfront what the customer can expect, and then deliver it. But even the best of systems are imperfect. That is why it is vital that you establish complaint, refund, and guarantee policies that clearly spell out what your customers can expect when things go wrong. But do not stop there. These clearly spelled-out policies mean little if the customer is unaware of them beforehand. Take steps to promote awareness of your complaint, refund, and guarantee policies just as you would sale information, your hours of operation, or any other benefits. Then when something goes awry, the customer will know what to expect, and you have changed the topic from "what went wrong" to "how it can be fixed." In this way, your mistakes will rightly appear to be opportunities for pleasing customers, rather than displeasing them.

Get Listed in Directories

Nearly every industry has business directories that operate much like the traditional Yellow Pages. Your company can have a free listing, or pay for a larger display ad listing. Take advantage of every free avenue for promotion available. Get listed in every business directory that is remotely related to your market niche. Hold off buying larger display ads the first year while you gauge the responses generated from your free listings. After a year of asking customers whether they found your business in a particular directory, you will have a good idea of which directories are most effective. Then, if your advertising budget allows for it, place a display ad in the better drawing directories.

Your Chance to Be Popular

Remember back when you were in high school there was always that guy or girl who seemed to know everyone. And know them by name. They were hardly ever seen alone, these types; always in a crowd, always the center of attention. These were the popular kids. Everyone knew them. They knew everyone.

Now that you are all grown up, it is your chance to be popular. But because you are not in high school any longer, you do not have to worry about whether you are "cool" enough to pull it off. Grownups in business look for other characteristics. More on that in a bit.

First, here is another secret: Networking is a three-step process. Step one, go to the places where people you need to know hang out. Step two, employ those oral skills we discussed above. Step three, begin the process all over again, which is to say, be persistent.

At formal networking functions like those sponsored by "leads groups," you not only do not have to be shy about giving your "Hi, I am . . ." introduction or your thirty-second elevator speech, you are expected to give it. These lead groups, like Le Tip International, a 450-chapter, 9,000-member organization based in San Diego, California, exist expressly for their members to network among themselves, and to send one another business referrals. But to be an effective member, you need to hone your "Hi I am . . ." introduction, your thirty-second elevator speech, and your telephone or in-person persona.

Less formal networking functions, those ostensibly for industry education, research, buying discounts, or political lobbying, also provide enormous opportunities for networking, particularly for entrepreneurs who sell business-to-business and whose potential customer base is well represented within the group.

Useful Groups

Other de facto networking organizations provide vertical as well as horizontal contacts. These groups, like the local chamber of commerce or service club, enable eyeball-to-eyeball contact with diverse populations that may involve the entire spectrum of business community, from manufacturers, distributors, wholesalers and retailers to service providers and consumers.

You personally should search out the networking opportunities most appropriate for your needs, join and attend regularly. And use those low-cost oral marketing tactics you have practiced in front of the mirror.

Your Company Can . . .

Having developed an infectious knack for being a confident oral representative of your company, now spread it like a virus throughout your organization.

Leading by example is the most sincere form of instruction, of course. But you have other things on your plate than personally instructing each employee in the skills of oral presentations and the knack of networking.

One way to underscore the importance of these low-cost skills is to incorporate descriptions of what is expected of employees in their job descriptions, and in their annual job performance evaluations. It is one thing to tell your shipping clerk and salesman they should make customers feel welcome and important, it is quite another thing to evaluate their pay raises based in part on how well they have done that.

One of the best reminders for employees is that the customers (and potential customers) they come in contact with are people, not numbers, and should be accorded the dignity and respect due people, not the indifference and disrespect of inanimate targets on a check list.

A Critical Difference

The difference between being served by an unsmiling clerk who avoided eye contact, who never uttered a "thank you" or a "please," and being served by a cheerful clerk who doted on you courteously is not lost on anyone—except apparently the unsmiling, impolite clerks of the world. The difference should not be lost on your staff either.

Go on the Air

After learning how to be comfortable in talking the talk, do not be shy. Talk to mass audiences. Nearly every metropolitan area is home to scores of radio and television talk shows. These programs generally are starved for guests and for material. If your company has developed something new, finds itself in the news, or has experts in newsworthy areas, you probably can arrange you or someone from your company to be interviewed on the air. Make sure you tape the appearance, or better yet, get a copy of the master recording from the station. Audiocassettes or videotapes of your appearance make effective and impressive handouts. Mail them to select customers or clients with an attached note, such as, "I thought you might be interested in our recent appearance on XYZ network."

Again, this kind of adjustment in attitude costs little, if anything, to implement. And the fruit of its labor is plentiful, not the least of which is a perceptible improvement in employee morale. Speaking of employee morale, there is another low-cost marketing tactic that works much better when nudged along by employees who are happy in their work. It is word-of-mouth marketing.

When most people think of word-of-mouth marketing they naturally think of customers talking to potential customers about businesses that served them well. But to think only of customers is to ignore the most pivotal people in the equation: your employees. After all, an admirable word-of-mouth reputation may be spread by happy customers, but they were created by, you guessed it, your employees.

Moreover, there is no need to sit back and hope that customers choose to speak well of you. Encourage them to, first by exceeding their expectations and then by coming right out and asking them to.

Spread the Word

Make it a policy for your employees to request that their happy customers mention how happy they are to their friends and associates. Some are likely to spread the word without being encouraged to, but many will simply file away their happy experience in their personal memory bank and never pass it on. But when these same happy customers are expressly asked, "If you are happy with your new widgets, please tell a friend," they almost inevitably are pleased to do so. It is a commendable trait of human nature that people are almost always willing to perform a favor for people that have pleased them—particularly if it does not cost them any money to do it.

Once your staff has become accustomed to representing themselves and your company orally and to genuinely reflecting a customer-first attitude, it is time to dispatch them

The Customer as Evangelist

If your business has been successful it has created dozens, hundreds, thousands of pleased-as-punch customers. And those happy customers each know dozens, hundreds, or thousands of other people—in other words, potential customers. This means you already have an army of evangelists just waiting to spread the word on your behalf. Solicit from these happy customers testimonials and endorsements, and use their own words of praise and their own smiling faces in all your marketing collateral. Nothing sells like a happy customer. People want to know that other people like themselves were pleased with a product or service before risking their own money.

en masse to venues where they can infect others with their contagious glee. Trade shows, conventions, and conferences are all high-profile, mass-exposure events in which your company has an opportunity to put its best foot forward and to market at low-cost to select, targeted audiences.

Attendance at these types of events is almost always low-cost, literally the price of admission and often even free. Participation and exhibiting in these settings can be more costly, although they still represent a good return on the investment if chosen wisely.

The Common Factor: People

The thing that all these venues have in common is that they are people-oriented, low-cost marketing opportunities. There are few occasions that provide as many face-to-face opportunities, and if you are discerning in which events your people attend, they can be wonderful occasions for making effective use of those low-cost oral and customer-friendly people skills you have encouraged your staff to develop.

The great thing about people-oriented marketing is that it combines the better of two worlds: extremely low-cost and highly effective personal contacts. Equip yourself and your staff to use it effectively, then use it as often as you can.

> **Chapter 12**

Hard Stuff: Marketing Collateral

The Nuts and Bolts of Marketing

Marketing collateral might be described as the nuts and bolts of marketing. In a strict sense it is the supporting material that corroborates your marketing message. But in a very real sense it is the everyday stuff probably most commonly associated with marketing in the public's mind. It is foundational, and it is almost always appropriate in some fashion for nearly every type of business. It is widespread and widely used for good reasons: It is relatively inexpensive and proven to be effective.

From Business Cards to Direct Mail

For almost every business—large or small, new or established—the question is not so much whether to have marketing collateral as it is a question of which types to have and how much of it.

Some of this material—such as business cards, brochures, and ad specialties—is so commonplace it has become virtually synonymous with the term "marketing collateral." Yet oddly enough, despite the ubiquitous image in most people's minds, these and other "hard" examples of marketing collateral are often neglected. And when they are neglected, it is almost always to a business's detriment. Moreover, hard marketing collateral is rarely neglected after thinking through the decision, but usually out of a benign forgetfulness. Some entrepreneurs just do not bother to give a passing thought to the countless types of hard marketing collateral that may be appropriate for their business.

Many of these marketing solutions come in the form of "leave-behinds"; that is, they are items that are intended to be left behind after a face-to-face encounter with a customer, client, or prospect. Their purposes are varied, but in general all this type of collateral is intended to be an ongoing reminder of that valuable marketing message you already have delivered orally.

You remember that message, the one in which you explained how you can benefit your prospect or customer? These reminders, when properly delivered and appropriately configured, can linger in the mind long after you are out of sight. Nevertheless, encounters with customers and prospects too often leave behind no "leave-behinds," which gives rise to another truism: "Out of sight, out of mind."

Point-of-Purchase Collateral

Other forms of marketing collateral are meant to be distributed or exhibited at a point of purchase or at an event, such as an open house or a convention. Marketing collateral also can be more than merely informational, it also can strive to be useful, such as logo-emblazoned plastic bags distributed at expositions, or mouse pads with company contact information printed on them. Such useful collateral can have prolonged life, meaning the reminder of your company's benefit lives longer too.

The variety of these types of hard marketing collateral is wide and deep. It can be designed to function as a simple reminder, like a real estate agent's photo on a leave-behind notepad, or as a more direct sales tool to bring a buyer closer to the sale decision, such as a presentation packet filled with brochures, white papers, specification sheets, product and company information, and, of course, an order form. It can be as innocuous as a ballpoint pen with your company's name and Web site engraved on it, or as elaborate as a trade show booth complete with multimedia displays, audiovisual demonstrations, and mounds of paper handouts.

As always, your guiding light in employing any of these solutions should be its appropriateness for your particular target market, and the precise message that you need to deliver. If your business is personal credit counseling, you will have little need for the trade show extravaganza, and even if you had a venue in which to use it, it probably is unreasonable to expect people to pull up a chair in public under a sign that asks, "Going bankrupt? Need help?" Similarly, rubber duckies with your company logo embossed on them probably are not the image that you seek to project if your business is heavy construction equipment sales.

> Your guiding light in employing any of these solutions should be its appropriateness and the precise message that you need to deliver.

Business Cards

If there is any marketing device that is universally applicable and utterly inexpensive, it must be the common business card. One good rule to keep in mind in business is never to be caught without your business cards. They

The Uncommon Business Card

Common business cards need not be common. Although you do not want to goop up your business card with a lot of gimmickry, at times the innovative and unusual can make an effective impression at low cost. The flap-over type of business cards in which the flap must be raised to read the information beneath are generally annoying, for example. A creative spin on this type for a minivan sales center might have the image of a rear trunk lid on the flap that when lifted shows the interior of a minivan with name and contact information inside. One caveat: Do not make business cards so expensive to produce that you are reluctant to give them out. You should distribute them as freely as smiles.

are as expected as a handshake and about as frequently used, and thank goodness, they are wonderfully low-cost. These 3½-inch by 2-inch cardboard tokens should convey all the vital and basic information needed to remind the recipients who you are, what you can do for them, and the innumerable ways they may contact you. When you think about it, squeezing all of this data on 7 square inches of real estate is one of the marvels of modern communication.

The Basic Card's Basic Appeal

A lot of attention has been given over recent years to making the old reliable business card more innovative. But resist the temptation to get carried away and too fancy. And do not fret that you did not have a high-priced graphic artist design your card. Many commercial printers are happy to provide a template for your card at no additional cost. Just ask. Keep in mind that the number one purpose of the card is to impart information. Every unnecessary jot and superfluous title, every pretty graphic or elaborate design runs the risk of crowding out the essence of your message: *who* (you are), *what* (you can you do for them), and *how* (to contact you). Some of the dumbest business cards sacrifice this critical message for the sake of looking fancy and innovative.

Commonsense Business Card Guidelines

Use common sense when creating your business cards. If accommodating fancy and innovative designs means that you must squeeze your typeface so small that you need a magnifier to read it, sacrifice fancy and innovative and increase the type size to something more legible. Another thought—make sure not to give short shrift to the all-important "what" factor when designing your card. That, of course, is your slogan, motto, or Unique Selling Proposition that answers the card recipient's number one question, "What is in it for me?" That is the only reason anyone would want your card in the first place, so make sure it is included on your card. A phone number and address are of no use without a reason to call or visit.

Stationery

Think of all stationery as business cards, but on different scales. The same information that appears on your business card should appear on all these individual pieces. The information should be uniform in appearance as well, so that things like type fonts and graphics do not vary from one piece to another.

As with business cards, the purpose of stationery is not merely to give information on who, what, and how, but also to reinforce your message by being familiar and repetitive. If every time a customer receives a letter or a mailer or a note from you it appears under a different logo, or in a differently arranged typeface, it undermines the goal of reinforcing your image. Imprinted stationery from letterhead to oversized envelopes is relatively inexpensive. You must purchase the paper products anyway, and the minimal added cost to pay a commercial printer to run off your logo, address, and so forth is well worth the investment.

Do-It-Yourself Basics

With the advances in computer technology and desktop color printers and increasing computer savvy among users, making your own stationery on the fly is a fairly straightforward and very low-cost alternative to having a commercial printer do them for you, particularly if the amount you need is modest. Many office suite software programs come with easily modifiable "templates" for everything from invoices and business cards to letterhead and shipping labels. When used in combination with today's moderately priced and extremely capable desktop laser printers and preformed paper products, your standard logo and familiar company information can be easily printed on demand.

In the long haul the cost is probably comparable to printing up a large quantity of the collateral commercially. But the do-it-yourself approach builds in a flexibility that may save you money if you decide to revise the logo or change your street address, something that renders useless an inventory of preprinted stationery.

Consistency Is the Key

The principles that apply to your business cards and other company stationery should be extended to all forms of your direct-mail contacts with customers and prospective customers. Indeed, the uniformity of your marketing collateral's look and feel is not only effective in reinforcing your company's image on repeated exposures, but it is definitely a low-cost approach. The same logo, the same letterhead heading, the same motto, expressed in the same fonts, colors, and relative locations mean that the design of each piece of this type of marketing collateral need not reinvent the wheel.

The uniformity of the look should carry over into your advertising, leave-behind collateral, and all other hard-stuff marketing solutions. The low-cost aspect of this approach is that you pay one time for one look and apply it to all your collateral, rather than paying to design each piece separately.

Create a Database for Relationship Marketing

In this era of computer literacy, it is inexcusable for any company not to capitalize on database capabilities for relationship marketing. There is software aplenty to do the job, and much of it requires only rudimentary computer skills. But even if your operation is staffed entirely by computer illiterates, you still should take whatever steps you must to have someone establish and maintain a customer database, even if it means contracting out or taking a computer course at night school. It is far from rocket science. Maintaining and operating a database requires the kind of computer expertise that many youngsters have acquired by the time they graduate from high school. And the return on investment should pay big dividends.

If you already own one of the popular software office suites of programs, you may already own database management software. If not, elementary database programs are available for about the price of a couple of months of lunches at the local diner. So even if you are on an ultra-low, low-cost budget, you can always eat less to database more. The point is, for

> In this era of computer literacy, it is inexcusable for any company not to capitalize on database capabilities for relationship marketing.

the minimal cost of software and a few hours on the keyboard learning curve, you can gain valuable control over the wealth of data that your customers represent.

Use Those Customer Records

Chances are you already keep computerized customer records of some sort. Consider these possible ways for mining, then applying, the data you have collected:

1. If you are a florist, at the time of every sale offer to give male customers advance reminders by mail or by telephone of their wives' or girlfriends' birthdays. Ask your customers if they know what their loved one's favorite flowers are and enter that along with the reminder date in your customer's database entry, and have your software remind you daily whom to call or mail reminders. Some customers may even prefer to preauthorize purchases on a credit card and simply have you remind them that the flowers are ready to pick up or to be delivered. This proactive approach is likely to increase sales many times over, simply because the customer has already agreed that the purchase is necessary, and that he is willing to buy it from you.

2. If your business rents videos, you probably already have a computerized system that correlates your customers' credit card information and address with each rental they make. If you categorize your movie inventory by genre, it is a minor database task to create reports of who rents what type of movie. When movies are added to your inventory, send personalized postcards to customers who have previously rented that type of movie to let them know you have something new in which they may be interested. You can even configure databases to set a threshold number that triggers the reminders when a minimum number of films have been rented in a particular category. The occasional adventure film renter may not be interested in being contacted every time a new adventure film is released in video. But a customer who has rented ten adventure films in six months probably will be.

Follow-Up Calls

A lot of consumers complain that the retailers they buy from are interested only in making an immediate sale, and not in whether the customer ends up happy. An elementary but effective use of your customer database is to follow up sales with computer-scheduled telephone calls or questionnaires after a period of time has elapsed to determine if the customer is pleased with the purchase. Obviously, such follow-ups are not realistic for every sale and every customer. But customers who purchase substantial products or spend significant amounts probably are worth checking back with after a reasonable amount of time has passed. If you sell draperies to homeowners, use your customer database to follow up on customers' satisfaction six months after the purchase. A telephone call or a one-page letter, with no overt solicitation for new business, can do wonders for customer appreciation. Chances are the customer is delighted with the purchase, and very pleased to say so. (In that case, you also might ask these customers if they will allow you to use them in a testimonial.) On the off-chance the customers are less than pleased six months after their purchase, you definitely want to know why and to do what you can to correct that bad image before the sourpusses spread the word to their homeowning, drapery-buying friends.

Packaging: Your Last Chance to Market

One very often-overlooked piece of marketing collateral is the package your product comes in. Although we are admonished not to judge a book by its cover, we all do. At best we are unmoved by unspectacular packaging. At worst, it delivers a dour image right at the time we hope to deliver our greatest benefit. Using packaging to reinforce and deliver your marketing message can turn these zeros and negatives into a big plus.

What Your Packaging Is Saying

Packaging can serve two meaningful marketing ends. One, it is your last chance to market when your product sits on the shelf next to your competitors' products. Not only does your packaging need to grab the buyer's attention, it needs to communicate your Unique Selling Proposition in the strongest terms because that is what those competitors' packages next to it are trying to do as well.

Two, it is a chance to remind the buyer that he has done the right thing by selecting your product, which is precisely what the buyer wants to know when he gets it home and begins to open up the package. This reinforcement can be accomplished by forcefully delivering your Unique Selling Proposition and addressing the customer's question, "What's in it for me?" on the exterior of the package. Use that valuable space to speak to these issues, much the way you would in an advertisement, direct mailer, or face-to-face conversation. Many popular products capitalize in this way by featuring bulleted lists of benefits on their packaging. Yours should too.

It Is What Is on the Outside That Counts

The outside of the packaging that encloses your product is not the time to stop touting its benefits. Indeed, it is a crucial time—whether on the shelf or in the customer's home—to underscore the best reasons that buyers want to justify having spent their money. In practical terms, this adds virtually nothing to your marketing costs because creating and printing the packaging for your product already is in your budget. What it does require, however, is that the package designer must work closely with your marketing department—or with you, if you are the one in charge of implementing your marketing plan. One last point on packaging: Just as a uniform image must be put forth in business cards, stationery, and direct mail, your packaging should appear to be very familiar to those already familiar with your other marketing collateral. A consistent look and feel does much to reinforce brand identity and image.

> Many popular products capitalize in this way by featuring bulleted lists of benefits on their packaging. Yours should too.

Logos

We have discussed "look and feel" in relation to your published and printed collateral, and mentioned in passing graphics and logos. These elements—the graphical as opposed to verbal representations of your company—in the long run probably do as much to identify your company as all the words you will use.

"The Envelope, Please . . ."

If you have talented employees, you may be able to get your logo for the cost of a salary you already are paying. Or even less. To obtain a logo that effectively captures the essence of your marketing message at an extremely low cost, hold a contest. Invite employees, their family members, graphic art students at local colleges, and anyone else with an eye for design to submit entries. Turn the logo creation contest into a marketing vehicle itself. Promote it in mailers, ads, news releases, on your Web site, in short, everywhere. Clearly specify what the winner wins if selected, and that the logo entirely becomes sole property of your company, regardless of whether you end up registering it or not. Hold a gala event inviting finalists and make the presentation to the winner a surprise, à la the Academy Awards show. "The envelope, please . . ."

Obviously, when a longtime Coca-Cola drinker sees the familiar Coke logo, he needs no words to tell him anything about the product. From years of satisfied use, he knows the drink tastes good, is relatively inexpensive, refreshes him on hot days, and is the brand that he prefers for all those and many other reasons. But if every other year Coca-Cola had revised its familiar logo, the happy customer would probably be hard-pressed to quickly identify his favorite drink from a host of imitators and competitors.

The lesson here is that an established "look and feel" reinforces the satisfaction that happy customers come to associate with a product or service. The danger therefore is in fiddling with that look and feel too often at the risk of offsetting all the good marketing created by hundreds of words and scores of exposures to thousands of customers.

Therefore, a logo and other identifiable graphic images are among the most cost-effective uses of your marketing budget. Better yet, they do not cost an arm and a leg—unless you are Coca-Cola and hire top-level design agencies, in which case it can cost you millions. Chances are you can get the same amount of ink on paper for a tiny fraction of what multinational giants pay for their logos.

Free Stuff: Collateral That Gets Attention

While in almost every case your marketing collateral is offered free to customers and prospective customers, the recipients are prone to view it as "sales material," something designed to persuade them to buy.

One category of hard marketing collateral does have intrinsic value, however. This collateral includes free samples, gift certificates, and ad specialties. Just like the collateral lacking intrinsic value, this material also must stress who you are, what you can do for the recipient, and how to contact you, although the message may be more subdued. But the main difference is that this collateral is useful or valuable in itself, not just in its message.

Free Samples

Free samples are a time-tested and proven method of not only introducing customers to what you sell, but also perhaps the best way to demonstrate the value of what you sell, because the prospective customers can experience it firsthand, rather than abstractly through words and images.

Free samples run the gamut. It can be a smaller version of the full-size canned baked beans, or a ride on a river-crossing ferry, or a financial analysis by a certified public accountant. In all cases, however, the idea is to permit prospective customers to actually sample the service or product that you hope to sell them, and to do it at no cost. Many free samples come with enticements to "upgrade" to the full product, such as offering a free one-month trial of a one-year magazine subscription.

Others entice purchases by offering limited time opportunities to buy the full-scale product, such as "If you liked our baked beans, bring the can's label within fourteen days and buy up to two cases for half off." And others offer free samples in the hope of establishing longer-term commitments, such as the CPA who tells a prospect that, "If you found my free financial analysis to be helpful, let's talk about how to reduce your tax liability and increase your savings."

Gift Certificates

Gift certificates are a form of free samples. You can either give them away, or sell them to others to give away. On one level, gift certificates enable your customers to buy gifts for their friends and associates without struggling to come up with something the recipient will like. This appeals to customers' longing for uncomplicated solutions. On another level, gift certificates enable you to reach customers who might otherwise never inquire about your products or services. In effect, the purchasers of the gift certificate are paying you to do your marketing when they give the gift certificate to people who do not normally buy from you.

Ad Specialties: Inane, Innocuous, Mundane, and Practical

Ad specialties differ from free samples in that they usually are not samplings of what you are selling, but they are similar in that they have intrinsic value. There is no shortage of ad specialty providers and their multifaceted offerings, almost all of which can be imprinted with your logo and other pertinent information. They are as limitless as the imagination. They range from the absolutely inane that have only entertainment value, such as an innocuous box that when opened sounds a loud alarm, to the most mundane and practical like a wall calendar or ballpoint pen, and even to those of relatively high dollar value like leather luggage.

The effectiveness of ad specialties hinges on two main factors.

1. They must carry your message to the recipient—the *who, what,* and *how to contact you.* Obviously, the more conspicuous the message, the more likely it is to be noticed, although if it is too large, it may discourage use of the ad specialty item. There is little reason to skimp on the size of your company name and phone number on ballpoint pens, but you probably do not want to emblazon your company logo three feet wide on travel bags. Not everyone likes to lug around de facto billboards for someone else's products.

2. The ad specialty must be appropriately useful. It makes little sense for stockbrokers to pass out garden tools with the brokerage's name and address on the handles. An imprinted fountain pen is probably more appropriate. The stockbroker certainly would rather his prospective clients be reminded of how he can serve them as they are writing checks to pay their bills than when they are planting petunias.

Signs and Placards

Another example of low-cost hard marketing collateral is ever-present signs and placards. This is another area where cost can be minimized by simply creating items in-house, although contracting out does not generally cost a lot either. Signs and placards are easily made even for those without computer skills or graphic arts training. And if you think they are ineffective, think again. The next time you are shopping, try to count how many placards and signs you see. You will run out of patience in short order. They are everywhere in vast numbers. That is because they work. Retail shopping is replete with sign after sign signaling prices, benefits, sizes, and brand names, whatever hot buttons work with their target markets.

Even service providers are aided by signs and placards, which can help tout benefits much the way the more intimate tools like brochures and direct mailings do. Another great benefit of signage of this sort is that customers are permitted to move at their own pace, rather than relying on step-by-step dialogue of a sales rep to nudge them closer to the sale.

Signage serves not only to motivate and inform, but also to direct traffic. It is counterproductive to make customers hot under the collar because they stood in the wrong line simply to ask a question that could have been easily handled if they were first directed to the appropriate department. Part of making it easy for customers to buy from you includes not frustrating them en route. Signs and placards are invaluable marketing tools in that regard. And, of course, extremely low-cost.

The Swipe File

Finally, here is an invaluable tip while loading up your hard marketing collateral arsenal. Steal. (Do not worry. It is perfectly legal and entirely moral.) Actually, the idea is more akin to borrowing, but we do not call it a "borrow file," we call it a "swipe file."

A swipe file is an accumulation of the kinds of hard marketing collateral that have struck your eye or otherwise seemed particularly effective. If you are not collecting examples of your main competitors' collateral, you are making a

Discount Gift Certificates

Here is a low-cost twist to the already low-cost marketing solution provided by gift certificates. Discount them. If you offer gift certificates, a certain percentage of them will never be redeemed. That is money in your pocket without having to deliver a product or service. If typically 10 percent of your gift certificates go unredeemed, try offering a 10 percent discount to purchasers of gift certificates. That is, sell a $10 gift certificate for $9. Since you pocket $1 out of every $10 certificate sale already without making a sale, pass on that largesse to your customers. But do not be shy about it. Advertise and promote the benefit, "Get a $10 gift certificate for only $9!" In this way, the purchasers can spend less and give more to whomever they give the certificates as gifts.

big mistake. Keep a watchful eye out for business cards, letterhead, direct-mail packets, product packaging, samples of logos and graphic design, free samples, ad specialties, gift certificates, signs, or placards that impress you or that have clearly been effective. While it is certainly improper to "steal" the material per se or verbatim, the ideas behind them cannot be copyrighted or owned. Ideas are in the public domain and indeed are "stolen" every day, probably even by the people who made the stuff you are collecting for your "swipe file." Build a "swipe file" of ideas that work and then draw on them for inspiration. It beats inventing the wheel from scratch, and it certainly is low-cost.

► **Chapter 13**

Conceptual Stuff: The Psychological Edge

Part One

Part Two

Part Three

Part Four

Part Five

Get Inside the Minds of Potential Buyers

In some ways marketing can be viewed as a meeting of the minds. The mind of the seller and the mind of the buyer come together from different perspectives to share a mutually beneficial common concept. What benefits one benefits the other. And as we have seen, benefits exist entirely in the mind. Since it is what is on the buyer's mind that determines the benefits, it is important to start there when marketing.

> Since it is what is on the buyer's mind that determines the benefits, it is important to start there when marketing.

Alas, what buyers perceive as benefits may have no basis in reality. That is all the more reason to begin with the buyer's point of view in mind when marketing. To do otherwise risks making incorrect assumptions and wasting your marketing efforts trying to answer unasked questions.

Take the case of a fleece sweatshirt. It is not the actual physical attributes of the fleece sweatshirt—soft, comfortable, and washable cotton—that necessarily appeals to the buyer. It is the idea that "everybody is wearing them," or that "it is really cool looking," or that "it shows what a rebellious and independent person I am."

It is irrelevant that what the buyer identifies as benefits does not mesh with reality. In fact, hardly anyone may be wearing fleece sweatshirts, and wearing one may cause the wearer to look dopey in the opinion of anyone with common sense and good eyesight. And obviously, anyone who believes he is being "rebellious and independent" because he is wearing something that he thinks "everybody is wearing" is not someone thinking logically.

So a marketing campaign that touts the "benefits" of "soft, comfortable, washable cotton" sweatshirts will send the wrong message and answer questions the target market is not asking. But any competitors who understand the real benefit of fleece sweatshirts from the point of view of the buyer's mind will easily capture that market by promoting their brand of "in," "really cool," "rebellious" clothing. The low-cost approach to marketing is to get that competitive edge by knowing the psychology of your target market. It is all in the mind.

As is the case with benefits, all other factors that drive your marketing campaign depend on what is in your target market's mind. And being able to identify what is on these peoples' minds and responding appropriately is the key to bridging that gap between buyer and seller and bonding in a mutually beneficial common purpose.

Ask for the Sale

Of course, it does not matter if you have clairvoyance or ESP and intimately know what your target market wants if you do not complete the marketing process. Once you have connected all the dots and persuaded customers that you can deliver the benefits they seek, you must ask for the sale.

Many otherwise effective marketing tactics seem to run out of gas simply because they fail to finish. After heaping tons of benefit-rich information on a prospective buyer, after overcoming every objection and justifying every dime of the cost, many marketers make the mistake of stopping. They maneuvered the buyer to the threshold but did not close the deal. The solution? Ask for the sale.

Tell Them Where to Go

Asking for the sale can be done in different ways in different situations:

- In advertisements: Direct the reader to where and when to go to purchase.
- In catalogs: Prompt the buyer by stating: "Enter prices here. Enclose check. Fill in your name and address here. Mail in enclosed envelope."
- In in-store promotions: Ask, "Can I wrap that up for you?"
- In direct-mail campaigns: End the letter with an unmistakable instruction to "Call today," or "Return this form for more information."
- In live radio and television promotions: Implore listeners and viewers that "If you call in the next fifteen minutes . . ."

Close the Deal

There is another potential breakdown en route to the sale. It can occur at the very end, once you have urged prospective customers to act, or at any of the innumerable steps along the way whenever a response from you is required to a response from them.

Perhaps you have noticed how conversations between two people tend to peter out when one of the two is sluggish in responding. It is very annoying to have to repeat yourself in a conversation because you have not had a response. Talking to someone who takes forever to reply generally signals that the unresponsive party is uninterested in the topic, not paying attention, or just does not want to talk with you. The same dynamics work in the marketing conversation you establish with potential customers, your target market.

The solution: Adopt a policy for communicating with customers who contact your company. For example, you might establish a rule that any telephone call that is not resolved when it is received must be returned by an appropriate employee within twenty-four hours. Some supermarkets responding to complaints about poor customer service instituted policies that if more than five customers are lined up at a cash register, another register must be opened. Waiting rooms at doctors' and lawyers' offices are experiences in drudgery. Tattered magazines and Muzak alone do not constitute good customer relations. If a patient or client waits more than fifteen minutes, a receptionist or other appropriate employee should be dispatched to the waiting room to personally apologize for the delay. Just saying, "We're sorry" in a timely manner effectively wards off grousing customers before it is too late.

Getting the Customer's Trust

There are two stereotypical sales types. One is the plaid-jacketed, greasy-haired, eager-to-shake-your-hand huckster. We will call him Mr. Slick. The other is the wholesome, believable, salt-of-the-earth type. We will call him Mr. Genuine.

When we encounter Mr. Slick we immediately erect another additional barrier to buying. If it would have taken twenty units of persuasion to move us from "just shopping" to opening our checkbook, the addition of Mr. Slick to the equation adds another five or ten units. Mr. Slick not only has to persuade us that we need, desire, and want what he sells, but he has to overcome his untrustworthy personality and pretentious "slick" image.

Our two hypothetical sales types are of course exaggerations, but only by degree. The more that sales personnel can appear to be like Mr. Genuine and less like Mr. Slick, the easier the sale is to make. As we have seen, marketing is really selling. We are simply selling desire, rather than widgets. But desire, like widgets, sells best when we appear more like Mr. Genuine than Mr. Slick.

Be Believable, Even If the Product Isn't

So in order to remove barriers to our quest, be believable. Even when the product is not.

Marketers—and salesmen—have acquired somewhat deserved reputations as snake oil peddlers. If we were all to be judged on a sliding scale, the public's perception of marketing probably begins closer to Mr. Slick's end of the spectrum than to Mr. Genuine's. What that should tell you is that you begin in a hole, and you have your work cut out for you to overcome a generally unflattering, untrustworthy image. Every advertising claim you make and every offer you proffer is tainted from the beginning in much of the public's mind simply because of those who have gone before you and more closely resembled Mr. Slick.

That is the bad news. The good news is that with genuine sincerity, transparent honesty, and by not trying to be what you are not, you not only can overcome this initial deficit, but once you do, you will appear to be head and shoulders above your competition—because you really are head and shoulders above your competition.

The Road to Believability

Unfortunately, there is no short cut to believability. That is to say that customer confidence is won incrementally and grudgingly, and takes time. Customer distrust can occur in an instant and immediately wipe out the valuable ground you have gained over months, even years. If there is a sub-plot here, it is do not push the envelope of sincerity. What temporary short gains you may make with phony claims or hyped promises run the risk of wiping out everything you have accumulated when you are found out, as eventually you surely will be.

So the lesson here is to be believable. Gaining a psychological edge with your target market is one of the lowest of low-cost approaches to marketing. It certainly costs no more than the slippery road of connivers and deceivers. The reputation you build pays off in customer loyalty, and

> Customer confidence is won incrementally and grudgingly, and takes time.

consequently generates delightful low-cost repeat customers who trust you because you have proven to be trustworthy, rather than you having to continually develop high-cost new customers, who have not yet discovered you are untrustworthy.

Full Disclosure

Sincerity does not require false modesty. You are allowed to state your case as forcefully as it warrants. There is nothing to gain from downplaying the benefits you offer customers or clients. In fact, it may even hurt your credibility to underplay your benefits. It is not too much for customers to expect that if you have got it, you would flaunt it.

Full disclosure should be your watchword. But full disclosure powerfully stated. It costs you no more to use power words than it does to use wimpy words. And power words are much more profitable.

Use Power Words

Consider the case of a personal coach who counsels clients on how to improve their attitudes and business demeanor in order to improve them in their respective fields. Let's assume now that our hypothetical personal coach can deliver on all the promises he makes in these statements (because we know that if he cannot, he is ultimately doomed).

If the coach were tepid and hesitant he might market to clients in this way: "I can help you achieve at no cost." Wimpy words.

But how would the coach come off if he used power words? Perhaps he would market to clients in this way: "Instant free success now." Power words, all of them.

The coach has improved his marketing approach immeasurably just by using power words rather than wimpy words. "I can help you achieve" has several wimpy flaws. First, it mentions "I" (the coach) and it mentions "I" before it mentions "you" (the customer). Customers do not want to hear the personal coach talk about himself. They want to hear him talk about them. "I can help you . . ." not only mentions our coach, but it mentions him before his clients. Very wimpy on two counts. Second, our coach is promising to "help you achieve." Help can be good, and achieving is better than failing. But compare "help achieve" to "instant success." Which would you prefer, help achieving what you do? Or instant success in what you do?

The difference between "at no charge" and "free" is vast. Even though they mean essentially the same thing, they do not connote the same thing. The emotional response is warm to "at no charge," but hot to "free." It is like the difference between "attractive" and "beautiful." Which one lifts your eyebrows?

The point of this exercise has been to underscore the difference between flat, cold, or even warm words and power words, the ones that elicit maximum emotive response.

It has been said that "free" is the most powerful word in marketing or advertising, perhaps even in the entire English language. If you can offer something for free, never offer it at "no charge" or "no cost." Always say "free."

Similarly, do not merely be "different," be "unique." And why settle for "traditional" when you can be "legendary"? Everyone knows "excellent" is good, but "the greatest" has to be excellent plus some. And if that is the case, "the greatest ever" must be even better.

When describing your offers and explaining your benefits, invoke power words like these at every opportunity. They cost no more than other verbiage, and they take about the same amount of ink. (But make sure you do not promise what you cannot deliver.)

Listen More Than You Talk

Even if your vocabulary arsenal is loaded with power words, not using as many words as your customers can give you a most effective psychological marketing edge. This boils down to listening more than you talk.

Listening is an art that unfortunately too few people have developed. It is actually more than just not speaking. In marketing, listening is not merely listening either. It is hearing.

Really, Really Powerful Words

Some power words—like "free" —work all the time, and some work all the time with particular markets. Do not assume that your market is generic. The odds are that it is idiosyncratic. Therefore when selecting the language to use in your marketing collateral—for example, before committing for the long haul—test for what works best with your particular market. If you are a woman's retail clothier and mail to 3,000 regular customers, use haute English for 1,500 of them and more commonplace lingo for the other 1,500. Only in this way will you know whether your crowd is looking for "glamour" or for "cachet." You may be surprised to find the low-end spenders prefer the high-end terminology. Similarly, and perhaps especially, testing is called for when marketing to young buyers. It is even more dangerous to assume you speak their language since what was hip yesterday is today's nerd-talk.

Ease the Uneasy Feeling

One way to ingrain the successful habits of your high-powered, savvy sales force in the minds of your marketing staff is to let the marketers tag along. Sales reps know what buyers bite on and what they turn their noses up at. Send one marketer along with each salesperson for a few days in the field, and, after any initial unease, your sales folks will probably warm to the idea of being mentors to marketers. Successful people often delight in explaining their success to admirers. And a marketer who wants to get inside buyers' minds can find no better route than through a good salesperson's experience and knowledge.

One of the best training tools for your front-line marketers, those employees who carry your message directly to the public and interact one-on-one in person, online, or on the phone, is to give them a quick course in how to listen, by which we mean "hear." Sales professionals know this, and many sales training classes emphasize the skill of listening.

In fact, if you have talented and successful sales personnel, you probably already have keen listeners on your payroll. A low-cost approach to instilling the art of listening (hearing) in your marketing staff would be to single out those champions of listening in your sales staff and have them conduct miniclasses on how to hear what customers are saying.

How to Hear

You will find that your better sales personnel probably will have recommendations like these:

- Close off all distractions.
- Make eye contact.
- Give the speaker your undivided attention.
- Repeat back to the speaker what you heard, but rephrase it in your own words to check for accuracy to make sure you have captured the speaker's intentions.
- Take notes, but not to the detriment of eye contact.
- Do not just look, but be observant and notice body language.

- Do not just nod and grunt, converse, preferably by asking open-ended questions that must be answered with more than a "yes" or "no."

These are all skills that cost little, if anything, to develop but that pay back many times in dividends. Marketers are in essence reacting to market conditions. Very few marketing campaigns have succeeded by trying to shape public opinion. Nearly all marketing campaigns that succeed do so by tapping into public opinion, then shaping the marketing message accordingly. To do that, your marketers must listen, and when we say, "listen" we mean "hear."

Offer Discounts and Promotions

A more nuts-and-bolts approach to gaining a psychological marketing edge involves an age-old proven technique: Offer discounts and promotions.

It is extremely difficult to compete on price in nearly any field, whether it's manufacturing, wholesaling, distribution, retailing, service, or professions such as law, finance, and medical. There is always someone who can undercut your price, and that someone does not have to be profitable to undercut your price. It may bankrupt the undercutter, but that is little consolation if it bankrupts you, too, trying to keep pace. Moreover, it almost requires a near monopoly to keep operating and supply costs at rock bottom to be able to afford to compete on a low-price basis.

So what are typical entrepreneurs to do if they cannot compete on price, since increasingly our commodity-driven markets have made customers so price conscious? The answer is to offer discounts and promotions.

The Impact of Discounts

Discounts provide a double psychological edge for the marketer. On the one hand discounts suggest that the price is inexpensive since it is below market value for what is being sold. On the other hand discounts suggest greater value for lesser price. After all, it is not the "regular" price. It is a price that has been "discounted" from the regular price, which clearly means that whatever is being purchased is worth more than is being paid for it.

Be prudent, however. Avoid phony discounts. There are some industries that have completely obliterated the meaning of "discount." The furniture store with the perpetual going-out-of-business sale clearly has blown its credibility. The "marked down" price that actually is the same as before the "sale" strains credulity. When you discount, make it genuine. Indeed, another low-cost method of getting extra mileage out of your "discount" campaigns might be to promote them as "genuine discounts," not like the phony marked-down sales prices of your competitors.

Regularly Scheduled Promotions

First cousin to "discounts" are "regularly scheduled promotions." Whereas part of the psychological appeal of discounts is that they seem to appear out of nowhere as a windfall benefit, part of the appeal of regularly scheduled promotions is that your clientele comes to expect and count on them. "Our annual summer parking lot sale" can be a regular event for a sporting goods retailer, complete with tent erected outside the store on the asphalt parking lot, mariachi band, and soft drink concessions celebrating the occasion. A year's worth of customers have left their mark on the store's customer database, so it is a no-brainer to mail each a simple flyer announcing the annual parking lot event where "prices are slashed" and "closeouts on popular brands" are plentiful for "our special customers notified by mail."

In neither case do discounts or regularly scheduled promotions hamper the image of a business that has chosen not to compete on price. Indeed, such psychological appeals to savings are generally well received even by upper-scale customers to whom price has not been a major factor. Everyone likes a bargain. And when companies with midrange prices or higher occasionally indulge in discounts and regularly scheduled sales, it can be viewed by loyal customers as a reward for their patronage, and viewed by new customers as a way to test the wares without paying the normal price.

> Such psychological appeals to savings are generally well received even by upper-scale customers to whom price has not been a major factor.

Rewarding Valued Customers

Discounts and regularly scheduled events also have other applications. While they work well as broadly based appeals such as to your entire customer base, they also can be effective for rewarding segments of your market, sort of the way Christmas bonuses can be used to boost employee morale. A wholesaler might offer particular retail customers discounts tailored particularly to their circumstances, for example. The psychological edge is enhanced if, when the discount offer is made, it is clearly customized for that customer. While discounts are always appreciated, "discounts especially for you" are even more so. Be sure when fashioning discounts to fit particular clients or customers that you communicate to them that this "deal" is for them, and them alone. And of course, make it so. You can offer others discounts too, of course, but the personalized psychological edge is lost if they all believe they are being treated identically to the same discount.

Bringing It All Together

The same thing applies to regularly scheduled events. A commercial printer might hold an annual open house with festive hand-addressed invitations, then on the appointed day give tours, gadgets, and refreshments to clients and suppliers in an almost party atmosphere, but not forgetting to tout the printer's new services and equipment for all to see.

Every attendee can leave with a belly full of hors d'oeuvres, a bag full of print samples, a good idea of what new benefits the printer has to offer, an armful of software samples and other hard marketing collateral, and have a feeling of having been treated like a VIP. The printer might tie in a discount campaign with the event, making sure every attendee also walks off with a coupon that discounts a printing job by 10 percent if orders are placed in the next thirty days.

Present Prices Favorably

If regularly scheduled promotions are first cousins to discounts, the next subject is probably not far removed on the family tree. Price setting is one part science and one part art, but a big part of it is psychological, too.

Decisions on what you should to charge your customers are beyond the scope of this book. But how to most favorably couch your price is something marketers should be aware of. Everyone knows that consumers respond better to ninety-nine-cent items than to items that are priced at $1. And the principle applies all the way up the price scale. $34,999 is clearly a

More "Free" Advice

It is hard to imagine that the word "free" can be overused, since it costs you nothing to use it and it almost always has a positive effect on the person who reads or hears it. But like anything else, it wears thin with repeated use. Most people have an intuitive sense that things are pretty much worth what they cost, and that you get what you pay for. Forever free suggests forever worthless. Just as you would not kiss your spouse without ceasing or eat ice cream 24/7, constant harping on "free" may be too much of a good thing. Do not run the risk of rending the most powerful word in the English language impotent. Use it judiciously to keep your psychological marketing edge.

better deal than $35,000, even though you cannot buy much for a buck these days (except at a ninety-nine-cent sale).

Beyond those simple examples, how to put the best face on your pricing strategy will probably always require testing. But the tests are worth it. As with testing techniques discussed in previous chapters, always restrict your tests to one element at a time. Will the public respond better to "Three for a dollar" or "Buy two for a dollar and get one free"? The only way to know is to test, and to test on identical samples under identical circumstances. Even though competing on low price is not advisable for nearly any business, as we discussed with discounting and regularly scheduled events, price still is a powerful motivator, even for upper-crust clientele, if handled properly.

The lesson here is to couch your pricing in the best possible language—determined by testing the attitudes of the very people you hope to sell to.

Train Clerks to be Salespeople

All the psychological marketing edges are not in your customers' minds. It pays to sharpen the edge for your sales personnel, too.

While successful professional sales representatives generally know how to develop that psychological bonding with the people to whom they sell, many low-rung sales clerks do not. Earlier we discussed employing your top sales reps to help your marketing staff understand how to listen. There is another low-cost opportunity for your marketers to educate your cashiers and clerks.

Train your clerks to be salespeople, not just cashiers. In those businesses in which sales culminate in person-to-person contacts, the lowly, minimum-wage, least-trained cashier is handed the final responsibility of making sure the customer leaves happy. All the marketing energy and expense that has led to this point is on the line. A sour experience at the checkout counter can nullify all your successful hard work. This is reason enough for your checkout counter employees to understand the psychology of sales. This is reason enough for your cashiers to cultivate the skill of listening. This is reason enough for clerks to understand the principles of marketing so they can respond appropriately to questions, complaints, and the unexpected. It may cost you hundreds or thousands of dollars just to develop one lifetime customer. One poorly prepared, ill-trained, gum-chewing, oblivious checkout clerk can obliterate all that in a blink.

The lesson here is that cross training can save far more dollars than it costs, and since the trainers are already on your paid staff, it ought to be manageably low-cost.

> **Chapter 14**

(Relatively) Low-Cost Advertising

PART THREE   PROVEN (BUT OFTEN NEGLECTED) SOLUTIONS

■ CHAPTER 11 Soft Stuff: People-Oriented Marketing   ■ CHAPTER 12 Hard Stuff: Marketing Collateral   ■ Chapter 13 Conceptual Stuff: The Psychological Edge   ■ CHAPTER 14 (Relatively) Low-Cost Advertising   ■ CHAPTER 15 Media Coverage: The Best and Lowest-Cost Advertising

Choose Advertising with Care

Let us be absolutely clear on the subject of this chapter—you can fritter away a lot of money on the options listed here. Employed liberally and without wisdom, these potentially low-cost advertising options can escalate quickly into stunningly high-cost options, and, worse yet, they can be tragically ineffective high-cost options to boot.

So tread carefully. You are about to navigate a minefield that can explode a marketing budget if you are not careful.

That said, there are genuine low-cost marketing opportunities among these more conventional advertising choices. Though recent years have seen advertising revenues decline in many sectors, billions of dollars a year are still spent in conventional advertising. It is true that advertising, particularly in printed media, often returns less on each dollar spent than do more innovative options, but it still is the grand old model of advertising that drives much of the communication between seller and buyer. And that is for basically one reason: It works.

There is no way around it. Ads are where many people look to find what they want to buy. The low-cost marketer, by spending a relatively few dollars prudently and wisely, can still buy a lot of bang for the buck in conventional advertising. The devil, as they say, is in the details.

Niche Publications

Perhaps the most endemic characteristic of the new age of media and communications has been the emergence of niche publications. At one time, broad national magazines served the needs of much of the nation's entire population. The age of specialization has changed that forever. Indeed, the nation's largest circulation magazine, *Modern Maturity,* appeals to a niche market of senior citizens and—are you ready for this?—it has a circulation of 17 million plus. That is some niche.

As enticing as it may seem to be able to reach millions of potential customers, for the vast majority of start-ups, small businesses, and other entrepreneurs, advertising even in a national magazine market as narrowly focused as one targeted to "senior citizens" is probably still not narrow enough. It is in this realm of niche publications that the demographic and psychographic data you have collected about your target market is so valuable, and this information will save you wads of cash by warning you away from buying ad space directed at people who really do not match your target market's profile.

For example, if you sell yarn and knitting implements, you may at first believe that a magazine catering to "senior citizens" would be a good place to advertise. But while knitting aficionados may be much more likely to be senior citizens than "younger citizens," not all or even a majority of senior citizens knit. Therefore, the considerable expense of advertising in a national publication with a circulation of 17 million is probably not a prudent use of your limited marketing budget since it is likely that only a small percentage of the readers you are paying to reach are likely to be knitting enthusiasts.

Smaller Can Have a Bigger Impact

A publication with a much smaller circulation devoted strictly to the hobby of knitting, or better yet, one that reviews or critiques knitting supplies, will ensure you that 100 percent of the magazine's readers are likely to be interested in knitting. These readers promise to be excellent targets for advertisements proclaiming the benefits of your knitting needles and yarn.

Before buying space and even before comparing advertising rates, there are two preliminary steps to take in choosing which niche publications to consider for your limited advertising dollars: First, find out the magazine's readers' profile, and then compare that profile to the one you have fashioned for your target market.

Ask not only for the publication's rate card, which explains how much you pay for different types of ads, but also for detailed explanations of who reads the magazine, broken down in terms of their income, lifestyle, age, occupation, and other characteristics. Many publications include such data on their rate cards and can provide even more specifics if asked.

The more your target profile resembles the magazine readers' profile, the more confidence you can have that your message is going to be seen by a receptive audience. But if your profile is a poor match with the magazine's readership, it is probably prudent to search for another publication whose readers have more in common with your target market.

First, find out the magazine's readers' profile, and then compare that profile to the one you have fashioned for your target market.

Interestingly, many times—though not always—the more narrow a publication's focus, the less costly its advertising rates, since it also probably tends to have a smaller circulation than more general interest magazines. So it is likely that as a publication's focus narrows, it not only increases the likelihood its readership will be interested in your ad, but also reduces the cost. Indeed, the ratio of interested readers per ad dollar can increase dramatically.

Dollars and Sense

A $1,000 ad spent to reach a million readers among whom only 1 percent are interested in your message means that you have spent $10 to reach each interested party. But a $200 ad spent to reach 20,000 subscribers to a very targeted publication, all of whom are interested in your message, means that you have spent only one cent to reach each interested party. If a typical customer buys $10 worth of knitting supplies, you must persuade 100 readers of that million-subscription publication to make a purchase just to break even. But you need convert only twenty readers in the specialty knitting magazine in order to pay for your ad.

If you cannot reasonably estimate or the publication cannot demonstrate how many of its readers match your target market's profile, why would you want to advertise in it? It would be an utter shot in the dark. For those magazines whose readership profile resembles your market profile, use this simple formula to determine how much it costs you to reach one interested reader and, therefore, which targeted niche publications are the lowest-cost options for your advertising dollar:

C (the cost of the ad) divided by
N (the number of readers who match your market profile)

It takes time—and therefore costs money—to compare, collate, and calculate relative cost-to-benefit ratios for niche publication advertising. But there is a wonderful time-saving, money-saving shortcut to this arduous task. Simply ask your customers what publications they read. Attempting to infer from demographics which magazines your target market may read is a good idea, but not nearly as reliable as getting it straight

> It is likely that as a publication's focus narrows, it not only increases the likelihood its readership will be interested in your ad, but also reduces the cost.

from the horse's mouth. You may be surprised at what you find. If you sell camera film and film developing services and you want to target Japanese tourists coming to America, you might assume that tourist magazines are the best venue for your ads. But by asking customers you may find that golfing magazines return a better ratio of cost-to-reader when it comes to reaching your Japanese target market, which also tends to include avid golfing enthusiasts.

Yellow Pages

Yellow Page advertising is nearly as ubiquitous as newspaper and magazine advertising, but it differs in several important respects. For one thing, you have little control over matching the demographics of your target market to the readership. Everyone reads the Yellow Pages. Well, not quite everyone, and that is one of the factors you must consider.

Some businesses are simply better suited to the Yellow Pages than others. If you need a plumber, the Yellow Pages may be where you start to look. But in these days of HMOs and prepaid health plans, if you need a doctor, it may never even occur to you to refer to the Yellow Pages.

Are the Yellow Pages for You?

The first determination for you to make when deciding whether to advertise in the Yellow Pages is whether it is where you target market goes to find what you sell. This is actually easier than comparing magazine demographics. Open the Yellow Pages to your business type and see if your competitors advertise there. Check the directory index to see if your business fits in any of the existing categories. Check previous years' books to see if the ads continue from year to year.

If there are no advertisers listed in your industry or type of business, or if they appear some years and not most years, it is a pretty good bet that the Yellow Pages are not for you. Unless your business is the very first of its kind, it is likely that competitors would be listed if the Yellow Pages were effective for them. Learn from their example. When it comes to Yellow Page advertising, you should not be a pioneer. There are more effective uses for your low-cost advertising dollar than trying to be the first widget distributor

Part 3 ■ Proven (But Often Neglected) Solutions

Lead Readers Through Your Ad

Make sure your Yellow Page ad conforms to basic tenets. Lead readers through your ad in the order you want them to travel. In our culture, people read from top to bottom, left to right. Also, the eye is attracted to the largest, boldest, and brightest items first. From that initial point, readers proceed down, working from left to right. Do not waste space in your limited space ad. Make the ad's entry point at the top and step your readers from left to right down the ad until they arrive at the exit point where your telephone number and other contact information is listed. If whoever is creating your ad cannot conform to the top-to-bottom, left-to-right, larger, bolder, brightest concepts, get someone else who can.

ever to succeed with Yellow Page ads. Do not waste your marketing budget advertising in Yellow Pages that your customers are not likely to even open.

Refine Your Ad

If, however, you find numerous listings for your type of business, it probably behooves you to advertise there, too. Be aware of the peculiarities of Yellow Page advertising. Unlike magazines and newspapers, Yellow Page advertisements have a long shelf life. That is, your ad in a daily or monthly periodical probably will be viewed once, or only until the next edition is delivered. Yellow Page ads generally last a year, until the next year's Yellow Page directory is printed. They can be viewed every day for a year.

For this reason the nature of your ad will be different than an ad that you may run in a newspaper or magazine. The Yellow Page ad must be an evergreen, which is to say it must be just as valid on January 1 as on July 4. Time-sensitive material, such as a "limited time only" offer that works well in daily or weekly publications, is inappropriate for a Yellow Page ad. Other perishable offers, such as closeout sales or promotions of products that may not be in stock all year, also should not appear in a Yellow Page ad. The Yellow Pages are suitable, however, for services or goods such as pet training and termite eradication or maternity apparel and sewing supplies—the kinds of things that will be the same tomorrow as they were today.

There is one other potential downside to Yellow Page advertising. Your company is going to be listed on the same page with most, if not all, of your direct competitors. That means at a glance your target market can compare you to your competitors, benefit by benefit, feature by feature.

Although this occurs to some extent in magazines and newspapers, it occurs big time in the Yellow Pages. It is the comparison shopper's dream. And for businesses that do not set themselves apart from the competition, it is like playing roulette. For these reasons it is important that your ad specifies your Unique Selling Proposition to clearly and emphatically set you apart from your competitors.

Free Ad Designers

Unless you have your own advertising department or agency that creates your display ads, feel free to draw on the expertise of the Yellow Page directory's staff. Generally, they will create a display ad for you at no extra cost and it will be about as effective as most other ads on the page, many of which they probably also created. Their no-fee service is a low-cost opportunity worth taking advantage of. The key is to give the Yellow Page ad designer the right information to include in the ad, and to present it in the right order of emphasis.

Recall the AIDA formula: get attention, create interest, arouse desire, and finally prompt action. Your ad should stand out from the others on the page, either in its graphic display or in its main headline. Leave the graphic appeal to the graphic experts. You can judge for yourself whether your ad jumps off the page or not simply by comparing it to an existing page in the directory. But do not leave the words to the whim of the ad designer.

Your product's or service's primary benefit, the underlying appeal of your company's USP, should be the main headline in your Yellow Page ad. Chances are your business's name is not the main benefit in the mind of your target market. A moving company probably should not make the most prominent words on the page "Widget Moving Company." So do not waste you biggest typeface on saying "who" you are. And lackluster or say-nothing blurbs, such as "We can move it" or "Moving and Storage," also amount to wasted space if they are used as the main headline.

The most prominent headline in your ad should deliver your main benefit in no uncertain terms, in language that distinguishes what you have to offer from your competitors on the page, such as, "Fast, Careful, and Guaranteed" or "We've never damaged anything."

Another critical factor to remember when crafting your ad is that all the benefits you offer should be enumerated. Because the Yellow Pages are a comparison shopper's delight, the ad that presses the most hot buttons is the ad that wins. Don't forget to include your company's name, which unless it is a major selling point, is almost incidental though obviously necessary.

And finally, your contact information should be displayed at the exit point of the ad, generally at the bottom, and nearly as prominently as the main headline is displayed at the entry point of the ad, which should be at the top. Unlike direct-mail pieces that should always instruct the recipient what to do next, such as, "Call today . . . ," the call to action is implicit in a Yellow Page ad and you need not waste valuable space spelling it out.

Coupons

Coupons are another low-cost advertising option, but also another that is not suitable for every business. You probably would not be enticed to do business with a brain surgeon who offered half-off coupons. On the other hand, a farmers' market might find coupons to be alluring for fruit and vegetable customers. Coupons generally serve one of two purposes: to establish an identity or branding campaign, or to offer discounts, special sales, or other savings-oriented messages.

Identity or branding coupons can often be found in direct-mail packets that group dozens of coupons from many dissimilar businesses. For relatively low cost you can have your business's message included and delivered to thousands of homes, where unfortunately thousands of homeowners will toss them into the trash. As a meaningful low-cost option, these branding mass mailings are not advisable for most businesses because the mailings are targeted too broadly.

Coupons with Real Value

Before committing a large chunk of your advertising budget to branding coupons delivered in untargeted mailings, you should look for other avenues that reach a higher percentage of your target market. For example, if you operate a diaper service, you might include your coupons in packets specifically targeted to new parents. But using coupons simply to establish a company's identity or brand to the larger market of homeowners is probably not the best use of your marketing and advertising budget.

The greater value of coupons is achieved when they are used as a form of currency, not merely miniature billboards. In this way, they have intrinsic value. They find their way into wallets rather than into trash cans. They are used, not ignored. They are effective, not a waste of your marketing budget.

Coupons used in this way can offer dollars off, percent discounts, two-for-one, or any variety of other cash-value offers. Since these real-value coupons simulate money, it can be very effective when they resemble money. In a world where everyone is swamped in a blizzard of ads, marketing collateral and other demands for attention, it is silly to downplay a clearly recognizable benefit.

Coupons that resemble dollar bills clearly send the signal that they are equivalent in part or in whole to dollar bills. Coupons that look like checks obviously tell anyone at a glance that they are to be used like checks. Coupons that mimic tickets are noticeably intended to be used as admission passes. Real-value coupons, therefore, have a substantial advantage over other marketing collateral. They communicate their message immediately, even before communicating the benefit of what it is they sell. It is as if you handed cash money to someone. But now you have to explain the limits on how it can be spent.

As with all collateral and advertisements, the main benefit should be the most prominent and the first message delivered. In the case of real-value coupons, this is their monetary or other transactional value. A large "$5 off" should be the main headline or graphic on a $5 off coupon for widgets. You have caught the target's attention and interest in one fell swoop. Next in the hierarchy of the coupon message should come the benefit of widgets. That creates desire. And finally, your real-value coupon should end with its call to action, which may include instructions for how to redeem the coupon, where to go to spend it, and whatever restrictions apply to it.

One more element must absolutely be included on your real-value coupons. And it should be prominently displayed, not relegated to tiny agate typeface. This element is the

The Flexible Coupon

Coupons are almost never inappropriate, whether in a neighborhood welcome basket of goodies for new arrivals or stuffed inside a direct-mail packet with a sales letter or questionnaire. But one very effective use is to include them with goods and services at time of delivery. A customer who has ordered a product probably is most receptive to ordering another when the first one arrives. As the old adage goes, you should strike while the iron is hot. If the product is as good as was promised, customers might never again be more ready to buy another than at that very moment. A discount coupon sweetening the offer even more can be just the nudge a satisfied buyer needs to buy again.

expiration date of the coupon. Every real-value coupon needs to expire at some point, and the sooner the better. The reason is that people use coupons first that have expiration dates.

Those coupons that are good forever are saved or stacked up for use later. If you want your coupon to be used, which is the whole idea, make it clear to coupon holders that they must use it by such-and-such an expiration date, or lose its value entirely. In this sense, real-value coupons burn a hole in your target market's pocket even faster than had you handed them real cash money, which of course does not expire. And best of all, they can spend the coupon only on your product or service.

Direct Mail

Entire volumes have been written on the practice of direct-mail advertising, or as it has euphemistically come to be known, direct response. Rather than cover the entire spectrum, most of which is beyond the realm of low-cost marketing anyway, we will discuss a few aspects of direct-mail advertising that can be beneficial to the small business owner or entrepreneur.

For most small businesses, it is far preferable to use mailing lists compiled by the business itself than it is to rely on renting mailing lists compiled by third parties. For one thing, you already have gone to the expense of compiling your own list, and to obtain a third-party list that you hope resembles your own, you must spend additional money.

If your business has created a good database of existing and previous customers, your list is made to order for direct-mail advertising. Your database may already show you the buying habits and preferences of your known customers, enabling you to fashion advertisements and offers that speak directly to these customers' preferences. This is information that a rented third-party list may or may not be able to duplicate.

Finding the Easy-to-Persuade Mailing List

Your list, needless to say, is comprised of people who are far easier to coax into repeat business than it will be to coax complete strangers into new business, no matter how much they may resemble your current customers' demographics or psychographics.

The best low-cost direct-mail advertising therefore is that which targets your current and previous buyers. Direct mail is suitable for keeping these known buyers apprised of new offerings, new pricing, and special promotions, all matters that they can reasonably be presumed to have an interest in because they already have purchased from you at least once.

Increasingly, direct-mail campaigns offer recipients the opportunity to opt out of receiving future mailings. Although this trend was born in consumer complaints about "junk mail," it actually is one of the more beneficial developments for those who use direct-mail promotions.

The last thing a low-cost marketer wants to do is to waste money sending costly collateral and advertisements to people who have no interest in receiving the stuff. While there was initially a lot of hand-wringing in the direct-mail industry over the opt-out debate, small businesses and entrepreneurs should view the phenomenon as a godsend. It is the very vehicle that can help them prune from their costly mailing lists those people who have no interest in receiving their mail. Deleting people who do not want to talk to you from your mailing list should translate into fewer wasted dollars and a greater ratio of responses to mailings—in short, more profit and less expense.

So if your company uses direct mail for promotions or advertisements, you certainly should employ the latest customer-friendly tact by offering recipients the opportunity to opt out of receiving future mailings. It will at once cut your costs and increase the return on your investment.

This cost-reduction method should be employed before even considering whether to rent third-party lists. Then, even if you are persuaded that one of the myriad providers of compiled mailing lists can adequately clone your target market, proceed cautiously. Most reputable list brokers will provide you a substantive sampling of names to use as a test mailing. It is in their interest to do so, since they want to make sure that what they eventually rent to you is effective so you will return and rent more from them later.

If a broker will not or says he cannot provide you with a free sample list for a test mailing, find another broker. Plenty of others will. After all, a test mailing still requires you to go to the expense of creating the mailing material and paying to have it mailed. All you are getting free in the test is the use of a few hundred names.

> The last thing a low-cost marketer wants to do is to waste money sending costly collateral and advertisements to people who have no interest.

Money-Saving Direct-Mail Tips

Direct-mail costs can easily run away with your budget if not controlled. Eliminate ineffective direct mail and cut your spending by doing the following:

1. Offer every mailed recipient an opportunity to opt out of your next mailing. They can use the same return mail device that you have included for other responses. This avoids repeat mailings to consumers who have no interest in your services.
2. Closely track your mailings to determine which ones fail to cover their costs. This simple cost-to-revenue comparison is definitely worth the time that it takes to perform it.
3. Continually test your mailings, changing only one factor at a time as you seek to maximize each mailing campaign's effectiveness.

Track and Evaluate

Use this as a steadfast rule: Unless the test mailing is profitable, do not rent a larger list from the same list brokerage. To calculate whether your mailing was profitable, do not forget to include all the costs. Costs may include at the least some or all of the following:

- Creation of the advertising or collateral (design and copywriting)
- Paper and other material that comprise the mailing
- Printing
- Postage
- Tracking (the time your staff spends or the fee an outside consultant is paid to evaluate the mailing's effectiveness)

To get an accurate estimate, also include what it would cost if you had to rent the names that you were provided for free. If you would normally be charged fifteen cents per name to rent the 500 names a broker provided you for a "free" test, include $75 (fifteen cents times 500 names) in your costs.

Once you have identified the entire cost of the mailing, it is a relatively simple task to compare it to the sales it generated. In the same way, you can compare different lists to see which return greater profit. (Remember when comparing mailings, however, to change only the list itself rather than any other factors like the nature of the offer, or the appearance of the material.)

Outdoor Advertising

Outdoor advertising has little in common with the type of advertising that we have mentioned so far, except that it too can be costly, and ineffective on top of costly if done poorly. There is a wide range of outdoor advertising, and certainly not all or even most of it is appropriate for all businesses. The options range from billboards, signage, sandwich boards, bus benches, and skywriting to large inflatable cartoon or animal characters.

For the cost-conscious entrepreneur, the lowest of the low-cost alternatives probably is outdoor signage. But because of the plethora of signs dotting the landscape, signs tend to get lost in the sea of signs, each almost indistinguishable from another.

Three ways to make your low-cost signage highly effective are to make it engaging, distinctive, or unexpected.

Engage the Viewer

The most successful signage involves the viewer. Consider the leasing agent for a high-rise apartment or office complex. As the building begins to fill its skeletal form from the ground upward, the leasing company hangs a new mega-sized banner just above the last completed floor with words to this effect, "Now on the third floor, seventeen floors to go. Lease yours now." After another floor is completed, a new sign goes up, "Now on the fourth floor . . ." and so on.

Day and night the passing auto and foot traffic is drawn to the developing story, simple as it may be. Passersby find themselves looking to mark the progress of what otherwise might have nondescriptly blended into the skyline. What might have become a routine sight, a building under construction, has been transformed into an ongoing saga that engages thousands of eyes daily, each time with the reminder that rentals are available, but obviously will not be forever.

Frequency Rather Than Size

Since frequency is such a critical component of advertising, it is probably worth sacrificing the size of your ad in order to increase the number of times you can afford to run it. Of course, it is not worth it to pay for any ad so small that it goes unnoticed. Test different size ads that deliver essentially the same message to determine the smallest ad that works; that is, that is profitable. The difference in ad rates can be dramatic based on the size of the ad. This is the case in nearly all media, from newspapers and magazines to billboards and outdoor signage. Reduce the size of your ad to its minimally effective size, then use the savings to buy increased frequency so your target market will have many more exposures to your message.

Distinctive Signs Catch the Eye

Distinctive outdoor signage is that which is unique and comes to be identifiable with one service, product, or company and only one. The best of this type of signage succeeds much like successful logos or widely recognized acronyms, such as NBC for "National Broadcasting Company."

They become instantly identifiable with the product, service, or company they represent. As distinctive signs go, few have been as successful as the elevated rotating bucket of Kentucky Fried Chicken or the golden arches of McDonald's. The key to their successes lies in consistent association with their products and their uniqueness. When striving for distinct outdoor signage, first make sure it represents you and only you, then be persistent. Do not change the image. About the time you begin to get bored with it, it probably is beginning to have the effect you want in your target market's mind: They are associating it with you.

Look for the Unexpected

Unexpected signage is just that, unexpected. It is found where it is unanticipated, or it says something equally unforeseen. Or both. Because of the unlikely juxtaposition with its environment and its startling message, the sign grabs attention, creates interest, and, depending on how effective its message, creates desire. Patrons of cocktail lounges and taverns probably least of all expect to see in such establishments a sign asking, "Is alcohol killing your sex life?" But where better for a psychologist who treats such ailments to buy signage on a bar's outside wall, or a nearby bus bench?

Eliminate What Is Unprofitable

Whatever your advertising venue or medium, whatever your message or your tact, the one thing to relentlessly apply in all your efforts is to regularly track and evaluate what you have done. There is no other way to know for certain whether your advertising is cost-effective or wasteful, or whether tweaking it can improve it or not.

Dip your toe in the water before taking the plunge. Sample on a small scale any advertising you buy, then expand the scope of the campaign incrementally, never advancing to the next stage until you have seen the current stage turn a profit.

One of the caveats to the wonderful world of advertising is that ad salesmen will admonish you that it takes seven impressions or more before a customer is moved to buy. Some mediums may take more. Some may take less. Some approaches more, others less. If you have firmly decided on these more conventional means of promotion—magazine, newspaper, Yellow Pages, coupons, direct mail, or outdoor advertising—rigorously track and evaluate their results. Then ruthlessly eliminate what is unprofitable.

> Chapter 15

Media Coverage: The Best and Lowest-Cost Advertising

Part One

Part Two

Part Three

Part Four

Part Five

The Many Benefits of Media Coverage

There is high-cost marketing, which is not such a good thing, and low-cost marketing, which is a very good thing, and then there is the very best and perhaps the lowest-cost marketing of all. This brand of marketing combines the benefits of tooting your own horn, having an advertisement in a respected publication, and receiving powerful testimonials all wrapped in one. Think of it as free ads placed by a third party. It is, of course, press coverage.

And when it happens the way you would like it to happen, there is not much better marketing available at any price. The downside is that when it happens in a way that you prefer it not to happen, there is not much worse marketing at any price.

A Source of Credibility

Press, or "media" coverage, as it has more recently become known, when done right presents something flattering or beneficial to you, but out of the mouth of an independent, unbiased source—a publication. It carries not only a message that something significant has occurred, but also the proof that someone other than you thinks so, and not just any old source, but a credible news publisher. You cannot buy credible crowing like that.

Of course, when the same publication mauls you or your business in print, it hurts as much as the flattering coverage helps. No one wants an investigative reporter to show up at the front door. Bad press coverage can be devastating. Unflattering press coverage only less so by degree.

The good news is that if you have cultivated good, aboveboard working relations with the press, you may be able to minimize or even reverse the effects of bad news, should you make some. That is just one more reason to develop this low-cost marketing solution.

Where Does Your News Belong?

News judgment varies from writer to writer and publication to publication. But it varies most from niche trade publications to general interest publications. The farther you get from narrow trade publications and the closer you get to general news publications, the more your subject matter

Get That Story

To get news coverage of your company, you must first know what writers and editors want; that is, what they consider to be news. Next, give them what they want. Do not forget to show how their readers will benefit from your story by linking your news to their readers' interests. And, of course, make it easy for them to publish your news by anticipating and answering as many of the questions that writers and editors will have. This last step improves with experience as you learn the nuances of each publication. But the better you become at anticipating questions, the better you'll be at getting your company written about.

has to conform to real news and the less it can look like in-house gossip. Your "news" belongs in the trade press if you have just started a new business. Your "news" belongs in the general press if your new business provided twenty new jobs in the community. Your "news" belongs in the trade press if your business has just bought another business. It belongs in the general press if the other business you bought was bigger than your own. Trade press news: Your business celebrates its first anniversary. General press news: Your business celebrates its first anniversary despite the hurricane that demolished your showroom.

Understand What the Press Wants

Obviously, it is important to make free press coverage happen the way you would like. That is not difficult to do if you play by the rules of the people who control the game—editors and writers. Your fate is in their hands. The good news is that in many ways they need you too. The key is working out a mutually beneficial relationship with the press.

The first thing to be cognizant of is that the press is similar in many ways to your target market. You cannot succeed with your target market by making demands of it, nor will you be successful by being condescending. The individuals or entities that comprise your target market are interested in you solely based on what it is you can do for them. "What's in it for me?" is what they want to know.

Exceptions to Consider

Most principled news organizations keep their moneymaking side segregated from their news-writing side. This is to avoid the appearance that advertisers are treated preferentially. Alas, this is not a universal ethic. You do not have to worry about finding those publications that mingle advertising and editorial. They most likely will find you. Often the offer is to run a "story" about you or your company of a comparable length to the size of an advertisement that you purchase. Previously, such swaps of dollars for coverage were confined to less respected publications, but in recent years they have included more and more upscale and reputable trade publications. Generally, the articles traded for ads are not the highest forms of journalism, and sophisticated readers recognize them for what they are—or are not. Whether you engage in these tradeoffs is your decision; just be sure to keep in mind any possible effects on your company's reputation.

Likewise, the press is interested in you entirely based on what it is you can do for them. As you have with your target market, you need to evaluate what the press wants. In a nutshell, the press wants to feed the appetite of its readers. Therefore, you need to feed the press what it can feed its readers. Luckily for you, readers' appetites are insatiable. They cannot get enough. Feed them today and tomorrow they are hungry again. Handle your press relations properly, and readers may end up getting a steady diet of you.

The principal mistake made by businesses seeking press coverage is to assume that what interests the business should interest the press. Rarely is this the case. Businesses tend to be interested in themselves and in their customers and prospects, none of which is particularly interesting to the press—unless those subjects happen to interest their readers too.

Identify the Outlets That Are Right for You

Your first crucial step is to identify the media that you must cultivate. Get this wrong and it will not matter how well you follow the subsequent steps.

There are literally thousands of press outlets. They run the gamut, including print publications like magazines, newspapers, wire services, newsletters; Web-based publications like online journals, e-mail updates, e-zines; and the conventional hot media, such as television and radio. They can have national, international, regional, or local reach. They can range from strictly hard news to warm and fluffy human-interest stories to a narrowly defined business focus or even to the weirdly eclectic. It is probably safe to say that there is a publication somewhere that deals with any topic you can imagine. Some have very rigid standards for what they will publish, while others rush into print virtually anything handed to them. But they all have this in common: They publish only what their particular readers want to read about. The Super

Bowl is not about to get an inch of press in *Dog Show Weekly*, and the latest gossip at the local women's club has not got a ghost of a chance of being published in the columns of the *New York Times*.

Therefore, if you want something published in a periodical in print, or broadcast on radio or television, or posted electronically online, you need to conform what you have to say to what that press outlet's readers want to read. Do not waste your time—or your money if you pay an outsider to handle your press relations—trying to break into an unrelated publication, one that has nothing to do with you or your target market or industry. Even if you succeed, you accomplish little more than ego gratification.

How to Build a Media Contact List

To build a media contact list, draw from three areas:

Publications read by your target market. If you have built your target market profile properly, you know where these people go for their information, what they read for pleasure and for business. If you want to reach them, target the publications they read.

Publications that focus on your industry. If you are plugged in to your industry, you know where your counterparts go for their information to keep abreast of the latest trends, news, and gossip. Even though your target market may never see these publications, they are worth cultivating. They provide you with a respectable presence among your peers, but also provide you with news article clippings that you can leverage with your target market later (an aspect we will discuss in how to create press packets). This segment of the press also is much more likely to be interested in what you have to say, making it easier to get your words into print.

High-profile publications. These media outlets certainly will be the toughest for you to crack, but if you ever do, they can create a domino effect felt throughout your industry and your target market. Because it is unlikely that you will succeed in getting press coverage here at first, if ever, it is not advisable to make these outlets a high priority. However, keep them in mind, because success in getting press coverage in the first two categories just may later lead to success here.

The first category, publications read by your target market, should be your highest priority. You may already have decided to buy advertisements in these publications to reach their readers. With rare exceptions, the fact that you pay the publication to print your ads will not help you get press coverage in its pages. In fact, most editorial departments resent advertisers acting as if they are entitled to press coverage because they have paid for an ad. If you suggest otherwise to an editor or a writer, you are likely to get lectured on the separation between the editorial and advertising departments, and to wind up on a list of people to be ignored, not written about.

The second category, publications that focus on your industry, is your next priority. You no doubt already are familiar with most of these publications (if you are not, you should be) and therefore you probably have some feeling for the type of articles they publish, their subject matter, tone, and perspective. This is important because it means you have much less of a learning curve than you face with your target market's favorite publications. That means you are much closer to getting published in these. It also helps immeasurably that you probably are already involved in something these publications are interested in since they publish what you and your industry want to read.

As for high-profile publications, for our purposes we mean any nationally recognized media that does not necessarily cater to either your target market or to your industry. You need not obsess about getting press coverage here, particularly in the early stages of any media campaign that you may launch. But keep these outlets in mind, places perhaps like the *New York Times* or *Christianity Today,* nationally syndicated radio talk shows, or one of the prominent television news magazines. For now, it is enough to know that these outlets are always a potential option, however remote. After mastering the technique to break into the lesser, more parochial media, you will better understand how to deal with the high-profile publications should the opportunity later present itself.

Read Them First

The way to prepare for a relationship with your target market's favorite publications and your industry's publications is to read them. You cannot know for certain what these publications like to publish unless you read them. Begin your media contact list by noting the publications' chief editors and the writers who seem to be assigned to key areas. Build a database of these contacts complete with e-mail as well as conventional mail addresses and telephone numbers. If the publication has guidelines for submitting news releases, note those guidelines along with each contact's name and other information. If the publication has guidelines for freelance writers from whom they buy articles, obtain these guidelines as well. The guidelines will explain in detail the type of material the publication accepts as press releases and the type it pays freelancers to create; this information can help you not only craft press releases that press hot buttons, but may also give you fodder for submitting articles that the publication will pay you to publish—the best of all possible outcomes.

Go through the same procedure with your industry publications, noting not only how to reach the key editors and writers, but also what their special interests are and how they prefer to receive news releases or articles that they may purchase. Plan to update these database entries periodically. Every six months is probably often enough. Employee turnover, promotions, and reassignments keep the editorial personnel churning at most news outlets. It also is worth noting when one editor or writer with whom you have developed a good working relationship moves on to another publication. Use the occasion to telephone or write to express your congratulations (or condolences, if called for). Do not lose track of valuable editors and writers. You never know where they may end up, or how they may help you later. Journalists are like everyone else. They tend to be more likely to do business with people they already know and like. Make contacts, and make friends.

> Plan to update these database entries periodically. Every six months is probably often enough.

Press Releases and Press Packets

There are four general approaches to garnering press coverage once you have determined which publications and which individuals at those publications to target.

- Press packets and news releases
- Becoming a respected source for the media
- Becoming a news tipster
- Becoming a writer yourself (or have someone on your staff do it)

Press packets and their little brothers, news releases, can help promote, position, and enhance your company and its reputation. Get writers and editors to act on your request for news coverage even though they are overwhelmed with similar requests from others by providing them with a press packet, or media kit, as it also is known.

How to Craft a News Release

Even after you have determined which publications may be interested in news about your company, you still need to make sure you send your news to them in a way that makes them want to give you that valuable coverage. The guide on the facing page shows how to write a press release that gets the result you want: plenty of press.

Two final notes:

Check grammar, spelling, and facts, especially names and places. Computer spell-check programs usually are not accurate for proper names.

Find out how your target editor or reporter prefers to receive press releases: e-mail, fax, or postal mail. Deliver it that way.

Putting Together a Press Packet

The press packet is a modular approach to assembling your message. It consist of all or some of these modules: a press release, a company history, a list of sources to expound on the story, photographs to bring the words to life, charts to illustrate facts, profile pieces to add personality, and any other modules that may be appropriate to give fuller context and richer meaning to your message.

Many of the modules can be created in advance and added to any mailing if appropriate. Others, like the press release itself or fact sheets to supplement the release, must be drafted new with each mailing to be current and germane.

The module approach allows you to mix and match segments of the packet when targeting different publications. The idea is to give writers what they need to make their job easy, but not to overload them with modules they do not require. A publication that never publishes stories about individuals may not need to see personality profiles. A black-and-white

> Many of the modules can be created in advance and added to any mailing if appropriate.

Company Name
Address, Phone
Contact:
Name
Phone
Cell phone
E-mail

Release date: Jan. 1, 200– *(or the words "For Immediate Release")*

Widget Labs Clone Santa Claus
(This is your grabber headline. Do not be subtle.)

Santa Claus donates DNA for Widget Labs to develop a new breed of gift-givers. Movie deal expected to follow.
(This is your grabber subhead providing more information to get the editor or reporter to continue reading, rather than throwing the press release in the trash.)

The body of the release includes the following:

1. The first sentence is the absolutely most important thing about the story stated clearly and in a straightforward manner. Do not put your company name or owner's name in this sentence, no matter how much he pays or threatens you. Not even if you are the owner. But include in this paragraph any times or dates, if applicable.

2. This is the second most compelling fact about your story. And so it goes throughout the rest of the release, which should be no more than two pages. Tell the reader who, what, when, where, why, and how.

3. Emphasize what the benefit is to the reader of the publication or Web site, the listener to the radio program, or viewer of the television show. If you have waited until this point to do that, you have waited too long.

4. As an addendum or "kicker" at the bottom of the release, mention graphic or visual material that you can offer if needed, or enumerate them if included already in the press packet. If the story you are pitching is about someone other than the person identified as the contact person, include in the final paragraph how the writer can contact that person. Be sure the contact's assistants are aware the release is being sent so they can make special effort to connect the reporter and news source quickly.

5. End your press release with either of these notations: "-30-" or "###"

newspaper does not need color pictures. A magazine that never features graphics has no use for charts.

If spoon-feeding the press is entirely new to you, think of it as assembling a good sales presentation. With preprinted press packet modules, you not only can be proactive, but reactive as well. You will be prepared to respond to press inquiries immediately by providing your company "backgrounder" or CEO's profile, for example. Resolve now to never again be forced to throw something together on the spur of the moment. Many press inquiries are time-sensitive, and reporters are delighted when their questions can be answered quickly. A prompt response may mean the difference between being mentioned in an article or not.

Press packet modules give perspective to your news. They give journalists alternate entry points, additional opportunities to find something newsworthy. For example, a news release about a new product line may not interest the writer, but he might find a feature story is suggested by the accompanying personality profile. Ideally, each module should be contained on a separate page. Be thorough, but do not belabor. Label each page at the top with an appropriate and informative headline, such as "Company Background" or "Frequently Asked Questions."

Press Packet Modules

Some of the modules you might consider including in your press packet are:

1. **News release**—This is the timely news or feature story idea that you are offering. It might be about a product launch or a strategic alliance, or opening a new branch office. Whatever it is, it must be concise, direct, and to the point. Keep the release to one or two pages, double-spaced. Keep supplemental information in the other modules. This should be written like a straight news story, including the story's five Ws (who, what, where, when, and why) and one H (how). There are many occasions they require only the press release, but make a decision now to always include some other module with it as a supplement. The company backgrounder, or fact sheet, is a good candidate to ride along with the news release.

2. **Fact sheet**—This is the at-a-glance overview of relevant information

about your company and its newsworthiness. Think of this module as a news release minus complete sentences. Use bullets to enumerate items. This information should be scanned quickly. Emphasize items with boldface type or with subheadlines. As with the news release, cover all five Ws and How. Use the key words such as *"Who:* Bob Smith, founder of Widget Retail Company. *What:* Named Chamber of Commerce man of the year. *Where:* Diamond Bar, California. *Why:* Opened two new stores and launched a community breakfast program for the homeless."

3. **Explainer**—This module is an invaluable addition if the topic of your news release is complex or requires more explanation than fits comfortably in the news release. Expand here on the five Ws and How. The news release may say that Bob Smith was named man of the year, but this module can explain how the honor was determined, who past recipients were, and the purpose of the organization that bestowed the honor.

4. **Photos**—Pictures increase the chance any story will be used in most publications. In fact, the story with the better accompanying art often gets the nod. Pictures can also dramatically improve the display and placement of your story if it is used. Some publications want color photographs, others want slides or transparencies, or black-and-white prints. Some accept digital files on disc or by e-mail. The best way to know a publication's preference is to ask. Be prepared to have some of each in your press packet, but if possible, send only those that the publication desires. Clearly label them with captions.

5. **Graphics**—Items like charts, diagrams, schematics, and artist's renderings pump up interest in a story. As with photos, make sure the publication you send these to can use them. If they cannot publish what you send, it is wasted effort.

6. **Trademarks**—Camera-ready art or computer files of any logos or other trademarked graphical representations such as product labels should be included when appropriate. You could end up with your logo on the front page of the newspaper as an illustration that refers to a story buried on page 35. Explain in an attached note that you have given your approval for your officially registered and legally restricted images to be reproduced in conjunction with a news article.

7. **History**—This module explains your company's background. It probably will not be used except to flesh out references to your company

Pictures can also dramatically improve the display and placement of your story if it is used.

in whatever story the publication is preparing. But the publication also may keep this document on file for future reference. The next time that publication chooses to write about your company, its staffers will find this document in the file and have more to say about you than they might otherwise.

8. **Testimonials**—Self-serving testimonials may be included, but do not hype them beyond the evidence. What you may feel comfortable using in a paid ad may be a bit embellished for a news story. It is entirely appropriate to include testimonials from someone bestowing honors on your company, but plaudits for plaudits' sake backfire. They signal gratuitous self-promotion that turns off many writers and editors. When in doubt, don't.

9. **Reprints**—Include reprints of previous coverage. They are regarded as stamps of credibility. Writers often feel more comfortable writing about a private company if another respected publication already has deemed it to be newsworthy. There is one admonition. You should get permission before using reprints of copyrighted articles for self-promotion. Most publications willingly grant permission. Some for a nominal fee will even provide you with slick copies or tear sheets rather than tacky photocopies.

10. **FAQs**—Frequently Answered Questions are the best friend to writers on deadline faced with digesting mounds of information. A single sheet or two that asks and answers the most common questions about your company or about your news event is extremely helpful for writers.

11. **Profiles**—One-page biographical sketches on people who figure prominently in your news release are helpful the way the backgrounder piece is helpful about your company. These profiles also may end up in a permanent file at the publication, increasing odds of subsequent coverage. Always include a photograph of the profiled company employee.

12. **Business card**—Do not forget the most obvious module.

13. **Brochure**—Not every publication is going to be interested in your brochure, which is probably a slicker, more marketing-oriented version of the company backgrounder. But trade publications often appreciate seeing your marketing collateral, particularly if it is germane to what they are writing about.

14. **Awards**—It cannot hurt to toot your horn, but do not be obnoxious about it. This information adds credibility when relevant to the news you are sharing, but it seems egotistical if it is not germane.

15. **Other story suggestions**—As long as you have caught the publication's interest, take advantage of the opportunity. Writers and editors keep story idea files. You might put a headline on this module that says, "You Also May Be Interested In . . ." Here you can suggest other stories that the publication may find of interest. List only credible suggestions—something you will be better able to do after working with the media for a while. With each suggestion, include potential contact persons at your company and elsewhere, and how to reach them by phone, mail, or e-mail. Something that you plant in this way may spring to life months later. Do not suggest stories that are inappropriate to a publication.

16. **Sources**—To demonstrate credibility, include a list of other sources that the writer can use to check on your character and reliability. A news release about your latest widget manufacturing improvement might include how to reach the National Widget Manufacturers' Association at its toll-free phone number as an independent source on the topic. Writers love when you make their workload lighter by making it easy for them to find "experts" in a field.

17. **Quotes**—This is something like a writer's cheat sheet. It is not that it is dishonest, but it certainly saves writers interview time in preparing their stories. Good quotes increase a story's readability, but not every source is glib enough to be quotable when a writer telephones unexpectedly. To make sure that you have something catchy to say, include the catchy quote in this module. Many quotes you read in news and trade publications are simply lifted straight from press releases and quote modules like this.

> List only credible suggestions—something you will be better able to do after working with the media for a while.

Become a Respected Source for Press

After dealing with the press for a while, you are ready to go the next step and become a respected source for news. This is a good direction to go if you have something to offer, such as an insider's perspective of your industry, or a particular expertise that is valued by publications. Go slowly, but definitely go if you are suited for this type of relationship.

The trickiest part is the initial step of offering to be available for comment in the future on a particular subject without seeming self-serving. A good time to make such an offer is when a writer has interviewed you about a story. Suggest to the writer that if he has questions in the future,

Exploit Your Good Fortune

When you are fortunate enough to get press coverage in a magazine or a newspaper, turn a good thing into a great thing. Mail copies of the article to select—or even to large—numbers of your customers or clients. Attach a personally signed (if possible) note such as, "I don't know if you saw Widget Company Ltd. mentioned Tuesday in the *Daily Gazette*. I thought you might be interested." The idea is to bring to the attention of your important clientele the fact that your company has made news. Even if the recipients had seen the article when it first appeared, you can reinforce the message by mailing them a copy, and you have made another personalized contact without trying to sell them something, while letting others brag about you.

you would be happy to discuss them with him, and not just issues dealing with your company. In this way you can win the confidence of important writers at the publications you target.

Keep in mind these are relationships built on mutual trust. If you genuinely seek to be helpful to writers in understanding topics and your industry, you probably will find that these writers will become more open to suggestions that you may have later for stories that deal with you and your company. One caveat: Do not abuse the relationship. Writers will drop you like a hot widget if they suspect you are manipulating them for self-promotion. The secret, as we have seen in so many other instances, is to be honest and sincere.

Be credible and objective in your dealings and you may well find yourself listed in many writers' Rolodexes as a leading source in your field. The practical upshot is that even in articles that are not written about your company, you and your company may be prominently mentioned simply by virtue of the press recognizing your expertise as a quotable, reliable source and seeking you out for comment.

Become a News Tipster

Another way to ingratiate yourself with your industry press is to become a news tipster. The news tipster differs from a quotable, reliable source in that he often is not identified in articles, instead serving as the catalyst for reporters to look into a subject. News tipsters benefit in other ways, however. They also earn credibility in the eyes of the press. Credibility, of course, is dependent upon how credible your tips are.

Once again we see that honesty and sincerity underscore this relationship. But if tipsters prove trustworthy, they can benefit in the same way as quoted sources in that writers are more inclined to listen to their story ideas and are less jaded when reviewing press releases submitted by them.

Moreover, many tipsters later graduate to full-scale quotable sources. And some are both.

The last and perhaps sweetest way to make the press work for you is to become a writer yourself that contributes to the publications you want to cultivate, or have someone on your staff do it.

Promote Yourself Through Your Writing

What could be better than getting your company name splashed all over the pages of your favorite trade publication, and getting paid by the magazine or newsletter for the privilege? This is low-cost marketing at its best. Obviously, not everyone is suited to writing for trade publications, general interest newspapers, or any other publications for that matter. But if you are capable of stringing coherent sentences together, this is an excellent option. It at once elevates you—or whoever is doing it on your company's behalf—to the exalted position of journalistic authority in the mind of many readers. It is keeping your company's name in the best light in your targeted publications. And it is providing fodder that can be reproduced as marketing collateral to add to your press packet, direct-mail campaigns, or leave-behinds. And on top of all that, you may be paid for it. It is tough to beat that competition.

Test the waters by submitting articles first to less demanding publications, such as your local chamber of commerce newsletter. But as you master the art of wordsmithing, pitch your pieces to more lofty publications, eventually moving up to those that pay, even if nominally, for freelance contributors. If the idea of pounding on keyboards does not appeal to you, perhaps it does to someone on your staff. Be sure, however, to retain tight control of anything written that leaves the building. Since staffers are identified by their affiliation to your company, what they submit under that aegis should be signed off first by you.

> Chapter 16

Innovative Low-Cost Techniques

Stay Ahead Through Innovation

nnovation is what gives new life to old ideas. It refreshes what has worked by invigorating it with what will work better. Innovation is not mere change, and certainly not merely change for change's sake. Innovation is the spark that denotes entrepreneurship. It is innovators who lead the way. They see something new in something old. They see opportunities when others see dead ends or disaster.

To innovate is to make more of less, and to envision something when others see nothing. It is vision as opposed to sight. It is the old saw, "When life gives you lemons, make lemonade." But innovators also make champagne from lemonade. Imagine that! That's why they are called innovators. They imagine what others do not, then make it happen.

When you apply the same inventive and creative energy to your marketing that you apply to your entrepreneurship, you squeeze out of the mundane and the routine something extraordinary and stimulating.

As an illustration, recall the last time you received extraordinary service. It is likely that you were surprised, perhaps not overwhelmingly surprised, but surprised nonetheless. That is because by definition ordinary service is what occurs ordinarily—most of the time. When service exceeds that expectation, it also by definition is unexpected. This does not mean that you must be a five-star hotel in order to provide extraordinary hotel service.

On the contrary, a five-star hotel is expected to provide extraordinary hotel service. It is the mom-and-pop bed and breakfast that more easily can surprise its guests with that kind of over-and-above service.

> When service exceeds that expectation, it also by definition is unexpected.

Exceed Expectations

Perhaps the most effective marketing solution you can employ is to exceed expectations. Sounds expensive, does it not? It does not need to be. Think about it. Most of us go through our days at something less than full speed. We do less than we could. We smile less than we should. We please less than we would have others please us. And for the most part, we treat ourselves better than we treat others. (If you are one of the rare exceptions, congratulations.)

Exceeding expectations can be viewed as the marketing Golden Rule:

Do unto them as you would have them do unto you. When you do, you will reap the benefits.

Taking Service to a Higher Level

Of course to exceed expectations, you must have some idea of what the expectations are. How do you know what your target market expects of you? Ask. Incorporate the question into all customer contacts when appropriate. It is important to establish this baseline of expectations. Otherwise, you have no clue as to whether you are falling short of or exceeding what your customers expect from you. You do not know whether you should be trying harder, or if you are doing too much.

A hotel may offer room service, and as is the common custom, its prices probably are higher than its restaurant prices downstairs. With the higher prices plainly listed on the in-room menu, patrons know in advance that they will be paying a premium to have dinner served to them in the comfort of their room, rather than pay less if they trudge downstairs to the hotel's formal dining room. Every guest in the hotel expects this. The in-room menu reinforces and confirms their expectation. Some are reluctant to pay the higher price, even though they long to eat with their shoes off and the television on. So when hotel patrons do order room service, they certainly expect to pay more than they would in the hotel restaurant, and depending on the hotel, substantially more.

This ordinary expectation to pay a premium for special service is an opportunity for the innovative marketer. Hotels vie aggressively for repeat business. They are service-obsessed, knowing that the degree to which their patrons are pleased has a direct correlation to whether they will return to that hotel or seek different lodgings next time. The noninnovative approach to this competitive marketing situation is to try to provide friendlier, faster, better room service.

The innovative approach is to deliver the room service meal and unexpectedly announce that it is free this time, or half price, or one-third off, or any other degree of unanticipated discount. Which hotel patrons are going to check out after their stay with warmer and fuzzier memories of their hotel—the ones whose room service dinners were served to them quickly with a smile or the ones whose room service dinners were served to them

Deliver Unrequested Service

Resorts and the businesses that serve them are crowded with vacationers in cars who have logged many miles catching bugs and debris on their windshields en route to their destinations. People on the road view life through their windshields. And a dirty windshield literally taints one's view. Here is how to build good will and do it inexpensively. Have an employee with a bucket and a squeegee go from car to car in your company's parking lot car washing windshields while the drivers and their families are enjoying whatever it is you sell indoors. Leave behind on the immaculate windshields business-card-sized notes thanking the cars' owners for stopping at your establishment. Make sure the notes include a mention that the window washing was a free, complimentary service of Widget Resort Destination, and that you hope it improves their view when they leave.

quickly with a smile at half the expected cost? Which marketing approach is more effective in generating repeat customers? Indeed, which approach is more likely to generate a second request for room service before the guests check out?

Unexpected Delight

The key to this type of innovative approach is, of course, that it is unexpected. That is, if the first night's room service is advertised in advance as "half off" or "free," it becomes the expectation. But if it is a marketing solution that arrives unannounced serendipitously, and takes patrons entirely by surprise, it exceeds their expectation.

The marketing of exceeding expectations therefore requires a stealth that overt, conventional marketing does not. Conventional marketing says to tout your benefits in advance, which is good, as far as it goes. But innovative marketing springs unexpected benefits on customers once they are in the door in order to exceed their expectations. It is the sneak attack of kindness that disarms and wins converts, and customer loyalty.

Just as asking your clientele can help you to add services, benefits, and features to your bill of fare, it also helps you to eliminate the extraneous. You may find that the amenities and extras that you offer customers now at some expense are really unnecessary and unappreciated, or in other words wasteful.

For example, a hotel may provide a restaurant on site for the convenience of its patrons. But hotel restaurants are notorious money losers. They often are entirely dependent on the number of people staying in the hotel. If vacancies are up, business is down. When was the last time you saw an ad for a restaurant located in a hotel unless it was part of the hotel's ad? An innovative approach to the dilemma of the money-losing hotel restaurant may be to eliminate the eatery and instead offer a free meal for each guest at an affiliated, off-site restaurant.

If the hotel's restaurant loses the equivalent of $30 per hotel guest, why not offer a $25 dining certificate to each guest redeemable at the restaurant across the street? Not only would the restaurant add a benefit (a free meal), but it would also eliminate a money-losing operation and be able to cut expenses substantially.

Certainly, this approach would not work for every hotel. Some hotel restaurants are profitable. Some hotel patrons prefer the on-site convenience to the freebie. Many hotel guests simply have an expectation of an on-site restaurant. But many others can just as well do without, as evidenced by the scant number of diners in many hotel restaurants on any given evening.

Why not simply ask hotel guests, "Please help us determine how to best serve you. Would you prefer a $25 certificate redeemable for a meal at XYZ restaurant conveniently located across the street, or would you prefer the convenience of a restaurant in our hotel at the prices on the attached menu?"

Don't Be Too "Creative" or "Original"

Innovation is such fun. Remove your marketing blinders and see the possibilities that previously were hidden from view. Push the envelope, as they say. Once you learn to market without stifling restrictions and conventional restraints, the opportunities are boundless. Anything goes.

Now that you have rediscovered the boundless potential of thinking outside the box, here is a reality check. Do not be too creative or too original. Creativity for the sake of creativity may win awards at your regional marketing convention. And originality definitely can put your stamp on what you do. But taking these otherwise admirable qualities to the extreme misses the point, and can do a disservice to your marketing efforts.

Some of the most clever and original marketing is some of the worst marketing in terms of achieving what it should achieve. It may win awards, but does it market effectively? The best illustrations of this are the advertisements that are so wonderfully creative and hilarious that the wonder and hilarity completely overshadow the marketing message. "Creative" ad agencies are among the worst offenders.

They crank out ads and commercials that move people to uproarious laughter or sentimental tears. But no one who views them can recall the product's name. It may garner awards and accolades. It may be enthusiastically received by the target audience. But unless it achieves your goals, it is simply good entertainment and bad marketing.

The lesson here is that you should think outside the box, and you should strive for creative approaches that will distinguish your company, product, or service from competitors. But apply real-world measures to your marketing solutions. Innovation in and of itself is self-indulgent and frivolous. Keep in mind the goals that are set out in your marketing plan. Measure all solutions—the innovative and the conventional—against your real-world goals. If they are not moving you toward those ends, abandon them regardless of how clever or original they may be.

When to Hire a Pro

One of the inherent characteristics of entrepreneurs is that they have a burning desire to do too much. Most of them are not born delegators. They are by nature just the opposite. It is difficult for most people who start their own business or who launch an entrepreneurial endeavor to unhand the reins and to allow others to take control. Entrepreneurs tend to micromanage. This is the principal reason that we often find the founders of businesses are paid off and shown the door once the business goes public and professional management is put in place to run the show.

Any small business owner or start-up proprietor should bear these facts in mind when crafting their marketing solutions. Their first tendency may be to do it all themselves. After all, who knows the business better than the people who created it? Well, for starters, marketing the business is an entirely different function than starting or operating the business. The skills inherent in creating a profitable enterprise are not necessarily the same as those required to promote it. Indeed, these skill sets may be diametrically opposed to one another. Quick decision-making and risk taking are innate to the entrepreneur. Few businesses would be launched, let alone succeed, without people at the helm who exhibit a willingness to take risks or the ability to act decisively, often based on their intuitive grasp of circumstances. But beware of the marketer who is predisposed to gamble, or who makes snap judgments before evaluating all the options.

Marketers, while creative and innovative, also are systematic plodders. At least they should be. They survey the market, they evaluate the data, they calculate the potentials, then they execute carefully controlled solutions. Imagine the disaster otherwise, such as a direct marketing campaign run on intuition or a hunch. That can get costly. Fast.

All of this is simply a way of reminding those of you who are more entrepreneurial than plodding that there may be people on your staff or in the consulting world who are more inclined or better suited to execute your marketing plan or perhaps some aspects of it than you are. The best course to follow is when you find yourself in uncomfortable water, or assuming marketing responsibilities that exceed your expertise, do not be afraid to delegate them to those who are better suited to the tasks. So when you find yourself operating above your pay grade, invoke the low-cost solution and hire a pro.

Think in Bullets and Think in Threes

While developing your innovative approach to marketing, be mindful that certain conceptual and structural fundamentals will always apply. One concept that seems universal and applicable to tactics and content alike is that three is an optimum number. Processes have a beginning, a middle, and an end. In other words, three stages. Children learn their A, B, Cs, *not* their A, B, Cs, and Ds. Things are as easy as one, two, three.

Spatial relations are up, down, and in the middle. Time references are past, present, and future. Values are good, bad, or indifferent. Yes, no, maybe. We could go on and on and on. (We just did.) The world seems naturally structured by threes. Whether this is a mystical universal law etched in our subconscious or merely the way we have come to think, it is a fact nonetheless. People approach reality with sets of three in mind, therefore, when dealing with people it is always wise to speak their language if we want to connect. And that is every marketer's goal.

Tread Lightly with Humor

One more cautionary piece of advice that innovative marketers should heed: Tread lightly with humor. For one thing, not everyone laughs at the same stuff. (One man's humor is another man's tragedy.) And even if your material is funny, humor may be inappropriate for promoting your product, service, or business. A humorous campaign should not conflict with the nature of the product or service. Funny marketing slogans to promote mortuary services are unlikely to score big with aggrieved families members hoping to lay their loved ones to rest with dignity and solemnity. Humor is difficult to pull off effectively, and even when it is funny the results may be unhappy. So when in doubt, don't.

Therefore, when crafting your marketing message, avoid wandering far afield from the rule of three. In terms of content, when your message tells a story, be sure it has a beginning, middle, and end. Leave one out and you risk confusing rather than communicating.

The same rule applies to structure. Group graphic presentations by the rule of three. Typefaces should be large, smaller, and smallest. Colors dark, light, and in between. Remember the design of Yellow Page ads in Chapter 14? The principal elements were the main headline, the bulk of the content, and the exit message. Three elements. View all your collateral in this way. Get the reader in, give him the message, and get him out with instructions. Three stages.

Nearly as effective as the rule of three is the bulleted approach to communications. Like the rule of three, bullets help to simplify a message. This is truer today than ever before. As our pace quickens and the demands on our time increase, it becomes more and more difficult to capture the time and attention necessary to convey persuasive arguments. How do you sell a complicated benefit to harried prospects? If you manage to catch their attention and stimulate their interest, how can you build desire if they do not pay attention long enough to hear the entire message?

This reality is what has given birth to the sound-bite culture. Brief snippets now serve where extensive explanations once reigned. In practical terms this means that you must be brief and to the point. You can always offer more later, but only if you have offered enough quickly enough to generate interest. The common shorthand for this approach is "bullets," so named because they often are listed with bullets preceding them.

Bulleted lists abound. They are an elegant and effective means for presenting benefits and also are an excellent means for guiding decision-making:

- Do this
- Then this
- Then this

Bullets allow the presenter to give snatches and the gist of a message without including all those bothersome parts of speech like verbs or nouns that fill the fat paragraphs so imposing to an increasingly reading-averse populace. In short, bullets provide a tidy, organizational structure that can simplify complex messages. Consequently, bullets are among marketers' best friends. Especially when used in groups of three. Use them liberally in your collateral, in your messages, in your communications.

Stagger Promotions for Efficient Response

It is conceivable that your marketing campaigns will deluge your company with responses, exactly what you hoped would happen. But too much of a good thing is counterproductive. For instance, the damage that can be done to a company's reputation may well outweigh the short-term benefits if a marketing campaign generates more responses than the company can accommodate. A marketer's nightmare is a campaign so successful the company cannot adequately respond. Instead of delighted customers, it creates grumbling, complaining customers.

One solution to this potentially costly problem is to stagger your promotions so they do not overwhelm your ability to respond. Staggering a direct-mail campaign, for example, may also permit you to gauge its effectiveness as you go, rather than being flooded with orders that back up and threaten to disappoint customers because they cannot be filled in a timely manner.

If you stagger the mailing, you can measure its response incrementally. If the response is far from taxing your ability to process orders in a timely fashion, you can mail a greater number in the next wave. But if your first mailing results in backlogging orders, you can reduce the number of direct mailings that go out in the next wave.

The innovative low-cost approach is to build a campaign incrementally so you can gear up if necessary to handle responses, or reduce the effort to bring responses into a manageable number. In this way, measuring and gauging as you go, it is possible to find the optimum effort and the optimum response without running the risk of souring customers in the process because you were unable to fill their orders in the way they expected.

> If you stagger the mailing, you can measure its response incrementally.

Ask for Letters of Introduction

For whatever reason, bold, confident entrepreneurs who shy from no challenge sometimes simply shrink like timid children when it comes to asking happy customers to market on their behalf. Why is anyone's guess. Perhaps it is the independent streak in the entrepreneurial personality that arrogantly (and wrongly) assumes they can do everything on their own without help from anyone else. This is where it is important to separate that valuable and essential entrepreneurial spirit from the more practical and more humble nature required of the marketer. The marketer knows he cannot do everything on his own, and is willing to seek help wherever it can be found.

One of the greatest sources of marketing help is the happy customer. Innovative marketers will devise innovative methods to tap that invaluable resource. One such method is to ask happy customers for letters of introduction. These letters are beyond conventional testimonials, such as might appear in advertisements or in brochures. And they are more than referrals because they more actively involve the customer in the marketing process.

Letters of introduction actually once played a far greater role in commerce than they do today. Before the computerized era of credit checks and background databanks, men of commerce were introduced formally to new business relationships by handwritten letters of introduction penned by a common, respected intermediary. They were endorsements of character and of suitability.

The author was saying in effect, this person has my trust and deserves yours too. It was a very personal and effective means of introduction. It still works, although it is employed far less frequently in most sectors. The tactic is so uncommon today that it is almost certain to get the recipient's attention, and can hardly fail to win respect. Those alone are a couple of great reasons to do it.

If your happy customers are willing to recommend you, but a little hesitant to put pen to paper, offer to provide them a draft letter they can modify as they like. One last thing: Be sure to have them print it on their stationery and to personally sign it and mail it to the prospect. After a suitable interlude, follow up the letter with a telephone call and/or a letter of your own to the prospect to arrange a face-to-face meeting.

Seek Customer Responses in All Contacts

Innovative marketers not only seek dialogue with happy customers, they also want to hear from as many customers across the happiness-unhappiness spectrum as possible. Listening only to happy customers is like listening only to your friends. How will you ever know why some people do not like you if you listen only to your friends?

It is delightful and necessary to know whom you please and why so you can do more of the same. But you also need to know whom you displease and why so you can stop doing whatever it is they find disagreeable. To this end, innovative marketers find methods of gleaning customer responses from every contract that is appropriate.

If you have order forms, include space for customers to register their complaints as well as their accolades. If you take orders over the telephone, incorporate into your telephone dialogue questions to determine whether customers are less than pleased, and if so, why. Your Web site should include some means for customers to register complaints or to offer suggestions, with an assurance that their comments are valued by you and will be taken into full consideration in shaping future policies.

Face-to-face sales personnel should be trained to incorporate requests for constructive criticism at the end of their sales encounters, such as, "We hope you found everything you needed today when shopping in our store, but if you did not, please share with us what it was you did not find so that we may consider adding it to the inventory."

Even though unhappy customers are more likely than happy customers to volunteer their opinions without being asked, most disgruntled customers simply will not bother to complain. They will just never return. It may seem to be an odd thing to do, going out of your way to ask customers if they are dissatisfied. But if customers are unhappy, it is better to know than not to know. You cannot fix what you do not realize is broken.

Turn Negatives to Positives

Finally, one of the underlying principles of innovative marketing is to capitalize on the unusual, to make silk purses out of

Perk Up That Business Card

Thrusting your business card at potential customers is viewed by some as intrusive and even obnoxious. Overcome this attitude by making your business cards irresistible. If you operate a mobile service such as tool sharpening or window screen repair or plumbing, invest in magnetic business cards instead of the paper variety. Magnetic cards are slightly more expensive than paper cards, but as you will see, they probably are more valuable to your marketing efforts. Cover the exterior of your truck with the magnetic cards, but leave room for the all-important instructions painted on the side, "Take one." You will find that people who otherwise shy away from an extended hand offering a business card will walk across the street to pluck one off the side of your truck. One caveat: Do not park near schools. Children will clean you out in short order.

sows' ears. The knack of turning negatives into positives is precisely that type of technique. What could be more innovative than making satisfied customers out of complainers or using complaints to develop successful marketing?

Here's one example of an innovative solution. When a long-awaited movie is finally being shown at a theater, moviegoers line up sometimes for hours waiting to get in. There is little in life that is more annoying than standing in long lines for a long time. How can you turn such a negative into a positive? Try wheeling out a cart stocked with beverages, popcorn, and other refreshments normally only sold inside the theater after patrons are admitted. Not only will you relieve the discomfort and boredom of customers waiting in line, you will probably boost your overall concession sales. By viewing customers' complaints as an opportunity to serve them better, you can please them and yourself.

This kind of innovative thinking is most effective when it becomes institutionalized. It is one thing for your marketing chief or even for your entire marketing staff to mull over how to turn negative experiences around as positive possibilities. But it is far more effective if that attitude pervades every department and every employee. It is the difference between instilling a possibility approach to your corporate mindset and wallowing in the same old cover-the-hind-end approach. When every employee sees customer complaints as potentials for customer satisfaction rather than potential for that employee's chastisement, you will have innovated your marketing to the nth degree. At that point, anything is possible.

> **Chapter 17**

It's Not Junk Mail When . . .

Standing Out in the Daily Stack of Mail

It is a long-established fact that the U.S. mail—not so affectionately known these days as "snail mail"—has proven appeal to marketers. Who among us hasn't waited with anticipatory glee for that particular letter or package to arrive?

The mere heft of the daily delivery denotes substance and significance. There *must* be something important inside. The pieces themselves have a certain tactile appeal—varying textures, colors, and shapes. Every envelope whispers mystery. Mail can be very enticing.

Alas, the flip side in contemporary America is that marketers have exploited the effectiveness and ubiquitous nature of the U.S. mail by flooding mailboxes with literally billions of pieces of the stuff annually. By anyone's measure, it certainly has been too much of a good thing.

Get Your Mail Opened

Unfortunately, we have become so saturated in unrequested and unwanted junk mail that most of us are jaded to the point that the preferred place to open one's mail has become hovering over a trash can. Worse yet, much of it isn't even opened before it's dumped into the wastebasket.

This is a monumental problem if you require the mail to market to current and prospective customers. Behemoth corporations with millions of dollars to burn can rely on sheer numbers. Even a tiny response rate can be an adequate return on investment for Big Corp. Inc. if it mails hundreds of thousands or even millions of pieces.

Use the Right List

Mailing to the wrong list is the surest way to waste your marketing budget. It doesn't matter how clever your pitch, how wonderful your product, or how enticing your offer if you are talking to the wrong people. Whenever you market by mail, be certain that every name on your mailing list fits the precise characteristics of your target market as you have identified it in your marketing plan.

But for the low-cost conscious among us, we require more assurance that someone will actually see what we've sent. Direct mail is one of the more expensive methods of marketing, and it can be disastrously costly if not done properly.

The question is, how do you distinguish your very important message to your critically important customers and prospects from all that "junk mail" your competitors and others are sending? There are a few tried-and-true techniques to getting your mail noticed and opened.

Even the most jaded junk mail hater will give a cursory look at the envelope before tossing it. The outside of the mail piece is your first opportunity—and maybe your last—to persuade the recipient to look at rather than discard what's inside. You have only a few seconds to win this first crucial encounter.

Two Killer Mistakes

Making either of the following two irreversible errors can scuttle any direct-mail campaign.

Failing to tell the mail recipient what you want him to do. Unless your mailing is designed simply to reinforce and enhance your identity (which is okay if that's your goal), you should make clear what the reader is supposed to do after reading your message. "Call now" or "Go to our Web site at . . ." or "Fill out the enclosed form."

Changing the look and feel of every mailing piece simply for the sake of change. One of the goals of your marketing collateral is to build a consistent image, a recognizable face to ingratiate yourself as a familiar old friend. If every mailing you send out is entirely different in its look and feel, you start from scratch with every mailing. Build an identity with a cumulative effect.

Make an Offer They Cannot Refuse

Don't waste the outside of your envelope when it is the only piece of the mailing that you can be certain will be seen. If you are mailing to 1,000 people on your targeted mailing list and the mailing is costing you $1 per piece

Nominal Cost, Sizable Benefit

Have sticky yellow notepads preprinted at nominal expense with the notation "For your information" or "I thought you might be interested" and with your initials or first name. Have your commercial printer use a script type of font to give it a personally hand-written appearance. For very select mailings, it is worth your time to spend five minutes actually writing the notes and signing them. There is nothing quite like a handwritten note to convey personal warmth and interest.

in creative services, stationery, marketing collateral, and postage, how much is it worth to you to guarantee that each recipient opens your $1,000 mailing?

Try this message on the outside of the envelope:

"Don't throw this away. It may have a $100 bill inside."

Now, include a $100 bill in one of the letters. Your $1,000 mailing just became a $1,100 mailing. But it will be much more effective for that 10 percent bump in cost. For a mere $100 extra stuffed into one of the recipient's envelopes you can be fairly well assured that every envelope in that mailing will be opened.

Postcards Instead of Envelopes

The great difficulty with envelopes is getting them opened. But postcards don't have that problem. The recipient virtually cannot help but read them, or at least scan them. In effect, when mailing postcards the threshold battle for attention—what's written on the outside of the mailing—becomes academic. What's written on the outside of a postcard is the entire message.

Not only do postcards avoid the problem of unopened mail, they are generally far less expensive to send. Moreover, postcards are low-cost ways to use photographs and color in a mailing, and photographs and color are proven enhancements to communication.

All else equal, a person's eyes will be drawn to color over black and white, and to bright colors over dull colors. All else equal, images like photographs draw the eye far more effectively than words. Postcards provide a low-cost means to employ these time-tested and proven readership enhancers.

Remember that mailing in which you included a $100 bill? Follow it up with a low-cost postcard that announces to everyone the name—but not other identifiable information such as address—of the lucky $100 recipient. This serves the multiple purposes of establishing your credibility and making it more likely your next such offer will be opened by anyone who did not open the first one. It also gives you a good excuse for one more pass at each of the targets on your mailing list to reinforce your identity without an overt, off-putting sales pitch. There is one caveat. It helps to know which recipient, chosen at random before the mailing, will receive the $100. As a hedge and to protect your credibility, have on file a certified document by an independent party attesting that the $100 bill was inserted into Joe Smith's envelope. Imagine Joe's reaction when he gets your follow-up postcard and realizes he threw away the $100.

Copywriting for Direct Mail

The art of direct-mail copywriting is a dark mystery to most outsiders. That's okay. Unless you intend to become a high wizard of this mystical art you can get by with a few basic rules of thumb whether it be for your personal correspondence, sales letters, or cover letters to accompany brochures and fliers.

- Write in a cordial tone.
- Write in a style appropriate to the audience.
- Write in short, declarative sentences.
- Indent paragraphs.
- Highlight in some way—underline, boldface, italics— the important points.
- Write it long or short, but base the length on what the reader needs to know to get him to do what you want him to do.

Above all else, make certain the bottom of your letter contains a "P.S."

Print in Bulk

Have your commercial printer prepare postcards in bulk, enough for several mailings to your customer base and prospects, but with one side blank. You can get a slight price break by printing in greater volume. Then, using your own office desktop printer and word processor's mail merge capabilities, address each postcard individually or run off labels. If you had your commercial printer leave the "picture" side of the postcard blank, you can customize as many as necessary with your office desktop printer to send particular offers that can change over time. Meanwhile, the consistent look of the other side of the card helps reinforce your identity with recipients.

Put Something Lumpy Inside

But as you know by now, no one will read the postscript if they don't open the envelope. Here's another surefire way to get the recipient inside your envelope: Put something lumpy inside. It can be as innocent as a writing pen with your company name on it, or it can be as unusual as an odd-shaped ad specialty.

What is important is that whatever it is, it is not flat paper. If it shakes around inside, all the better. If it bulges, great. If it is unidentifiable from the outside, better yet. The point is to raise the curiosity factor to the level that the recipient simply cannot put aside your envelope without opening it.

The postscript is one of the most likely to be read portions of any letter. Letter readers are like newspaper readers, and readers of billboards and advertisements. They scan before deciding to read. They are looking over the document for an entry point, the hook that pulls them in to the message. Finding no hook, they go no further.

Those of you who remember the police detective played by Peter Falk will understand why the P.S. might be called "the Columbo Effect." The postscript is a way of saying, just as Columbo often did, "Oh, by the way, just one more thing . . ."

The real significance is that the postscript is far more likely than the body of the letter to be read first. Use the postscript to underscore your offer, or to add a sweetener to your offer.

Use Press Coverage as Collateral

Far too many businesses that have gotten favorable press coverage take that very positive event no further. It's as if the marketing department assumes everyone in the target market profile also subscribes to the *Daily Gazette*. Don't assume.

The value of favorable press coverage is that an independent, credible third party has portrayed you in a positive light, and noted that you are doing something significant. Why keep that a secret?

Photocopy your press clippings as they occur. Mail them to those in your target market mailing list who are likely to be impressed.

When possible, include a personal note. But at the least, attach sticky notes that say something to the effect of, "I thought you might be interested . . ." Of course, make sure the sticky note also includes your name.

Piggyback on Mailings of Related Professionals

Another often-overlooked low-cost marketing solution is cooperative efforts by noncompetitors.

If you sell personal lessons in how to use accounting software, approach computer retailers and explore the viability of piggybacking your marketing collateral with their mailings. Often, such joint mailings come at fairly substantial cost when large chain stores are involved.

But for mom-and-pop retailers, the cost can be much more manageable, and the retailers may well see that including your services with their mailings is a value-added service that enhances their offer.

> **Chapter 18**

Low-Cost Marketing Tools

PART FOUR   INNOVATIVE (BUT OFTEN NEGLECTED) SOLUTIONS

CHAPTER 16 Innovative Low-Cost Techniques ■ CHAPTER 17 It's Not Junk Mail When . . . ■ **CHAPTER 18 Low-Cost Marketing Tools** ■ CHAPTER 19 Low-Cost Marketing Tactics ■ CHAPTER 20 People Need People

Tools You Can Use

So how can you make use of your valuable research to aggressively target an audience while ensuring that you do not waste your limited marketing dollars? There are many cost-effective tools available for innovative marketers that can substantially reduce the strain on your budget while still setting yourself apart from competitors and appealing in a unique way to your customers.

One proven path to success is frequently traveled not by choice, but out of necessity. That path is taken by entrepreneurs who have no other option but to adopt "do it yourself" marketing simply because they cannot yet afford to pay someone else to do it for them. Ironically, those who can afford to pay someone else would benefit greatly if they also had done it themselves when starting out (and perhaps later as well).

It is always unwise to take on responsibilities that you cannot perform satisfactorily. But none of the following is rocket science either, and until you can afford to pay someone else to do it for you, plenty of marketing tools are well within your abilities. Besides, nothing is quite as enlightening or educational as learning on the job what works and what does not. What one learns firsthand in the school of trial and error is likely to remain an indelible lesson. After you are profitable enough to pay others, what you have learned from doing it yourself will be invaluable in evaluating the effectiveness of what others do for you when you can pay them to do it.

First, we will discuss three generic do-it-yourself tools that require a small amount of common sense and an even smaller amount of money.

> Nothing is quite as enlightening or educational as learning on the job what works and what does not.

The Letter

Tool number one is the ubiquitous and multipurpose letter. When writing a letter, for the most part the same fundamentals apply whether it is written as a sales letter, a thank-you letter, a response to an inquiry, or any other similar direct-mail piece. There are, of course, no hard and fast rules. Whatever works, works. But there are a few pointers to follow that make it much more likely your letter will work—that is, achieve its end.

How Long?

A letter should be as long as needed to effectively communicate what the reader has to know. But no longer. Some copywriters hold to the theory that a letter must never be longer than one page because readers have limited attention spans. Others insist that the longer the letter the better because readers need to know every last argument if they are to be persuaded. But common sense tells us that just as readers' desires and needs vary in breadth and depth, letters must be of different lengths in order to adequately address those desires and needs—but certainly no longer than necessary. The key here is knowing what it is your reader needs from you.

For example, if your reader is the editor at a magazine and your letter is suggesting that the editor should assign a reporter to write a story about your company, one page is long enough. Editors want only the essence of your story pitch, not elaboration or embellishment. Plus, you probably are putting flesh on the skeleton in companion pieces to the letter, such as the backgrounder, fact sheet, or perhaps even an entire press packet that will address any questions the editor may have. But those supplemental pieces come into play only if the letter does its job, which is to pique the editor's interest. Such a one-page appeal should look like a business letter, without garish embellishments or outrageous, eye-grabbing graphics. This letter is calm and businesslike, and appropriately so. It needs to present concisely the best reason that the editor should be interested in assigning one of his reporters to your story.

Close the Sale

If your letter is a sales letter that hopes to close the sale by the time the reader finishes reading it, then it is likely to require several pages. It will need to:

- Cover all the hot button issues
- Detail all the benefits
- In some cases, list the features that make up secondary sales points
- Give thorough and unmistakable directions for how to place an order, or otherwise contact your company for assistance in making the purchase

Such a sales letter will often include garish embellishments or other eye-grabbing graphics. It probably should have a headline that touts the major benefit you are selling, and the headline may be graphically enclosed in a box to emphasize it further. The letter may include subheadlines to break up the long text and provide optional reader entry points to the copy as well as underlined, boldfaced, or italicized words for emphasis. It is certainly likely to contain bulleted benefits that give the reader at a glance a good summary of the selling points. Other effective eye-grabbers are pull quotes or blurbs—key phrases from the content repeated and highlighted in boxes or in different colored type—in the margins or inserted between paragraphs. The letter also should repeat several times the main points you want to make to reinforce the major benefits of your offer. This letter is loud and verbose, but for good reason. It needs to grab, then hold for a relatively long time, the readers' interest to provide enough motivation to close the sale.

Stick to an Appropriate Tone

Whatever type of letter you write, it always must be appropriate in tone for its purpose and its recipient. If you have a long-established relationship with the letter's recipient, the tone of the letter should be friendlier and less formal than if the letter is your first contact. Despite relaxing of the rules of etiquette in contemporary mores, most people still are put off by feigned familiarity. Even if you trick readers into thinking that you know them by referring to them by their first name in the salutation, the trick will be short-lived, and consequently more likely to leave a distrustful attitude than a receptive attitude for the rest of what you have to say.

Just as you would not address a stranger by his first name unless invited to, you should not presume that it is all right to do so in your first contact in a letter, particularly if your letter is uninvited. The recipient is likely to think that you are presumptuous, perhaps even rude. Rather than ingratiating yourself, you probably will add another barrier to overcome.

Just as you would not be stilted or rigid when talking to an old friend, you should not put on airs of phony decorum when writing customers who have become longtime associates. They are likely to think they are getting an automated form letter, instead of a warm letter from an old friend. By being overly formal you waste the advantage of that close relationship that you have cultivated for years, and perhaps even damaged it. To recap, always have the appropriate tone.

Get to the Point

Your letter also should always get to the point immediately, then expand on the point fully, then summarize the point finally. Or, as the old saw goes, tell them what you are going to tell them, then tell them, then tell them what you told them. The theme here, of course, is repetition. No matter what the length of your letter, it should touch home plate at least three times. The opening sentence or paragraph is where the readers go to find out what the letter is about. Do not disappoint them or beat around the bush, or they probably will not go much further. The end of the letter is where they go to find out what the letter was all about. So tell them with a tight, concise summary. And the body of the letter is where readers expect to find the meat of the message. So feed them amply. Oddly enough, the body of the letter is often the last place readers go for information. Instead they go to the top and bottom, a headline, a subheadline or a postscript, seeking a reason to read all that fat verbiage in the body of the letter. No matter what you have to say in the body of the letter, it will not matter if you do not hook the reader at one of those entry points.

The P.S.

Speaking of postscripts, your letter should always have one. The postscript—the P.S. at the bottom of the last page—is one of the first portions of a letter that readers look to. Because the postscript is located at the exit point of the letter, at the very end, it also is a perfect place to plant a reminder of what you want the reader to do, such as your call to action like a telephone number to call, or a reminder that the offer you have made is good only until a certain date. Another

Questions Invite Curiosity

The question mark is a marketer's best friend. Part of the challenge of all marketing is to involve and engage your target market in a dialogue that leads to sales. One of the best ways to do that is to ask a question. Want to get an envelope opened? Ask a question on the outside and explain that the answer is inside. Want to get a block of text read? Put a headline above it that asks a question. If your target market looks at a declarative statement like "Our widgets are waterproof," the communication may end there. But when the same people look at a question like "Are there any waterproof widgets?" they will at least attempt to answer it. And, wanting to know if their answer is correct, they will then open the envelope or read the article.

effective use of the postscript is to sweeten the letter's offer by adding a bonus or extra benefit, such as: "Call before June 25 and get a free widget."

Do Not Put on Airs

Perhaps the most common error in letter writing is pretentious affectation. Snootiness. An example is using the words "pretentious affectation" instead of using "snootiness." Another example is using two words, such as we just did, when one word will do. This is not to say that you should talk down to your reader. But it is a reminder that the shorter your words, the shorter your paragraphs, the shorter your message, the more easily and more likely they will be understood. Highfalutin words run the risk of sailing right over your readers' heads. These days it is difficult to use language that is too simplistic. The typical newspaper is written at about a sixth-grade reading level. Unless you are selling dissertation-editing services and your target audience are all Ph.D. candidates, you are almost always better off saying whatever you have to say simply. Then everyone—even the Ph.D.s—will understand.

Advertisements

Tool number two is the ever-present advertisement, whether an ad for a newspaper, a magazine, a Web site, a direct-mail flyer, or a billboard. All ads have several things in common visually and verbally.

Be Seen

The first visual challenge for an advertisement is to be seen. This can be difficult in a sea of other ads that are each seeking the same threshold accomplishment.

So how to be seen? Think large, bold, or colorful. Better yet, think all three. Regardless of the size of your ad, it should have a large, bold, or colorful focal point, and a disproportionately dominant element that can be either type in a headline or a graphic or a photograph but must draw the eye before the rest of the ad is read. As we discussed in Chapter 14, people start reading at the top and proceed down, moving from the left to the right as they go. So unless you want to waste words, do not bother putting anything of substance above the large, bold, or colorful eye-attracting graphic or headline. Chances are, readers' eyes will be drawn to the largest, boldest, most colorful element in the ad, then proceed down, not up. Almost never up.

Be Read

The next visual challenge for an ad is to be read. Much like a sales letter, an ad should offer multiple entry points for readers. One way to do that is to use subheadlines and bulleted lists. Advertising design would be an utter no-brainer if everyone began at the top and read every word religiously until arriving at the bottom. Alas, ad readers are irreligious in that regard. They do not read. They scan, looking for something to read. Give them as many excuses as you can for them to read further. Use benefits as blurbs, subheadlines, and bullets to draw the reader in. Questions work too, especially when separated from the body of the text. Who can resist a question hanging in the margin without reading the text to find the answer?

Move the Reader to Action

The greatest challenge for an ad, visual or verbal, is to move readers to action. Needless to say, you should never forget the call to action in your ad. What is it you wish to accomplish with the ad? Do not be clever or coy. Tell readers flat out what you want them to do: "Visit our store at 123 Main Street from 9 A.M. to midnight, Monday through Saturday" or "Bring this ad for 25 percent off a case of widgets. Offer good only until Thursday." Clever and coy can be misunderstood. Do not risk being misunderstood after you have worked so hard to get them to read the entire ad.

> Needless to say, you should never forget the call to action in your ad. What is it you wish to accomplish with the ad?

Easy Navigation

Another visual challenge for an ad is navigation, or moving the reader from one point to the next logical point in your presentation. You can simplify the readers' task by putting things where common sense says they should go. Do not sprinkle your contact information all over the page. Put telephone and fax numbers in the same block with your address and e-mail

The Cumulative Effect

Ad salesmen will tell you that you need to repeat your message many times before most people will react to it. Of course, they want to sell you more than one ad, but they also happen to be correct. The most effective ad campaigns can be repeated many times. Even when the ad itself changes, by retaining the same general look and feel, you are able to obtain the reinforcement that builds familiarity and understanding. Indeed, you can capitalize on the idea of repeating ads by varying them enough to generate added interest. One way to do that is to clearly identify each ad in sequence, such as "Number two of four." This technique engages the reader in an ongoing story. If your ads are informational, you can also reprint them as small booklets for marketing collateral—"Numbers one through four in our series of the many uses of waterproof widgets."

information. That is where people expect to see them. Do not make it difficult for the reader to respond to your call to action.

You also can aid readers in navigating your ad by keeping in mind that they work from the top down, left to right. But they also work from large to small, bold to faint, colorful to drab. In creating the hierarchy of your ad's appeal make its most important messages the largest, boldest, most colorful and move down the gradation ladder as the messages become less compelling. In that way you ensure that readers are unlikely to read a minor point before a major point. This would not be a problem if readers read every word. But as we know, they do not. So make sure that if the readers leave your ad before digesting your entire message that they got the most important stuff first.

White Space Shouts

Finally, do not be afraid to leave blank spots in your ad; strategic blank spots, that is. These holes in the design are the air that breathe life into your message. Known as "white space," these pictureless, textless expanses powerfully emphasize the dark stuff on a page, the stuff you want readers to pay attention to. If everything in the ad is shouting, nothing gets heard. Silent, strategic white space is a magnet that pulls the eye to the adjacent headline or picture. A headline surrounded by white space appears to be larger and therefore more eye-grabbing than a headline crowded by type. A page without white space asks the reader to find a needle in a haystack. So do not camouflage your message by crowding it. Give it some air to breathe.

The Trifold Brochure

Tool number three is a trifold brochure, the business card on steroids. Trifolds can vary in size, but they commonly are made from an 8½"-by-11" (or smaller) piece of paper folded into thirds the long way so they can easily be slipped into a regular number 10 envelope, or a breast pocket.

The temptation with trifold design is to do too much. Resist that temptation. Some contemporary design is wonderful eye candy. It's attractive, emotional, inspirational, introspective—and as hard as a Picasso to figure out. The trifold brochure is already a powerful communications tool. Do not neutralize its power with a lot of cutesy goop that distracts from your message. As with the letter, the format or look and feel of a brochure should always be appropriate to its message and audience. But it need not be fancy to look expensive, for example. High-quality paper conveys a high-end ambiance more easily than fancy graphics that cost a lot to create or buy.

Have you ever noticed people who are handed a trifold? More often than not, they look at everything. They open it, fold back the next layer, close up the folded layers and turn it over, then turn it over again. A trifold is like one of those Chinese finger puzzles that you stick your fingers in then tug on and relax, then tug again trying to figure out how to release its hold so you can withdraw your fingers. A trifold has the same engaging quality because it is interactive. It is more than words and pictures on paper. It is a page-turning adventure always enticing the reader to unfold just one more flap, or turn it over just one more time. Its appeal is nearly irresistible regardless of what is printed on it. With six panels, only two of which are visible until the reader engages it, the trifold is an enticing and appealing tool. It is very sticky marketing collateral.

Six Panels to Use

You have six panels to work with, but the most important one is the one everyone sees first, the front cover. Do not waste it by splashing your company's name or logo all over it at the expense of your message. Use the front panel to tout your number one benefit. Relegate the company name and/or logo to the bottom of the cover (if you must have it on the cover), but definitely subordinate it to the message of the large headline and/or graphic that delivers your number one benefit: "The most reliable, longest-lasting widgets you can buy."

Think Small

Try a mini trifold brochure. The appeal of this innovative low-cost marketing tool is in its puny size. While most trifold brochures measure roughly 3 inches by 8 inches in folded form, a mini trifold can be as small as you like, and the smaller the better. Obviously, you are not going to be able to squeeze the same amount of compelling prose and enticing graphics into a package that folds up in, say, a 2-inch by 3-inch rectangle, but a mini trifold does not need as much information because it serves a different purpose. Use the novelty-sized trifolds as teasers that prompt recipients to go to the next step—telephone, visit a Web site, mail for information. If conventionally sized trifolds are engaging because of their multipage format (and they are), a mini-sized trifold is that much more engaging.

The back page of the trifold is a good place for your complete company name, location, contact numbers, and a reminder of the message on the cover, to reinforce the most important benefit you offer the reader. Keep it clean, free of clutter. Just the facts. Since all your contact information is there, you should consider it a call to action and spell out what you want the reader to do next.

The remaining four panels are flexible tools to accommodate your message of benefits, features, and company information. But when you open a trifold there is still one flap folded over, covering two inside panels. A good use of that folded-over panel is to give a more detailed breakdown of the benefit mentioned on the cover. Consider this the introductory information that lays out the details of your Unique Selling Proposition and a teaser for the inside three panels, which can be devoted to even greater detail. The deeper the reader goes into your trifold, the more detailed your message should be. But remember, it is a trifold brochure, not a catalog. Keep it simple and concise. As we have discussed with other forms of collateral and advertising material, bulleted items work well in a tightly confined space like a trifold panel.

Each panel should have a headline, but none as large or as prominent as the headline on the front cover. If you use more than one headline per panel, vary the size according to importance. If each headline is the same weight in size and in density, readers sense no hierarchy in your message, which is fine, if you have none. But if you want to step readers through from most important to least important, help them understand what is most important by giving your page elements, like headlines, a priority ranking. Larger, darker, and brighter say "look at me first." Smaller, lighter, and duller get lower billing. If everything inside is of equal import, but you still need to step the reader through sequentially, number the elements. Even folks who read at the sixth-grade level can figure out how to follow the numbers.

Do Not Overdo the Fonts

When considering typefaces for your trifold brochure, bear in mind that variations give emphasis. If every line or every word is emphasized with a different font, a different color, a different size (ten point, thirty point, etc.), a different weight (bold, italic, bold and italic), and a different orientation (askew, sideways, curved, wavy), the viewer is likely to be overwhelmed. When everything is emphasized, nothing is emphasized. You cannot go far wrong if you pick one font for body copy and another for headlines. Pick readable fonts, not fonts made illegible by curlicues and flourishes. You might consider an italicized or boldfaced version of one of the two fonts you have chosen to emphasize pull quotes or blurbs. But unless you are purposely trying to achieve a wacky or wild look for a particular effect, be calm. Use fewer font variations rather than many.

Leading the Reader Through

Writing the content for your trifold brochure is a good exercise in learning how to condense to its essence the information that best sells your product or service. The cover reflects your main benefit. The first inside panel is the detailed summary of your main benefit. The three inside panels may step the reader through the successive stages that they need to travel or may list of your three greatest sub-benefits, or list features that help to sell the main benefit on the cover. The back page is the exit point where you remind readers of what is in it for them and how to contact you. The trifold brochure is a tidy summary of just enough information to attract attention, create interest and desire, and call to action in an irresistible hands-on package.

One last point: Unless your product or service can be sold better with images than with words, resist the urge to clutter up the six-panel package with a lot of graphics and photographs. And, as we discussed about preparing your own advertising, you should leave white space to make your headlines and bullets more effective.

Now for some more specific, innovative low-cost tools.

"Who Do You Know Who Needs . . .?"

Simply asking customers and clients to refer their friends, associates, and neighbors to you is good as far as it goes. But it leaves the ball in the customer's or client's court. Invigorate the process. Do not simply ask for referrals. Ask instead, "Who do you know who needs (fill in the blank)?"

By phrasing the request in this way, you have relieved your customers or clients from connecting the dots. They no longer have to imagine how you can benefit someone they may know. You have specified precisely how you can benefit that third party. Moreover, you relieve your customers or clients from the trouble of initiating contact with those third parties to refer them to you. Instead, all they need to do is provide you a name, something much easier to do than to go out on your behalf and recruit new customers and clients.

If you get a name, be sure to ask your client or customer if it is permissible for you to use their names when contacting the referral. You want to be able to approach the referral by saying, "Our mutual friend so-and-so suggested that you may need the reliable widgets that I sell." Such an entrée provides three things that reduce your cost of marketing by increasing the likelihood of its success: one, it prequalifies the target; two, it reduces resistance because of a mutually respected intermediary, and three, it matches up a target with a specific service or product. Not bad work for a simple question, "Who do you know who . . ." And it costs nothing for you to ask it.

Giveaways to Win Them Over

If you are confident in your product or service, you probably believe that all it takes to sell is for potential customers and clients to experience the benefits firsthand. If that is true, all you need to do is get the strangers who comprise your target market to become familiar with your benefits. But how? Giveaways.

Giveaways are normally associated with ad specialties, which serve a valid marketing purpose as well. But the giveaways we are discussing here are more like free samples. And if your product or service is as good as you believe it is, these giveaways should go a lot farther in winning new customers and clients than trinkets and doodads engraved with your company name.

The great flexibility of giveaways is that they can be whatever you can afford. But whatever they are—miniature servings of your baked beans, or temporary access to your subscription Internet service—they must be enough to whet the potential customer's appetite, or else they are wasted. Giveaways are not limited to products or commodities. Personal and professional services also can be offered. A free body massage might be a giveaway offered by a spa that sells beauty treatments. Or a free business evaluation might be offered by a business broker who specializes in the purchase and sale of businesses.

Giveaways can be offered solo as teasers to get new customers in the door, or as value-added bonuses to curry favor with existing customers. One key to making the giveaways effective is to play them up. Do not be modest. If you treat your giveaway as if it is of little value, that is the impression you will leave with your targeted customers, regardless of how much they may appreciate the giveaway themselves. If you want customers to perceive your giveaway as something valuable, represent it as something valuable.

FAQs and White Papers

One of the most important goals of marketing is to tell your customers everything that they might want to know about your business and your industry before making the decision to buy. Two ways to fulfill this need for information are FAQs and white papers.

What's a FAQ?

The Internet opened a world of new opportunities to marketers. It also introduced a new acronym: FAQ, which is short for "frequently asked questions." FAQs work offline too. Some of the best marketing tools you can employ are the ones that resolve your customers' questions and calm their

Giveaways That Keep On Giving

Giveaways allow your target market to freely sample what you offer, but they can do even more. Make them redeemable for discounts on subsequent sales. In this way you can combine the double whammy of free and discount—two irresistible lures in the low-cost marketer's arsenal. A movie theater can offer a free pass to get people in the door, then get them to come back by printing on the back of the pass, "Keep the stub of this ticket for half off your next visit to the Bijou Theater." For the cost of an otherwise empty theater seat, you have introduced new customers to the comfort and enjoyment of your theater, then rewarded them again to bring them back. You already have a repeat customer, who no doubt spent about as much as a ticket's price at the concession stand.

qualms. It is difficult to address every customer's question simply because it requires so much time for them to ask and for you to answer. But many sales are separated only by the number of unanswered questions that remain in customers' minds. FAQs enable you to answer those questions and to move customers that much closer to the sale, and to do it without extensive face-to-face time that can be better spent in closing the deal.

As you would offer a FAQ page on your Web site, you should also include a FAQ handout among your leave-behind marketing collateral. If you have not got one yet, begin today and list all the common questions your customers ask. Keep it updated, because as time goes by inquiring minds will have new questions that demand new answers. The FAQ sheets are inexpensive to create and can be run off quickly on a desktop laser printer. Include them in all mailings and handouts, and make them available on countertops and in product packaging. Every question you answer in this way eliminates wasted time with inquisitive customers and brings a sale one step closer.

White Papers: FAQs on Steroids

White papers are FAQ sheets for thinking customers, not just the inquisitive ones. If you sell baked beans, you probably have little use for white papers. But if you sell technical products or professional services, white papers give an academic credibility to your marketing collateral. An accountant might offer a free white paper on, "New tax law changes that will impact small businesses in 2003." A Web designer could offer a white paper on, "The benefits of XTML programming language over HTML."

White papers go beyond the scope of customary marketing collateral in that they purport to offer a more independent, authoritative assessment than more self-promotional marketing collateral, and they may not tout a particular service or product. If you belong to a trade organization, you probably have access to white papers that can be reproduced royalty-free. Other white papers can be fashioned from government reports on particular industries or trades. Government publications are not copyrighted, meaning you can reproduce and distribute them freely.

In the event that you or someone you commission writes a white paper that might be useful as a giveaway, be sure that it strives for an objective view on the subject and does not overtly hype your product or service.

Survey Your Customers

If you are not surveying your current customers, you are missing out on one of the lowest-cost, most innovative tools at your disposal. As we have seen in previous chapters, surveys are invaluable tools for gauging potential customers' inclinations, for learning how current customers regard you, and for adjusting to changing market demand. Surveys are great tools to serve you.

Effective Surveys

Surveys provide an opportunity to show customers and potential customers that you value their opinion and, better yet, that you respond to their opinion. Since it is an inconvenience to customers and would-be customers to ask them to fill out detailed surveys, or even to give a few minutes of their time to answer questions orally, it is best to couch the request in terms that clearly show them how they, not just you, will benefit.

Always precede or introduce your survey request with an explanation of why it is needed and how it will be used. When people believe they stand to benefit, even if not immediately, they are much more likely to cooperate, and to answer honestly. Try approaches like this when requesting someone to fill out a survey, "We want to improve how we serve our best customers," or "We are considering a major change in our delivery policy, but first we want to know your preference."

Not only can surveys help to understand and define your customer profile and help you to adjust to changing market conditions, but surveys used in this manner also serve the double duty of customer service tools, not just market research tools. And as we know, the best marketing, and ultimately the lowest-cost marketing, is that which creates satisfied customers.

> Always precede or introduce your survey request with an explanation of why it is needed and how it will be used.

Focus Groups

The customer survey has evolved to a more intense and targeted form, the focus group. In a focus group, a representative sampling of your target market—or of a segment within your targeted market that you wish to learn more about—is gathered and treated like guests in an informal, friendly, but controlled atmosphere. The format might include snacks and beverages, an opportunity to review the product, and usually a facilitator, who asks questions from a prepared list. Typically, the session is recorded either on audio or videotape, and a transcript from the recording is made. Guests may be given a small token of appreciation, but not to bribe them. You want to know their sincere opinions.

The focus group is much more a dialogue than a survey. Its benefit is that you are able to assess respondents' reaction in real time, and ask follow-up questions, or ask for expansion on comments. And as in any dialogue, one respondent's answer may prompt a reaction from another, and your learning experience can take unanticipated paths. A focus group is a good way not only to assess customer satisfaction (or dissatisfaction), but also to mine for previously unknown nuggets of information or discord. Other than the cost of refreshments and a token gift, a focus group is a low-cost means of mining your market's sentiments, and it can offer glimpses of customer attitudes that otherwise might never be seen.

Some businesses are more suited to the focus group approach than others, but companies that frequently deal on a person-to-person basis with their customers can particularly benefit by learning directly from the customer, rather than indirectly from the employee, how that relationship can be improved. Other companies, such as those that rarely have personal contact with customers, also can use focus groups to close the inherent distance between them and the people they serve by learning what they really think.

No matter which type of company yours is, be sure to take advantage of the customer-service image that is created when conducting focus groups. Many people are flattered just to be asked to participate. Flatter them even more. Let them know the process is designed so that you can serve them better. Therefore, as you should with written and oral surveys, always overtly couch your focus group promotion in terms of how the customer will benefit, not just how your business will. Let customers know the focus group is intended to benefit them.

Toll-Free Numbers with Limits

There is another innovative low-cost tool that can be effective, but it may not occur to all entrepreneurs as being appropriate for their business. It is the toll-free telephone number. Toll-free numbers can be a great boon to customer service, but particular caution should be exercised. When used inappropriately or simply too liberally, toll-free numbers can become a money-sucking drain on a small business budget without providing commensurate offsetting benefits. So be careful. You are in essence inviting everyone who knows of the number to use your phone at your expense.

Toll-free telephone numbers send one of the most important marketing messages you can deliver to your target market: You care enough about customers contacting you that you are willing to pay the cost. But good image-making aside, toll-free numbers also clearly boost responses. After all, they invoke the most proven and successful of appeals: They are free. Toll-free numbers also employ another proven route to success. They make it easy for your customers to do business with you by removing barriers. A toll call, even an inexpensive toll call, is definitely a barrier. When all else is equal, prospective customers scanning Yellow Page listings will telephone the company that does not result in a toll charge on their phone bill. When customers are on the fence, a toll-free number can be the nudge they need to pick up the phone.

But be prudent and judicial. Overpromotion of toll-free telephone numbers can run up expenses as quickly as they can ring your phone. As with any marketing tool, toll-free telephone numbers should be employed only when they create more profit than they cost.

Indeed, that is great to keep in mind for all innovative marketers employing tools, low-cost or otherwise. Never use them if they cost you more than they earn you. That is definitely not low-cost marketing.

Too Much of a Good Thing

Toll-free telephone numbers are great incentives for getting people to call you. But before you get one, weigh the consequences of too much success. One organization offered members a toll-free number but made the mistake of including the number on its letterhead, which appeared on all its communications, including press releases. A national magazine published the toll-free number among a list of "sources to contact for more information" in an article of marginal relevance to the organization. The phones rang off the hook for days, and the bill was astronomical. The organization not only incurred the expense, but it had to field hundreds of phone calls from people who wanted "more information" about a lot of topics about which the organization had nothing to offer. Worse yet, organization members were unable to get through by phone for days because the lines were tied up.

> **Chapter 19**

Low-Cost Marketing Tactics

PART FOUR   INNOVATIVE (BUT OFTEN NEGLECTED) SOLUTIONS

CHAPTER 16 Innovative Low-Cost Techniques ■ CHAPTER 17 It's Not Junk Mail When . . . ■ CHAPTER 18 Low-Cost Marketing Tools ■ CHAPTER 19 Low-Cost Marketing Tactics ■ CHAPTER 20 People Need People

Tactics That Set an Example

For the innovative marketer, there are tools and there are tactics. Tools, which we discussed in the previous chapter, are for the most part concrete things that you can touch, like a letter or a trifold brochure. Tactics, on the other hand, generally are the ways in which you use those tools; indeed, the way that you market rather than what you use to market.

One of mankind's failings is that we are inclined to seek our salvation in things. In business, that flaw often is manifest as, "If I could only get a great looking, snappy trifold brochure, all my problems will be solved, and I could push wheelbarrows of profits to the bank day in and day out." Alas, tools, for all their utility, are only part of the solution. An even bigger piece of the marketing puzzle is found in the way that you market.

Regardless of whether you are the boss, or merely the marketing boss, or even just an employee, there are things that you personally can do to help achieve your company's marketing goals. Of course, the higher up the ladder you are, the more what you personally choose to do is likely to influence others in your organization. It is one thing for a line employee to adopt winning marketing tactics. That may or may not carry much weight with colleagues. But when the boss does it, whatever winning marketing tactic is employed sends an unmistakable message to the rank and file: "This is what the person in charge believes is good for the company." All but the most hopelessly uninspired employees are likely to be moved to some extent by such a message. Despite all the current thumb-sucking about egalitarianism and democracy in the workplace, the fact remains that what the boss does sets an example for everyone else. The boss is just not another face in the crowd. This is an unavoidable reality of leadership.

So, if you are the boss, or one of several bosses, be mindful that you can leverage every innovative tactic that you employ simply by setting the example for those you supervise and who look to you for leadership.

Leverage Your Customer Relationships

As a leader, one of the things that you can leverage is your relationship with customers. As we have seen previously in so many contexts, developing attentive, sincerely caring relationships with your target market and your existing customers is one of the best ways to market effectively. Person-to-person encounters are the real test of customer relations, and they represent a forum where complaints and concerns are best discussed and overcome. You could call this the tactic of close encounters.

Just Ten Minutes a Day

As an innovative marketer employing imaginative tactics and creative tools, your time is probably pretty full. It can be difficult to add additional time-consuming tactics to an already demanding schedule. So rather than overloading your schedule with a lot of frantic items for your already busy daily to-do list, try this tact instead: Personally contact at least one customer every day with no other motive except to find out if the customer is happy with you. For the vast majority of customers, this can be handled with a telephone call, and on the average should not take you more than five to ten minutes. Even the busiest of executives have a five- to ten-minute gap in their day. If you do not, make room for it. A five- or ten-minute personal marketing foray is an absurdly modest demand on your time.

> Personally contact at least one customer every day with no other motive except to find out if the customer is happy with you.

Two Types of Customers

There are two types of customers you may talk with, those who know you well, and those who do not. Imagine the second type of customer, who probably has never met you, or if you have met, it was likely a fleeting encounter. Imagine those customers getting a telephone call out of the blue from the top executive of a business whose product or service they purchased. Then imagine that the top executive of a business whose product or service they purchased is actually expressing a personal interest in whether the customer is happy. You might call this the "Wow, they really want to know if I'm happy!" effect. Your company is likely to be elevated in the esteem of even an unsatisfied customer, who gets such an unexpected call from a top executive showing personal interest.

Of course, some people may be put off by receiving unsolicited calls at home from business people they do not know well. To avoid annoying the very people whose repeat business you are hoping to maintain, make it clear at once that you are simply calling to ask if your product or service has been satisfactory, not to garner an additional sale. You may also want to make a "do not call" note next to the names of any customers who appear to be bothered by such extra personal attention.

As for the customers you know well, including them on your one-call-a-day phone list serves a somewhat different, but no less beneficial, purpose. These customers will probably react with less "wow," but doubtless with no less gratitude. You might call this the "They really do want to take care of me!" effect. It is difficult to imagine a customer regularly contacted in such a way that can ever deteriorate to an unsatisfied state. Your periodic "Are you happy?" telephone calls if nothing else are likely to serve as early warning systems for any potential unhappiness, and to help you to avoid problems before they fully develop.

Clearly, the effectiveness of these tactics will be in direct proportion to how much business the customer being contacted represents. If your product is nail polish, it does not make much sense to make these one-a-day telephone calls to the end user, the lady who buys the $2 bottle of nail polish. But it makes proportionately much more sense if you make those calls to the wholesale buyers of thousands of cases of your $2-a-bottle nail polish. As with any marketing tactic, the "Are you happy" one-a-day phone calls must be applied with reason and targeted appropriately.

Moreover, when the boss exhibits such regular, ongoing customer service, the attitude should permeate your entire organization. With every sales, marketing, distributing, and other type of employee that has customer contact employing similar one-a-day calls, you will leverage the "Wow, they really want to know if I'm happy!" and the "They really do want to take care of me!" reactions many times over, to say nothing of the potential problems that will be averted.

Use a Mentor as a Guide

One largely overlooked tactic for leaders and followers alike is using a mentor. A mentor is someone who has traveled the road before you and can serve as a guide, an early warning system and advisor. The relationship with a mentor can be formal or informal, but it is generally unpaid, unlike a personal coach or consultant. Many entrepreneurs and owners of start-up businesses let their exuberance and independent attitudes blind them to the reality that

Mentor Marketing Savvy

Getting a mentor can be of immense help in advancing your marketing savvy. But being a mentor can be even more help in marketing yourself at little, if any, cost other than time. One of the hidden values of being a mentor is the almost immeasurable enhancement it brings to one's reputation. A mentor who has done his job well leaves behind an extremely grateful apprentice. Like a happy customer, an extremely grateful apprentice can be one of your best marketing advocates. And with a little urging from the mentor, the apprentice will be happy to spread the word.

they do not know everything, and that there are others whose experience and skills can benefit them. If there is one essential nonemployee that you should consider, it is difficult to imagine one of more value than a mentor.

Some people find that mentor relationships last virtually forever. Others find them useful for particular stages of a company's growth. But what is important is that mentors have experience and knowledge that can help you, particularly in those areas you might be lacking. Find mentors by networking, researching, and seeking referrals from third parties you know and trust. Mentors are most likely to be helpful in guiding you when their business is complementary, rather than competitive to your own, so they can be open and honest without fear of you using what you glean from them against them.

One last piece of mentorship advice: Be ready to persuade your potential mentors that you are worth their time. Many mentors are happy to give of their time and experience with nothing in return expected other than the feeling of giving back and nurturing inherent in the role. But no mentors want to feel like they are wasting their gratis efforts on ingrates or hopeless cases.

Become a Writer

As we discussed in Chapter 15, one of the most gratifying marketing tactics is to make the press work for you by becoming a writer yourself, contributing to targeted publications. But the tactic does not have to be restricted to full-blown articles, which are relatively difficult to get published, depending on the publication.

While it is certainly worthwhile to become an acknowledged expert in your industry and be published in respected industry journals, for most entrepreneurs this can be very daunting, and difficult to achieve. An alternative with nearly as much credibility but perhaps an equally high profile is to be a contributor to the "letters to the editor" section of strategic publications. The "letters" section of any publications is one of the most read features, and one in which the name and affiliation of the letter writer is displayed in nearly equal prominence to what the letter writer may have to say.

If long, drawn out dissertations are not your thing, pithy, memorable letters to the editor are a good alternative. Plus, they take a lot less effort to write.

Conduct a Seminar

No discussion of how to share your industry insights would be complete without mentioning two related and very similar marketing tactics: teaching a class and conducting seminars.

Both of these tactics can help you to establish yourself as an authority in your field. You can offer a class or seminar at your place of business, through continuing education programs in public schools, or in conjunction with industry gatherings or professional training. Some people are intimidated with the idea of standing before a room full of industry colleagues, novices, or even the general public. But more often than not such stage fright is rooted in the mistaken belief that one must be an expert in order to teach, when in fact it is teaching that in effect bestows the title of "expert" upon whoever is doing the teaching.

How many times have you sat in a class or a seminar at an industry expo or a convention listening to some so-called expert prattle on only to think to yourself, "I already knew that"? The fact is, you already do know more about something than most people do, and most likely what you know has to do with your line of work. The thing to keep in mind is that you need not know more than everyone in order to teach. You simply need to know more than someone else to be beneficial to that person. The "experts" who know more than you do may not be impressed with what you have to say, but consider the nature of their objection. They most likely are unimpressed for the same reason you occasionally find yourself unimpressed—not because the teacher is wrong, but because they already know what the teacher has to say. So if your ego can stand the possibility that a few of the folks who sit in your seminar or class may already know what you are talking about, you can be on your way to elevating your status among the rest of the audience as "an expert."

When marketing within your own industry, the authoritative image you establish can be leveraged in many ways. When marketing to the buying public, your authoritative credentials become additional features to bolster your credibility. The buying public may even view these credentials as benefits if they regard expertise as a crucial selling point. After all, when picking a brain surgeon and all else is equal, you probably would opt for the one who teaches brain surgery to brain surgeons, no? The same can be true for widget makers and nail polish sellers.

What Your Company Can Do

There also are things that your company can do to help achieve its marketing goals.

One of the threshold decisions you must make in business is whether your edge over the competition is achieved by selling at a lower price or in some other advantage of benefits. It is immensely difficult to be the low-price leader, particularly in an increasingly competitive and commodity-modeled marketplace. It seems there is always someone who can come along and undercut your price, including the lunkheads that do not realize they may be low-pricing themselves into bankruptcy. So how can you justify your higher price? By adding value to the equation. (Incidentally, value also can help you to distinguish yourself from competitors even when you have managed to match their low price, or if your offering and theirs are identical in other ways.)

Handouts and Take-Backs

When you teach a class or a seminar, have plenty of course material to hand out, and be sure that every piece carries your name, your company name, and contact information. Encourage attendees to retain what you pass out by providing low-cost binders or folders, which also should carry your identifying information, as well as the title of the class or seminar. Finally, be sure to capture the names and contact information of everyone in the course. Then six months later send each a letter asking if they found the experience helpful, and if you can be of further help. If your course was filled with industry colleagues, this is a very nonintrusive means of cultivating networking partners. If the course was filled with potential clients or customers, it will have served as a best-foot-forward introduction, and the follow-up letter will be viewed as a professional and proper offer of assistance.

Hawk Value-Added Benefits during Slowdowns

As we have mentioned before, marketing is a matter of persistence and consistence. Add one more concept to that principle: Tout value-added benefits during slowdowns. While customers and clients always like getting a little something extra, when the economy declines, sometimes a little something extra can persuade suddenly reluctant consumers to buy. One approach is to add inexpensive but beneficial add-ons or modifications. There are many value-added services that might give enterprising entrepreneurs an edge over the competition. Try drive-up service for laundries, or home delivery for video rentals, or free car washes with any purchase of new tires. In any of these situations, the operators who aggressively market their advantages over their competitors may well find that little things mean a lot—at least when they are perceived as value-added benefits.

Low Price, but High Value

When competing with lower-priced competitors, to achieve the advantage of better value, you first must determine what it is that your target market is willing to pay more for. And remember, even when you end up in a head-to-head tie with a competitor, adding value will give you the edge. Competitors may deliver as quickly as you do, or quicker. They may be as reliable as you, or even more so. They may be as friendly, or even friendlier. But if you can add "value" to your list of benefits, it may be the difference between being an also-ran in the competitive marketplace or the winner. It can move you ahead of a competitor who may otherwise have an edge such as low price, and certainly ahead of competitors whose offerings are otherwise undistinguishable from yours.

Assess your target market's desires. If you have researched them properly, you should know what benefits they want. Even if your competitors have the same market research, you still can set yourself apart as the preferred provider by adding value. Add one more ounce to the package. Add one more widget to the contents. Sell a baker's dozen of thirteen instead of a regular dozen of twelve. Deliver overnight at the price of two-day delivery. Extend your warranty an extra month more than your competitors. Offer thirty-two flavors instead of thirty-one. And once you have added value to your list of benefits, do not be subtle. Hawk it as a significant advantage since it can be the single most important factor in distinguishing yourself from the competition. In short, add value to get a marketing edge.

Do Not Disappoint

The most direct marketing to your customers is when you serve your customers. Therefore, whenever your customer service bogs down or self-destructs you have delivered the ultimate ugly marketing message: We cannot help you.

Disappointing customers is inevitable to some degree. No business is perfect and not all customers are reasonable. Of course, you should minimize these disappointing marketing encounters. But it is just as important to handle them properly when they occur. If your employees are encouraged to apologize when the customers' reasonable expectations have not been met, they have only traveled half the road to redemption. Unless they can make good on the broken promise, make right the wrong, the best you have is two unhappy people who can commiserate with one another. The customers still have been disappointed, and you still have broken whatever promises the customers expected you to fulfill.

The next step in fully healing this customer-service wound is to fix what went wrong. If your employees are not empowered to fix problems, you create other unhappy problems instead of a happy solution. For those solutions that require costly fixes, low-level employees should be fast-tracked to whoever is high enough in the chain of command to take remedial action. For those solutions that are within the employees' jurisdiction, procedures for ready remedies should be in place and followed reflexively.

The bottom line is, be willing to say you are sorry, but do not stop there. Fix the problem. Win long-term customer loyalty by quickly and humbly fixing short-term crises. There is no better low-cost marketing than high-quality customer service.

Develop Strategic Partners

Another low-cost approach for your company is to develop strategic partners. These partnership relationships can range from cooperative mailings to reciprocal referrals and any other efforts that jointly benefit your company and another. For instance, you might cut your direct-mail costs by piggybacking your material along with that of another closely related but noncompetitive company. The company that sells window tinting may find a common target market with a window cleaning company. If the markets' demographics and psychographics are close enough, the two companies can halve the cost of a direct-mail campaign by splitting the costs and making one joint mailing.

A company that prepares tax returns for small businesses may have a target market that also is in need of computer and software services. Since the tax preparer is not in competition with the computer and software service company, it stands only to gain from a strategic alliance. It is a small matter to mention the computer and software company as a service that tax preparation clients may benefit from. And the same goes for the computer and software service company when dealing with its clients. Such referral marketing tactics can be used to build a network of trusted third parties, each with noncompetitive but supplemental recommendations they can make to their own clients. These recommendations via strategic alliances can come to be viewed by customers and clients as a definite value-added benefit. A small business client may come to view the tax preparation service as not just the company that prepares its taxes, but also as an invaluable resource for recommending other sought-after services.

Marketing cross-promotions work well in these kinds of symbiotic relationships. A car mechanic may attach coupons to receipts good for a discounted car wash and wax at a nearby car wash. Video rental receipts may double as coupons for large-size pizzas from a local pizza delivery restaurant. A gardening nursery may include fliers with potted plants promoting a gardening service. The secret to these marketing promotions is that the buyers of the first services or products have preidentified themselves as likely candidates for the other services or products. The shoe can fit on the other foot, as well. The car wash can promote the mechanic, the restaurant can promote the video rental shop, and the gardener can promote the nursery. The reciprocal nature of these cross-promotions can cancel out any expenses involved other than whatever it costs to print up the coupons or fliers. On the other hand, the promotions can be offered by any of the related companies for a nominal charge, much the way that advertising is bought. Either way, the cost of finding and rooting out prospective new customers can be greatly reduced by cross-promotions.

> The reciprocal nature of these cross-promotions can cancel out any expenses involved other than whatever it costs to print up the coupons or fliers.

Put on Outrageous Promotions

There are promotions, and there are promotions. And then there are outrageous promotions. Just because your promotion is outrageous, it does not have to cost an outrageous amount. It just has to be outrageous because that is what makes it work. In this realm, let your pocketbook and your imagination be your guides. Here are some suggestions that are guaranteed to generate responses far in excess of their cost.

A photography studio can hold a "look-alike" contest. The more outrageous the person—or thing—to look like, the better. Promote the contest with mailers, fliers, and entry forms distributed at neighboring stores and shops, through press releases, and similar low-cost means of getting the word out.

Elvis look-alike contests are old hat. But Abraham Lincoln look-alikes are few and far between. Or how about the latest public figure dominating the news? But there is no reason when being outrageous that one needs to stop at people who look like people. The photography studio might hold a sheep dog look-alike contest, that is, a contest for people who look like sheep dogs. Or how about people who look most like their pets? The possibilities are endless, and certainly abound with outrageousness. But the idea is the same: Attract people to your place of business, product, or service by eye-popping or at least eyebrow-raising promotions that are hard to ignore or delightful to enjoy.

Strike While the Iron's Hot

A couple of other low-cost tactics your company can employ are accomplished by taking advantage of the "strike while the iron is hot" phenomenon. In short, follow up. Neither tactic is costly, and both take advantage of the psychological highs reached when customers have just purchased something they want or need.

1. Include order forms along with all sales, whether at the counter, in the mail, or at the customer's venue. If their purchase pleased them, do not let time pass before they can consider another purchase. Give them the means for instant gratification, should they be so inclined. Put an order form in with whatever it is they have purchased.

2. It is not enough to simply answer inquiries when customers or clients have them. After you have responded in person, by phone, e-mail, or regular mail, be sure to follow up again. It is likely the

initial response whetted the appetite, but the customer still needs more prodding. For example, if a customer or potential customer has asked for information on a product, you should promptly respond. But after a respectful interval, respond again. Since you were invited to respond initially, link your next unsolicited response to the first one by recalling the initial invitation to open this dialog. Use words like, "following up your request . . ." and "here is more information about what you asked . . ."

More Effective, Low-Cost Tactics

The following low-cost tactics can be employed at no or little additional cost, but they lead to substantial results. Generally these tactics are matters of attitude and psychology.

Use Exciting Facts

One overlooked approach is the use of exciting facts, rather than bland boasts. For example, quantify your claims. Instead of blandly claiming, "We make the best salami sandwiches," say instead, "*Salami Magazine* rated our sandwiches number one." Rather than saying, "Ride bicycles for good heath," be specific, "The National Institute on Physical Conditioning found that regular bicycle riding lengthens lives by seven years."

Surprise! Unexpected Customer Bonuses

While being specific can persuade by mustering evidence, surprising customers persuades by real-life experience. Make it customary to surprise your customers with unpredictable, random customer bonuses. If you sell guitars and drums to rock bands, calibrate your cash registers to kick out bonus surprises randomly, but on the average of one every 200 sales. Little bonuses when delivered unexpectedly carry big benefits. The musician who has just bought a new amplifier for his guitar will be delighted to know that as a random bonus he has a choice of guitar strings or a guitar stand. Take his picture with the freebie and post it near the cash register next to the sign, "Will you be our next random winner?"

Limited-Time Offers

One of the secrets of success with coupons is that if they are undated, they generally go unused, at least in comparison to those that bear expiration dates. The same philosophy applies to any offers that you make. Always make "limited" offers. "Good until . . ." or "expires on . . ." or "good only with the purchase of . . ." Time limits prompt action sooner, rather than later. Term limits direct buyers to particular actions. As a restaurateur, do you want to increase the lunchtime business? Limit buy-one-get-one-free coupons to lunches, rather than dinners or breakfasts.

Term limits direct buyers to particular actions.

Creative Pricing

There is a very effective alternative to reducing prices to increase purchases. Offer installment plans instead. Rather than cutting the price of your widgets from $99 to $89, offer them for "four convenient payments of $24.75." You are likely to find that $24.75 is much more appealing than $89, even though the buyer must pay $24.75 four times and $89 only once.

Exploit Competitors' Weaknesses

Your low-cost approach does not always have to deal with what you sell. It can address what your competition sells, and do so very effectively. In politics this has come to be known as "negative campaigning." But just because politicians do it does not mean it is all bad. In fact, there is great appeal in the negative appeal, simply because buyers want to avoid mistakes at least as much as they want to do the right thing.

Apply the negative campaign principle by exploiting the weaknesses of your competitors. By implication you are saying to the prospective buyer that what you have is not only superior to the competition, but you also are establishing that regardless of your quality, the competition's product or service is flawed. A video rental store may perceive a weakness in its competitor's policy of one-day rentals and respond with a campaign that says, "You don't have to return our video rentals the next day. Take two, or three. No extra charge." The operator of a health-food store may run ads comparing the "contents" portion of a processed food with the same portion of a label from a nonprocessed food alternative.

Market to Their Pain

The "negative appeal" approach has a lot in common with the next tactic, which is to market to your customers' pain rather than to their pleasure. Some products and services are best advanced by touting the good that they deliver to their purchases. Others, however, are best advanced by pointing out the bad that they help their purchasers avoid.

Tax preparers, for example, have two choices. They can "help you pay your taxes" or they can "help you avoid tax penalties." Being helped to do something you are not crazy about doing in the first place has limited appeal. Being helped to avoid something you direly wish to avoid has great appeal. Many products and services fall into this category. Antiaging cream is not beauty cream. Heart-attack prevention diets are not health regimes. Federally insured savings are not high-interest investments. Some things simply sell better because they appeal to peoples' fear of what can go wrong, rather than appeal to their desire for what should go right.

Pander to Greed?

Finally, there is one last low-cost tactic that sadly seems to work very well. This is not a recommendation. It simply is an acknowledgment that in this day and age, marketing to greed rather than to need can be extremely effective. Moderation is increasingly an outmoded notion, while lust and covetousness are more and more commonplace on both sides of the buying and selling equation. We would hope that your desire for profits does not invert your moral compass. But the fact remains, greedy marketers can capitalize on customers greed. We will not offer any tips on marketing to greed. But we do suggest that you ask yourself whether you are willing to pay that price for such success.

> **Chapter 20**

People Need People

PART FOUR   INNOVATIVE (BUT OFTEN NEGLECTED) SOLUTIONS

CHAPTER 16 Innovative Low-Cost Techniques ■ CHAPTER 17 It's Not Junk Mail When . . . ■ CHAPTER 18 Low-Cost Marketing Tools ■ CHAPTER 19 Low-Cost Marketing Tactics ■ **CHAPTER 20 People Need People**

The Keys to the Kingdom

One reason that innovative marketing solutions are so often overlooked is because they are so obvious, hiding in plain sight, as it were. They may be little things, or large. They can be part of the things that you already do, or things that you would do, if only you had thought of them. Nevertheless, all too often they are not performed, or even considered. In this chapter we deal with some of these obvious, yet paradoxically hidden, large and small opportunities that frequently lie dormant among your everyday options.

We can take a clue from successful schmoozers. The best sales reps and the best newspaper reporters know who holds the keys to the kingdom. And it is not the security guard at the front door. More often than not, it is the secretary, or if you prefer the more politically correct and euphemistic title, administrative assistant. All good sales reps and aggressive newshounds know that if you want to see the boss, you must ultimately get past the boss' gatekeeper: the secretary.

Cultivate Secretaries

Woe to those who take the secretary for granted, or worse yet, those who snub the secretary. That would be tantamount to burning your bridges before you cross them. As a rule, the more important the person is that you need to reach, the more protective you can expect that person's secretary to be. Secretaries are not merely letter writers, dictation takers, and paper shufflers. They are the last line of defense between important businesspeople and the rest of the universe. If important businesspeople are among your target market, secretaries are one of the last hurdles you must clear.

The executive, the boss, or the manager who navigates the business world without a secretary (or without an adequately protective secretary) is a vulnerable target for anyone who wants to make contact, be it for good or for ill. For that reason alone, secretaries to people who are in great demand do not get their jobs by being doormats. Padlocks would be a more appropriate image. So the question arises of how to ingratiate oneself with secretaries, who are more inclined to say "No" than "Hello," and whose chief professional duty is to keep you from seeing the very person that you want to see.

(We will take a moment here to point out again an obvious truism: Be sincere. Secretaries entrusted with important screening responsibilities invariably come equipped with superb detection skills when it comes to phonies and con men. It is all but written into their job description. As we have recommended before, never try to be something or someone that you are not. There is no sense in waving unnecessary warning flags at the gatekeepers. They are tough enough to get past without emitting the smell of a phony.)

Little Things Count

Have you ever noticed a change in peoples' demeanor when they suddenly figure out that you are important to them? It can be pretty irritating. The same people who one minute are treating you as if you did not exist, or worse yet, as if you existed solely to serve them, the next moment suddenly burst into spontaneous, albeit insincere, smiles and gush with syrupy salutations when, oops, it dawns on them that they need you to achieve what they want to achieve. Take a lesson from those boors. Do not take secretaries for granted, and do not treat them as if they are second-class players in your life's drama. That will help you avoid the fatal and embarrassing "oops" phenomenon.

Clearly, if your marketing target today is the secretary's boss, eventually you must don your marketing-friendly disposition, even if you did not get your coffee that morning and a car splashed gutter water on your shoes. A dour demeanor can sour a face-to-face marketing opportunity faster than a limp handshake. Consider the secretary your warm-up. Do not wait until your audience with the boss before turning your lips into a smile and putting a smile into your voice.

> Do not take secretaries for granted, and do not treat them as if they are second-class players in your life's drama.

Be a Friend

Get to know the secretary as closely and intimately as appropriate. You probably send birthday cards to people much less important in your life, so add the secretary to the list. Secretaries have families, hobbies, favorite leisure activities, and yes, they even have lives away from the job. The time you spend cooling your heels in the outer office can more profitably be spent learning who that secretary really is. It is likely that after you have

Never Make Demands

When dealing with secretaries, never demand, but always apologize as if you have demanded. Put another way, be courteous. The secretary is not there to serve you, but to serve the boss. If you have a request or a question, always be considerate of the secretary's time and respectful of the secretary's duties. A few decades ago it might have seemed peculiar to point out the benefits of common courtesy. But these days you will be surprised how uncommonly welcome you will find common courtesy if you practice it. "Excuse me . . ." and "I don't want to interrupt what you are doing but . . ." and similar de facto deferences and apologies cost you absolutely nothing to use, and they pay big benefits in the all-important sphere of secretarial relations.

learned something about the secretary, the secretary will want to learn something about you. Sooner or later, maybe after as few as two or three visits, the relationship will transform from the antagonistic secretary and someone who wants to see the boss into a pair of friends. Friends are precisely the kind of gatekeepers every marketer prefers.

A Heavier Hand May Work—But Not with Everyone

In some cases you may find that more overt efforts at ingratiating yourself with secretaries may be effective. Flowers, small gifts, lunches, dinners, personal favors. All of these expressions of friendship and respect can be effective with the right people, and certainly are appropriate in many cases in which genuine friendships have developed. But walk softly here. The ice is thin. Not every secretary is amenable to overt gestures like flowers or an invitation to dinner, no matter how platonic. And not every secretary's boss is either.

When in doubt, do not venture into these more personal and intimate relationships. But when your doubt is not quite as strong, it may be appropriate to request permission first, sincerely and respectfully. Indeed, it might be appropriate to run an idea past the secretary's boss first, just in case the boss has reservations about how chummy the secretary and you should be. The last thing you want to do is be accused by the boss of trying to bribe your way past the secretary. But when your relationship with the secretary is aboveboard, deep friendships can be a result and can be mutually beneficial. For instance, it may be entirely appropriate to buy the secretary a lunch—with the boss' permission—in order to seek advice about your upcoming decision to hire a secretary of your own. What are friends for if not to offer advice? And what better way to demonstrate the high regard you have for a secretary's professionalism?

The bottom line with secretaries is that whether you go

the dinner and flowers route or the more reserved handshake and smile path, befriending secretaries is almost always worthwhile when marketing to their bosses. Secretaries are like other marketing targets, except they are probably more important than most. And every marketer's ultimate goal is to befriend a marketing target. People do business with people they like.

Get Personal Coaching If You Need It

If you have never made friends with a secretary, and if your marketing relationships are less cordial than your relationship with the cable TV repairman, you might be a candidate for personal coaching. In fact, you can even be glib and gracious and still benefit a lot from personal coaching.

It is particularly important for small business executives, especially those who must wear many hats, to hone their interpersonal skills. If you are one of those who do not naturally make friends, or even if your social skills are up to par but you just seem to have trouble making small talk, a personal coach can guide you through uncharted realms of etiquette and charm—or at least help you from sweating like a teenager on a first date.

Practical skills like how to get along with others, when to speak and when to listen, how to know when you are overbearing, or why you are such a wallflower are the kinds of aptitudes that come second nature to many people. But not to all. Some of us simply are not conversationalists, or not naturally effusive. But as a small business entrepreneur, you do not have the luxury of living with such shortcomings. Your need to master rudimentary personal skills may sound like a frivolous indulgence, but if your marketing necessitates face-to-face relationships with people you need to cultivate, there is nothing frivolous about it. So indulge yourself by getting a personal coach. The fees run the gamut from pleasantly low to painfully expensive, but do not judge their worth by how much they charge. A good rule to apply is whether you are comfortable in the presence of the personal coach. Chances are you will learn more from a coach who makes you feel comfortable than from one you are uneasy with.

Many coaches offer much more than basic how-to-play-well-with-others skills. Indeed, there are coaches who can guide you through the intricacies of every level of interpersonal relationship-building, up to and including advice on how to give speeches and even acting lessons designed

Speaking Solo

If you need to polish your public speaking, one way to improve is to join your local Toastmasters club (more on this in Chapter 21), where you can hone your impromptu and prepared speaking skills alongside others like yourself. Another option is to join a local community theater company, where small speaking parts allow you to dip your toe in the sea of public speaking with minimal attention. In some regions of the country oratory still thrives, and indeed is performed in clubs and associations that allow people like yourself to learn the tricks of the trade and have an opportunity to engage in the honorable, ageless practice of public speaking. Most programs and organizations that offer such training and participation have nominal costs, if any. For those who may not want to pay for one-on-one coaching, these group venues may be less expensive and also may provide more peer support.

to bolster your self-confidence and public showmanship. The idea behind all of this personal coaching is to transform you from a figurative lump on a log into an actual vivacious and interesting human being.

Recruit a Panel of Advisors

Other people outside your company can play an important role in your marketing strategy, but few if any entrepreneurs bother to ever draw on this valuable resource. In some sense we all have advisors, people whom we listen to and whose opinions we value. But rarely do we bother to formalize the relationship. One way to do that is to establish a panel of advisors.

Outside Experience

When put together thoughtfully, a panel of advisors can bolster a small enterprise by bringing to it direly needed expertise at virtually no cost, or at nominal expense. Typically, advisors serve gratis or are paid nominal stipends. If your personal coach has been effective, you may even be able to sweet-talk some experts into serving as advisors for the price of a good meal two or three times a year. Most advisors agree to participate essentially as unpaid consultants because the request to do so is flattering, and they already want to give something back to an industry from which they have benefited. There also can be marketing advantages for advisors to serving on your panel since you clearly will be a meaningful contact for them, and can make referrals and testimonials on their behalf.

Filling the Gaps

You can use advisors to provide the kind of know-how that may be missing in your company's management team, or to supplement areas where you need more wherewithal than you can afford to pay for. Do not be overanxious to add advisors just to add bodies to a flow chart. Pick them carefully based on what they can offer in the areas you need help, and always be mindful that the more knowledge they have of your industry the greater their worth. Although your panel should represent a variety of expertise, you definitely want advisors with marketing savvy.

Schedule periodic meetings with your advisors. You might conduct the meetings over luncheons or dinners. Be sure to keep your advisors updated by providing concise marketing campaign summaries and, if appropriate, updated versions of your marketing plan and your business plan.

Camaraderie is great, but do not let your panel of advisors deteriorate to a good old boy's (or girl's) club. Keep a business tone. Provide brief outlines or agendas for your periodic meetings, and make sure that business is conducted. The whole point of a panel of advisors is to get their valuable advice. Make sure you get the advice. If you were to put out bids for consultants to provide you this kind of advice, you would pay a lot. So treat your low-cost or gratis advisors with the respect and gratitude they deserve. Not only would their advice be pricey if you had to buy it, but you are gaining the added benefit that the advisor is free to give you a sincere opinion uninfluenced by a paycheck or consultant's fee.

Become an Advisor Yourself

You can use personal advisors to help you hone your marketing skills, but you also can turn the tables to do a little marketing. Be ready to mentor others as their personal advisor. The entire cost is easily controlled since it boils down to how much time you are willing to invest or able to afford. Not only do you gain the favor of the person you help, but in the process you also effectively recruit a willing walking testimonial in your behalf. Of course, the testimonial will be only as good as the advice you provide the people that you mentor. So put your heart into helping another and watch the payback come back many times over in the good word the other spreads on your behalf.

Charitably Speaking . . .

Here is one way to show off your community-minded or charitable involvements. Prepare a handout or a data sheet that you can distribute as a stand-alone document or that you can include with the rest of your marketing collateral, and perhaps even in your press packet. The handout should itemize all your charitable activities, the extent of your involvement in each one, and the dates that you first became involved in them. Most important, however, is to be sure to explain how you came to choose those causes that you support. Also be sure to use the opportunity to tout the greater good that is accomplished by the work of these charitable or civic causes, as well as the populations they serve. This is the opportunity for you to look good by association, and to do so in an acceptable venue without appearing too self-serving.

Perform Charity and Pro Bono Work

Beyond the obvious moral and ethical reasons to be charitable, there are direct marketing advantages to be gained as well.

One of the primary roles of your marketing is to create a favorable or admirable image of your company or product in the mind of your target market. Even in our age of cynicism and skeptics, it is difficult not to be perceived as commendable when donating time or money or anything else of value to a worthy cause. Your options here are limited only by your imagination, and can range from extensive and expensive to very modest and low-cost. Here are just a few possibilities:

- Sponsor a youth team and get your company or product name mentioned in their banners or uniforms.
- Provide your facilities to host civic or charitable group meetings, and be sure to have a company representative participate or at least be on hand as a greeter.
- Include a nonprofit organization's fund-raising mailer in your own mailing with a note to recipients that the group has won your support.
- Donate supplies or the use of equipment to a charitable group, and in return ask only that you be permitted a small notation of your gift be printed on their material.
- Encourage your employees to become involved with reputable community groups and to seek high-profile positions.
- Become an organizer or sponsor in an annual event like a 10K run on behalf of a worthy charity, then promote the event vigorously.
- Donate your personal time to a cause that has a need for your kind of expertise.

Capitalizing on your selfless contributions is a two-edged sword. Be careful not to overly hype your involvement, or to seem exceedingly self-promotional. Otherwise the impression you create will be self-serving, rather than selfless. Still, it is entirely permissible to make sure your target market and the general public is aware of your charitable and pro bono work.

Say Hello Without Overt Sales Pitches

No matter how much you have managed to ingratiate yourself with your best customers and your target market, if every time they see you coming they expect a sales pitch, eventually you will be greeted with grimaces and flinches rather than smiles. The secret of this little-used solution is that it disarms that potential hostility in your target market.

No Sale

Make a point of having periodic contact with your target market without making overt sales pitches. There are a number of ways to accomplish this. When the contact is in-person, it is simply a matter of not discussing sales or even bringing up the subject of what you can do for those to whom you are speaking. But when your contacts are made through mailings, telephone calls, or other similar hard marketing collateral, it is more difficult—and in the long run costly—not to appear to be selling or promoting. In fact, few small businesses can afford to spend money on mailings, telephone campaigns, or other hard collateral if the contacts are not in some way seeking the ultimate response: a purchase.

Your challenge is to interject as many nonsales or low-pressure contacts as you can afford. One way is to use thank-you letters or telephone calls. Both of these options permit you a legitimate reason for contacting your customers or clients, and it is entirely appropriate for both to be devoid of high-pressure tactics. Even when such contacts solicit market research, such as including a questionnaire, it is entirely fitting that they not overtly promote at the same time.

A Low Profile Can Loom Large

In addition to saying "thank you," other opportunities for contact with your target market can be accomplished through the venues such as we discussed above, including charitable involvements and when endearing yourself to personal contacts like secretaries and other gatekeepers. The successful marketer is the one who can distinguish the settings that call for overt promotion and those that call for toned-down, low profiles. Certainly, an aggressive marketer never should miss an opportunity to market, but there are times when low-profile contacts serve your long-term interest by providing the target market with a more moderate, less self-promotional image.

Every Sale Is a Solicitation for Another

Now that we have cautioned you about being too aggressive, it may seem incongruous to remind you not to miss an opportunity to ask for another sale. When backing off your marketing aggressiveness, you should choose situations appropriate for more low-key contact. But when we talk about not missing an opportunity to ask for another sale, we are talking about circumstances that are already high-profile, aggressive contacts. The best example of this circumstance is when you have just completed a sale.

There probably is no time in the marketing cycle in which the targets of your efforts are more disposed to purchase what you sell than at the precise moment that they make purchases. Consider what has occurred when buyers buy from you. They have traveled the entire marketing route. You have gotten their attention, piqued their interest, created a desire, prompted them to act, and now they are all but salivating at the prospect of enjoying all the benefits that you have persuaded them you can provide. It is nearly inconceivable to think they will ever be more inclined or more desirous of purchasing from you.

What Should You Do?

So what should you do? Wait for another marketing cycle to begin? Give the buyer time to cool off? Hardly. You should, of course, strike while the iron is hot.

The obnoxious caricature of this situation is the tiresome fast-food cliché, "Would you like fries with that?" Sure, nine out of ten customers probably decline the offer to add French fries to their fast-food order. But even that means that 10 percent bite, so to speak. Is a 10 percent response worth it to you to sell more than you would sell otherwise? It is hard to imagine that it would not be.

A People-Oriented Solution

Even if your business does not sell from a drive-up window, you too can employ this people-oriented solution. Build into your marketing and selling cycle one last additional request or offer while the emotions are high. Like the fast-food customers whose appetites are whetted by the prospect of adding fries to their orders, your customers' appetites likewise are primed for a sweetening offer. Do not miss the opportunity. Make them an offer they cannot refuse, or at least an offer that 10 percent of them cannot refuse.

To accomplish this, have your salespeople offer your equivalent of "Do you want fries with that?" Include in every shipped or mailed order an enticement for an additional purchase such as a catalog or discount coupon, or at the least an order form for ordering more of the same. If your customers place orders by phone, be sure that your telephone crew has a script of the day to read from that concludes with one more offer before totaling up the sale. If you sell products, include in the package a form for ordering more of the same, or supplemental or similar products. If you sell services, include with your invoice an offer for add-on services, or an opportunity to get more of the same for an additional term.

The underlying theme is that when people have been moved to buy from you they are probably more likely to buy more at that time than they will later.

Definitely No Fries with This

Some situations are not well-suited at all for asking customers and clients if they want to make an additional sale. Here are a few:

- When a customer has canceled a membership or a subscription
- When a buyer is leaving your store empty-handed
- When a caller telephones to complain about your service
- When you mail a shipment to a customer and it arrives late
- When a client says your work has been unsatisfactory

Although trying to add another sale in these circumstances is probably going to do more harm than good, it is always worth finding out what went wrong so you do not make the same mistake again.

"Do You Want Fries with That?"

Here are a just a few of the many situations that are well-suited to asking your version of "Do you want fries with that?":

- When a customer has renewed membership or a subscription
- When a buyer wheels a shopping cart up to the checkout stand
- When a caller telephones to compliment you on your service
- When you mail a shipment to a customer who paid extra for overnight delivery
- When a client expresses gratitude for the work you have done
- Whenever an existing or potential buyer has gone out of the way to consider your product or service

These happy encounters present you with customers and clients who already have been persuaded that you can please them. Build on that while they are still smiling at you.

> **Chapter 21**

Develop Personal Speaking Skills

Marketing as Conversation

In its most fundamental form, marketing essentially boils down to you and your target engaged in conversation. Certainly, these conversations can be figurative like e-mail, billboards, or magazine advertisements. But at the heart of the matter is a dialogue between you and the people you need to persuade. When we carried clubs, wore loincloths, and lived in caves, marketing was far more direct. With the exception of violent encounters, the cave dweller who could engage in conversation without boring, frightening, or disgusting the other was the cave dweller most likely to succeed.

We have discarded our clubs, dress better today, and have crawled out of our caves, but the challenge remains.

The point is that there are certain fundamental skills that come into play for the successful marketer seeking a dialogue. And perhaps the most fundamental of these skills may be the ability to say something to another person that persuades, and to do so without being boring, frightening, or disgusting. If you think that you do not need this skill perhaps because you rarely come face to face with your target market, you should think again. At some point in your entrepreneurial endeavors you will be required to actually utter words to another human being. But more than that, your ability to master this most elementary form of communication carries over into all more technically sophisticated exchanges, including e-mail, billboards, and magazine advertisements. The skillful speaker, the marketer able to speak effectively, is invariably the same marketer who can make all those other more figurative manners of speech equally effective.

So it is wise to learn to speak well. It is an inexpensive investment that will bring you endless and disproportionately happy returns.

Join Toastmasters

How did you learn to ride a bike? By reading a book on bike riding? Nope. By having a bike rider explain the intricacies of balance, momentum, and gear shifting? Nope. By watching others ride their bikes? Not quite. It may have helped a little, but no matter how closely you watched, you still were not yet a bike rider. You learned how to ride a bike by getting on one and pedaling.

And so it is with speaking to other people. You can read a book (including this one), discuss the fine points with accomplished speakers, and even observe great orators in action. But until you engage in the practice, you will never master the art of speech—and by that we mean speech that is effective in persuading others.

There are many groups formed just for this purpose, and we do not necessarily mean to endorse Toastmasters International over any other. But since most people are familiar with Toastmasters, it is a good frame of reference.

In these types of groups, every participant is expected to stand and speak as if others actually wanted to listen. And the rest actually listen, like it or not. The great benefit of this routine is that the venue is nonthreatening, or at least as nonthreatening as speaking in public can be, and everyone is there to help everyone else improve. The camaraderie helps overcome the stage fright. And just as you gain confidence in bike riding the more you ride, you will find that you gain confidence in speaking the more you speak. Would-be bike riders probably wish they had groups like these. You learn from your mistakes in bike riding with rather painful pratfalls, banged up knees, scraped shins, and broken bones. But for would-be speakers the pain is much less in a group of similarly situated souls who definitely empathize with your oral pratfalls. While egos still can be bruised, for the most part your colleagues will not be overly harsh in their criticism of you since they know their turn at the podium is coming up next.

So much for where you can go for help in learning to be glib and articulate. Now we will touch on a few techniques that may help you overcome your orally challenged nature. Feel free to try them out. It will not cost you a dime (in most cases).

Take a Breath

Arm yourself with these secret weapons in your war against insecurity. If you find yourself extremely tense, imagine the person you are speaking to is your closest friend. If you are terrified of speaking before groups, pick spots to the left, right, and in the center of the audience just above the heads of the people to whom you are speaking. As you talk, pan left to right and back again, focusing on those inanimate targets rather than directly into the faces of the crowd. If you find yourself speaking faster and faster, force yourself to pause, take a deep breath, slowly exhale, then continue. The "pregnant pause," that quiet stillness that you permit yourself, is like underlining the last thing you said. You allow it to sink in and have an effect because you are not shoving a new subject down your listeners' throats.

Quiet!

One of the most important keys to successful speaking is knowing when not to. Keep in mind that the goal of your speaking is to engage your audience, to create an atmosphere of dialogue, not dictation. For these reasons it is important to know when to shut up and listen. This is as important in group settings as it is in one-on-one dialogue. It is irritating and annoying for people to try to speak back to you only to have you interrupt, talk over, or simultaneously chatter back at them. Regardless of whether it is one-on-one conversations or speaking to a group, this flaw is easily detected. Pay attention. You can certainly notice when you interrupt or speak at the same time as the person to whom you are talking. When you catch yourself doing it, apologize and invite the others to complete their thoughts before you resume talking.

Speak Conversationally and Cordially

One of the first and most deadly errors novices make when they dare to speak in unfamiliar venues or in public settings is that they affect a personality that even their own mothers would not recognize. We have mentioned this before. Repeatedly. But it bears repeating again. *Be yourself. Relax.* If you think they will not like you for what you are, just wait and see how much they will not like you for trying to be what you are not. You are not going to fool anyone.

When it comes to speaking effectively, speaking cordially and conversationally may be the most difficult hurdles to clear, even for supremely confident entrepreneurs and self-made successes. For some reason, probably deeply rooted in insecurity, we all have a tendency to put on airs when speaking to strangers or in strange venues.

How Do You Talk to Friends?

But think about it. When you talk with friends what tone do you use? Do you try to sound stilted and formal? Imagine your friends' reactions if you did. Imagine your reaction if your friends talked like that to you. Consider the people you talk to as your friends. Even if they are not yet, making friends with them is certainly part of your marketing strategy because people do business with people they like. So talk to them as you would talk to a friend—casually, cordially, and conversationally. Avoid feigned formality, which keeps your audience at arm's length instead of handshaking closeness, and avoid stilted etiquette, which tells them you and they are not really very chummy.

Be Humble—Even If You Normally Aren't

One caveat: Be humble. This may be the exception to the "be yourself" rule. If being yourself means being boastful, prideful, arrogant, and obnoxious, it is probably worthwhile to assume a different persona. And not just for communications purposes. Shedding your boastful, prideful, arrogant, or obnoxious demeanor not only will help you communicate better, but it will make you a better person as well. The first step is to identify those flaws in yourself, then deliberately change them. Interestingly, over time your changed behavior will change those traits within you and it will become natural for you not to be boastful, prideful, arrogant, or obnoxious because you no longer will be. This illustrates the phenomena of marketing tactics as personal improvement tools. Who could have imagined such secondary benefits?

Interact, Don't Lecture

One danger everyone with a little knowledge faces is giving the appearance of ranting or sermonizing. It is an easy trap to fall in to. If you did not think that you had something of value your audience lacked you probably would not be speaking to them in the first place. And the inclination to position yourself as an authority is well-founded. After all, you want the audience to look up to and respect you for what you are telling them. If they do not, they are not likely to accept what you have to say as being valuable.

The problem occurs when you assume the role of lecturer, rather than being a participant in a dialog. This problem is particularly damaging when speaking one-on-one. "What a self-absorbed bore" is likely to be the thought you create in your listener's mind. But the same problem exists when speaking before a group, whose members are even more tempted not to pay attention. So do not be a lecturer. In the first place, it makes you responsible for carrying the entire conversation. Most of us are not so accomplished that we can hold up an entire conversation from start to finish without losing our listeners' attention. In the second place, a lecturer is all about the lecturer. And your purpose, as a marketer, should be all about your target, not about you.

The solution to this problem is to invite and encourage your listeners to participate in what you have to say. This does not mean that if you find yourself at a podium addressing a group you should invite free-for-all discussion. You would surely lose control of the situation if you did that, and since you are using your public speaking opportunity for marketing purposes, you definitely want to retain control. But there are a few tips for engaging your listeners that work whether you are speaking one-on-one or one to an audience.

A Half-Dozen Tips for Being Engaging

1. Ask questions. And allow answers. "Please tell me what you have found to be the value of using widgets."

2. Ask questions that do not require oral responses, such as "Has anyone here ever used widgets? Raise your hand if you have."

3. Ask questions that engage dialogue with one member of the audience. "Do you use widgets?" (allow response) "Have you found widgets to be worthwhile?" (allow response) "What went wrong (or right)?" (allow response) "What were the standards that you used to evaluate the success or failure of your widgets?" (allow response)

4. Before speaking to a group, place your business card on each seat. This ensures that everyone will pick it up and look at it. Then during your speech announce that the lucky folks who have your business card with an X written in blue ink below your name have won (fill in the blank). Everyone will take a second look at your business card.

5. When speaking to a group, leave the podium and go down into the audience if only to introduce yourself to a few of the listeners and to shake their hands. Incorporate this maneuver into your speech, such as "Does anyone here have widgets at home?" Then walk down to the closest acknowledged widget owner and shake her hand and thank her profusely for the benefit she provides to the widget industry.

6. At the end of your speech personally distribute a form asking your audience to critique your presentation. At the least this invites them to revisit in their minds what you have said. But as you are distributing the questionnaire it provides an opportunity for impromptu questions and answers. "I recall you did not raise your hand when I asked if anyone had ever used widgets. Why haven't you?"

The point of engaging your audience is to create a sense of dialogue, not dictation. You want your listeners to feel that you are speaking with them, not to them. You want to overcome their tendency to ignore you by giving them reasons to pay attention beyond the content of what you have to say.

Have Responses Prepared for Hecklers

It has been said that the greatest fear for more people than anything else is the fear of public speaking. The second greatest fear is said to be the fear of falling. This logically must mean that the absolutely greatest fear is the fear of falling off the stage while public speaking. But in actuality there is one fear even greater for those who have experienced it firsthand. It is the fear of hecklers.

No matter how innocuous your subject, you are bound to come face-to-face someday with someone who is bent on vehemently disagreeing with you, personally attacking you, or otherwise making your public speaking engagement an unmitigated disaster.

To be forewarned is to be forearmed. And to be forearmed means to be prepared. Have a strategy for dealing with hecklers. They are acting impromptu. If you are prepared, you have the advantage. You can undercut their disruptiveness because they have to think on their feet while you have a strategic plan. Here are a few tips for how to forearm yourself against the very rare, but very real, possibility of hecklers at your public speaking engagement.

1. If their comments require response, respond politely, but terminally. That is to say do not invite them into a dialogue. Do not ask them questions or answer their wisecracks in a way to invite a response.
2. Do not lower yourself to their level by exchanging brickbats.
3. Make a sincere request, "Rather than taking up the

Engage Your Listeners

To give your audience an incentive to pay attention, provide ways for them to interact with you during your presentation. For example:

Take a poll. Before beginning your speech, pass out a form containing a simple question that pertains to your subject. Make it is easy to understand the question and easy to add up the results. Have an associate collect the forms and tally the results as you speak. Use the totals to illustrate a point at an appropriate juncture in your speech. Be prepared with something to say whichever way the vote goes.

Hand out a game or a puzzle for the audience to complete. Then at an appropriate point during your presentation give the correct or most common answers to the game or puzzle so your audience can compare themselves to the "national average," or whatever other source you have.

audience's time, if you would like to speak to me privately after my presentation, I'd be happy to meet with you." This not only gives you the high ground in the eyes of your audience in this unpleasant confrontation, but it can be sufficiently disarming for all but the most obnoxious.

4. Ignore them. Most hecklers are seeking attention, and when they do not get it they eventually throw in the towel. Plus, ignoring them effectively passes the problem on to those seated around the heckler, and those people usually can be counted on to deliver glaring stares of disapproval, if not a few words of admonishment.

5. If you have reason to believe based on past experience or the nature of your talk that there may be hecklers, make prior arrangements with the host of your presentation to take steps to firmly request any heckler to refrain from interrupting, and also have a plan for physically removing the heckler if he does not quiet down.

One thing that we do not advise is to try to outshout your heckler. This escalation is more likely to feed the heckler's ego-driven motive. Unilateral disarmament in this case is preferable.

Your Speaking Persona

You already know not to pretend to be someone you're not when faced with a group. But how can you put your best foot forward and present yourself as the most likable, engaging person possible? Here are a few things to keep in mind when constructing a speech.

Don't Try to Be Funny If You're Not

"Have you heard the one about . . .?"

Have you noticed that when anyone begins to tell a joke, most people roll their eyes or groan or grimace? Have you noticed that after most people tell a joke how much more intense the eye rolling, groaning, and grimacing becomes? The reason for this is that it is very difficult to be funny, let alone to be funny to a diverse audience. The reasons are many, but they include the following humorless facts of life:

- Very few people are funny all of the time, or even are capable of being consistently funny.
- One person's belly laugh is another's pain in the posterior.
- Even funny people are not funny to everyone.

So unless you are a proven laugh-getter, the best course of action in your public speaking is to avoid humor. Skirt along its edges if you must, but avoid going for the big laugh. Nothing flops like an unfunny joke. And nothing is as difficult to recover from as the dull, dead silence and furrowed brows of an audience that did not get it, or worse yet, got it and hated it. Play it safe. Leave the joke telling to accomplished jokesters.

> Skirt along its edges if you must, but avoid going for the big laugh. Nothing flops like an unfunny joke.

Be Sincere

As we have seen in almost every other aspect of marketing, sincerity is one of the fundamental underpinnings. The same goes when you open your mouth to speak one-on-one or to a large group.

We live in perhaps the most cynical and skeptical age in history, which alas in no small measure is due to marketing excesses. Even children are inclined to disbelieve much of what they are bombarded with every day. So why should you expect that whomever you are speaking to would be more naïve than a child? People have reached the point that they even doubt the message when their instincts tell them it is sincere.

The only way for a marketer to overcome this increasingly ingrained distrust is to be sincere and prove the validity of your sincerity over the long haul of experience. When caught or suspected of being disingenuous, it can take a long, long time to undo the damage to your marketing reputation.

But when you are speaking to a marketing target, or to a group that you have targeted as part of your marketing strategy, you do not have a very long time frame to work with. This compressed time frame means that if you exhibit any hint of insincerity you will probably blow the entire encounter. For no other reason than this, it makes no sense to risk insincerity.

Be Self-Effacing

Another, more subtle clue to success at the podium is to be self-effacing.

As we discussed above, being boastful, prideful, arrogant, and obnoxious are surefire ways to shoot yourself in the foot. Humility goes a long way in establishing rapport with an audience. It is a very human tendency to swell up with self-importance when the spotlight is shone upon you. And there is a very human tendency for others to recoil at a speaker's puffed-up self-importance.

In this regard, there are few specifics to guide you. Self-effacing humility is an entirely subjective quality. But like art, even though it is difficult to define, people know it when they see it. If you are going to speak publicly, be it one-on-one with a targeted prospect or one-on-many in front of a room full of potential customers, one of your goals should be to find that comfort zone for you and for them, that area where you are self-assured but not self-important, confident but not arrogant. It may be an elusive goal at first, so we suggest you err on the side of too much humility rather than not enough. It will be a trial-and-error process, but be assured that if you are receptive to your audience, they will let you know how you are progressing.

Plain Talk Tips

To speak conversationally and cordially, use plain language, not pretentious five-dollar words. That is to say do not use "rodomontade" or "fustian" when you mean to say "highfalutin." Here are some other wrong ways and right ways to guide you when you verbalize your oratory, which is to say, when you talk:

- *Wrong:* "interface with"; *Right:* "work with"
- *Wrong:* "inoperative"; *Right:* "does not work"
- *Wrong:* "feedback"; *Right:* "response"
- *Wrong:* "at the present time" or "at this point in time"; *Right:* "now"
- *Wrong:* "effectuate"; *Right:* "bring about"
- *Wrong:* "they indicated"; *Right:* "they said"

Holding an Audience with Visuals

One of the secrets of magicians is how they misdirect their audiences' attention. They take their onlookers' eyes off their right hand by a diversion with their left hand. Your public speaking skills can be enhanced by drawing on the magician's secret.

There is little in life that can be as boring as a talking head. Even the most compelling subject matter begins to weigh on the eyelids if all the audience has to focus on are the moving lips of the speaker. Boring. Television news realized this long ago (though not necessarily to the benefit of mankind). The talking head on TV news has since been replaced by film at eleven. If it moves and can be filmed it virtually does not matter what it is, television news considers it to be more attention-getting with the audience than a newscaster reading deadpan from a teleprompter.

Use Props and Visual Aids

Do not get the wrong idea. We do not under any circumstances endorse the deceptive practices of the magician or the pandering of television newscasters. But there are common techniques that they use that can also aid you. Like them, you need to hold your audience's attention. Like the magician, you can direct the audience away from your yammering mouth with the use of props. Like the newscaster, you can rivet attention by employing visual displays.

Use props and other visual aids to supplement what you have to say, not as a replacement for what you want to say. A simple chart on an easel and a pointer stick is guaranteed to draw eyeballs. Samples of your product held up as you speak about them are guaranteed to be looked at. A demonstration of how widgets function on a tabletop is sure to be keenly observed.

On top of the value of drawing the spotlight off of you, props also can be very effective in explaining things that are difficult to put in words. One warning: Don't overdo it with props. Too much clutter is worse than a boring talking head.

Effective Visual Aids

Here are a dozen ideas for props that can be useful in supplementing your public speaking:

- Charts
- Graphs
- Diagrams
- Photos
- An easel with pages that can be turned as your talk progresses
- Sample products
- Live demonstrations
- Model replicas
- Videotape clips
- Point out an item covered by a drape and promise a surprise later in the speech, then with a little fanfare eventually unveil it.
- Ask a volunteer from the audience to join you at the podium to show how a product functions.
- Award gifts at key points during the presentation when members of the audience respond appropriately.

PowerPoint Presentations

Perhaps the pinnacle of props is the PowerPoint presentation. For those of you who have been sequestered in caves for the past decade, PowerPoint is a software program made by Microsoft that has virtually revolutionized the presentation genre.

It performs what used to be performed by mechanical film slide projectors, but does so with the panache and flair of cutting edge high-tech wizardry. About anything that can be created or displayed on a computer can be included in a PowerPoint presentation, including special effects, motion, and sound. This means the old, less than enthralling slide shows used by public speakers now can be transformed into virtual multimedia extravaganzas.

The "slides," such as they are, can be remotely controlled, timed, or synchronized with music, other video or film, and, of course, with your oral presentation. The caution here is, once again, not to overdo. Computerized presentations projected onto screens or onto video displays should not be the centerpiece of your public speaking unless you are selling computerized presentations. Use them instead as supplemental tools to help you interact with your audience. Let them provide strategic diversions, instructions, and breaks in your oral presentation. Keep it real. Use the gadgets to enhance, not replace, what you have to say.

Hand Out Handouts

Perhaps the first visual aid used by public speakers was the handout. A measure of its effectiveness is that it is still around, though not always used effectively or wisely.

Handouts are usually printed material that reflects the subject matter of the presenter's speech, although they can go beyond the limits of what the speaker has to say, providing additional information.

On the plus side, handouts allow your audience to follow along a little more closely than if they relied entirely on their attention span and on your spoken words. On the negative side, handouts can do the opposite of what you desire by being so diverting that they take the audience completely out of your control.

Here are some tips for how to use handouts:

1. **Use them in moderation.** Do not overload your audience with stacks of paper.
2. **Make them available incrementally.** Wait until a subject comes up in your presentation before distributing the corresponding handout. Otherwise you risk the audience reading ahead and leaving you behind.
3. **Make them brief.** There is no need for handouts designed to supplement a speech in process to be a verbatim account of what you have to say. Make it an outline so the audience still must rely on you for the fuller meaning of the subject matter.

Speaking engagements, when done well, leave the audience wanting more. The end of your presentation is a good time to make available to the audience the fuller, more detailed handouts that you should not pass out during the speech. You can pretty much gauge the success of your presentation by how much demand there is for the after-speech handouts.

> **Chapter 22**

Do You Need a Web Site?

The Unfulfilled Promise of the Internet

When the Internet exploded onto Americans' desktops, a lot of people imagined that technology had finally brought everyone as close as a mouse click to capturing the happiness they had forever pursued. Okay, so they were wrong.

Limited Sales Potential

The Internet and its business- and consumer-friendly offspring, the World Wide Web, have indeed changed the way many of us buy and sell, communicate, do research, and even how we spend our leisure and work hours. But as the burst of the dot-com bubble around the turn of the century demonstrated, the Web is no panacea. In fact, a lot of entrepreneurial types—to say nothing of millions of investors—lost their proverbial shirts.

To be sure, it is not an exaggeration to say that most companies are unlikely to find sales success online, at least in the near future. The few companies that have turned out to be the exception to the rule and found the Web to be profitable usually are uncommon types such as those with deep inventories of hard-to-find, rarely stocked goods like radio-controlled toy cars, unusual neckties, or out-of-print books and records. Some professional

Be Enticing

Entice your Web site visitors into a long-running relationship. Among the incentives to offer visitors in order to get them to register or to sign your "guest book" are these:

- Discounts
- Notices of when you update your Web site
- Notices of when new products or services are available
- A free e-zine
- A free report or white paper

- Coupons redeemable online or offline
- Sales notices and other offers
- An entry in a lottery
- A free sample
- An offer to answer a question

services, such as stock brokerages, have fashioned ways of delivering their services to customers for a fee online at secure Web sites. But for most businesses, the Web is not yet the route to big profits.

Online Marketing Possibilities

This does not preclude companies from using the Web as an effective marketing tool, however. Indeed, nearly every type of company can find some form of marketing edge by having an online presence. The company Web site has quickly evolved into the online version of a brochure, a press packet, a market research vehicle, a customer service venue, and virtually every other interaction with target markets, customers, and clients. Indeed, even if the Web is not profitable in and of itself, potential customers have come to expect your company to have a Web site as much as they expect you to have a business card. You are about as likely to be asked, "Do you have a Web site?" as you are, "May I have one of your brochures?" Still, the key to Web marketing success is no different than successful marketing offline.

Reflecting Your Goals Online

When you drafted your marketing plan you clearly specified the goals you wished to accomplish. The same should apply to your online presence. Moreover, your online goals should advance your general marketing goals. Just because the Web is such a different medium is no reason to depart from your basic marketing and business plans. Consider the Web just one more tool in your marketing arsenal rather than an alien appendage, and your chances of success will be much greater. If you become enamored with chasing goals that are esoteric or off-point, you will fritter away a lot of money for little gain. In short, use the Web to advance what you have determined really works and to obtain what you originally set out to achieve. Just because it is possible to have a Web site with animated visual effects and stereophonic sound, you should only go to that expense if it advances your basic marketing strategy. Do not do it simply because you can.

Before hiring that costly Web-design company or signing a Web-hosting contract, plot out in black and white what your Web site should accomplish.

As always, make your goals reasonable, achievable, measurable, and affordable. And most of all, make the Web site's goals entirely compatible with your overall marketing strategy.

Some online goals to consider:

- Brand identification
- Corporate identity
- Sales
- Lead generation
- Product promotion
- Customer service
- Employee internal communication
- Supplier or distributor communication
- Customer communication

- Advertising
- Affinity or co-op marketing
- Press relations
- Referrals
- Association with kindred industry sources
- Dissemination of the history and culture of your company

The point to keep in mind is that your online presence is just another way for you to accomplish the same things that you identified as goals in your marketing and business plans. Do not let the Internet become a goal in and of itself, and you will find it to be a useful tool. Otherwise you will find it hollow and costly.

Online Basics

Here are some basic tips for establishing an online presence:

1. Choose a Web site URL (Universal Resource Locator address) that is memorable and meaningful. If you sell widgets, ✎ *www.widgets forsale.com*, is the kind of straightforward approach that also delivers the necessary message it in a way that widget seekers are likely to recall. Avoid if you can esoteric or multisyllabic URLs. Simple and straightforward works better than overly clever and drawn out.

2. Record your Web site with the United States Copyright Office by copying it to a CD, filling out the necessary forms (available from the agency's Web site at *http://lcweb.loc.gov/copyright/*), and mailing both to the agency, along with a check for the nominal filing

> Choose a Web site URL (Universal Resource Locator address) that is memorable and meaningful.

fee. Update your filing when you make substantive changes to the site, at least annually. Copyright infringement is an increasing problem online, and the best proof in disputes over who owns what is to have what you own registered with the government.

3. Add your Web site and e-mail address to all your marketing collateral from letterheads to labels. Let your offline presence promote your online presence and vice versa.

Free Access? Registration? Premium? All Three?

If you have determined that a company Web site can advance your marketing plan, one of the threshold decisions you must make is what type of Web site access you will provide. The vast majority of Web sites can be accessed at no cost, and this has given rise to the almost universal expectation of Web users that what is on the Web should be free. Your company's or product's Web site probably should be readily accessible at no cost to anyone surfing the Web, since that is what most people expect. But there is free and there is "free."

It is unlikely that you would leave a stack of your printed brochures sitting on the curb for any passerby to take. Likewise, it probably is unwise to leave your Web site sitting on the Internet for any Web surfer to click to. Curbside or Web side, neither practice is the most efficient or effective way to distribute your marketing collateral. Although you do not normally charge people to give them your brochure, you do normally capture something of value in return. Often it is as little as a face-to-face contact, or a name and address. But at least you obtain something in return for handing out your brochure. The same principle can be applied to your Web site.

Capture Visitors' Names

One of the best marketing uses of your Web site is to capture the names of people who have expressed an interest in your company or product. Your Web site is a perfectly unobtrusive, noninvasive vehicle for accomplishing this. While access may be free, the price you extract can be the capture of your Web site visitors' valuable names, and more. Accomplish this by asking visitors to "please register" or to "sign our guest book" or some other invitation to share with you at the least their identity, and at the most their burning desires.

As an incentive, you can offer value-added benefits not available to the hit-and-run Web site visitors, those who click to and then click away from your site without leaving their names behind. One of the most effective incentives is a promise to notify the visitors automatically by e-mail if there is a change in the particular subject of their interest. For example, your online registration form may ask visitors not just for personal information like name, address, telephone, e-mail, and so forth, but it also might include room for them to note their desire for future product information, or particular areas of interest, or maybe their wish to be told of future sales. This tact is best accomplished with check-off forms, which can more easily be filled out and more easily tallied in a database than can free-form questionnaires.

E-zine Sign-ups

A particularly effective means of capturing the identities of visitors and then further developing them as customers is to ask them to sign up for your periodic e-mail newsletter, sometimes called an e-zine. Your e-zine can be as elementary as a notice of when your Web site has been updated with new information, or it can be as elaborate as an online magazine, chock full of news, promotions, advertisements, and other information that can be tailored to the particular interests of the registered visitor. While you are at it, be sure to ask your registering visitors if they are interested in being contacted periodically by regular mail or even telephone in order to be kept apprised of their particular interests. Keep your registration form as brief as possible, but be sure to include all the options for capturing these self-defined interested prospects.

How about Premium Access?

While most Web sites feature free access or the increasingly popular registered access, you can also consider the still-infrequently used option of premium access, which has yet to blossom as a widespread revenue-generating model. But just because it is not profitable for every type of business does not mean it cannot be profitable for you.

If you can offer online products, services, or information that visitors are willing to pay for, you should consider a premium access option on your Web site. Information-intensive Web sites have pioneered this genre with mixed results. For example, some news publications offer free access to a limited sampling of their content, while charging a premium fee for access to their complete range of content. This model seems to work for information-intensive sites that can offer online samplings of their wares as a lure to purchase ongoing online access to fuller data or information.

Pencil Out Costs and Revenue

It is conceivable that your Web site could feature all three levels of access—free, registered, and premium—but if so, be sure to pencil out each element to determine how the costs of providing each compares to the revenue each generates, or the value each creates in terms of lead generation, prospect list building, or customer relations. Again, do not add an element just because you can.

Submit to Search Engines

Having a Web site for your company does little good if no one ever visits it. Some businesses use their Web sites simply as online brochures or order forms or means of communication with very targeted populations, those they individually refer to the site. These companies do not want to be bothered or inundated with a lot of incidental visitors. But if you are like the vast majority of other businesses online, you want to be found by people who may not know that you are there. In that case, you must be sure to submit your Web site to the major—and in some cases the niche—search engines and search directories.

Among the most popular of these types of online services are Google, a search engine, and Yahoo!, a search directory. The search Web sites operate by allowing Web users to

An E-zine Tailored to Your Customers

Your customers may have diverse interests, but in the old days of paper-and-ink communication, it could be impractical to print up a different edition of your newsletter for each market segment. A customer interested in product A had to sift through all the information about products B and C and D. But with the relatively low costs of online publications like e-zines, it is a small matter to "publish" a different version of your electronic publication to suit each market segment. Database-driven information can be sifted to send people who make inquiries about product A only the information that pertains to product A. It is conceivable to tailor e-zines even further to address each individual's taste rather than to a group's interests. So instead of one publication with everything in it, you may end up with as many different flavors as you have different customers.

Search Engine Musts

A few search engine and search directory services are indispensable, but there is no need to pay extra to have a Web-based service submit your site to hundreds or thousands of search engines. Many of the so-called search engines you pay to be listed on probably get meager Internet traffic themselves. If you opt for one of these, test their effectiveness by inspecting your Web logs that show where Web surfers came from right before visiting your site. Save the trouble and get your Web site listed on the following widely used search engines:

Alta Vista
www.addurl.altavista.com/sites/addurl/newurl
FAST/All the web
www.alltheweb.com/add_url.php
Google
www.google.com/addurl.html
Inktomi via
www.hotbot.lycos.co.uk/submit.html
Yahoo!
www.yahoo.com

type in terms and then receive the URLs or Web addresses of sites that match. Many of the search services do not require submissions, but instead rely on their own "spiders," which are automated Web searching software that logs millions of Web sites and categorizes them based on their content. Others, for a fee, will give your URL a higher ranking when particular terms are searched for. But for the most part, online searches work by matching up the appropriateness, frequency of visits, and other factors that make your site a good match for the term or terms being sought.

High Rankings Do Not Just Happen

Some people have made careers out of keeping abreast of the ever-changing algorithms and other arcane formulas and rules that search engines use to match up queries with URLs in attempts to crack their codes and get higher rankings. Unless you have personnel to devote to such time-consuming research, it is better to simply to follow the instructions provided by each individual search engine or directory, then to submit your site as frequently as each one recommends. (Some search engines will penalize you in the rankings if you submit your site too often.) There also are services that will handle the submissions for you, and other services that will assess your Web pages to advise how to optimize them for high search engine results.

Maximizing your exposure and elevating your ranking on the search engines is important if you hope to attract Web visitors who are unaware of your company's URL, and particularly those who are unaware of your company's very existence.

For those of you bold enough to want to understand firsthand how search engines and directories work, and how you personally can tweak your Web site to take full advantage of them, Search Engine Watch is the online authoritative source. It is updated continually with the latest in fine-tuning advice. It is located online at ✍ *www.searchenginewatch.com.*

Offer Free Downloads

Once people have found your Web site, it is a good idea to have something for them. In fact, your Web site's benefit can be measured in part by how long your visitors hang around. The longer they stay, the more likely you are to achieve your Web site's goals, whatever they may be. Apart from asking visitors to read or print out the content on your Web pages, another effective means of holding their attention is to engage them interactively. One of the most effective interactive techniques is to offer items that are free to download.

The downloadables can range from white papers and brochures to software programs or software samples. They can be ready to use or view upon downloading them, or they may require running an executable program to transform them into usable form. Whatever your downloadable goodie bag contains, it will be most effective if it costs the Web surfer nothing to obtain it other than the time it takes to download.

Free downloadables are an excellent means of introducing prospects to new products, such as a scaled-down version of new software, or to a chapter excerpted from a new book. They also work well to distribute marketing collateral that may be too time-consuming to read online. But the key appeal is that whatever they are, these downloadables are free.

Sell Online

Free downloadables will work in keeping your Web site visitors on the site longer but also can serve as teasers for online sales. Virtually anything that can be sold can be sold online, as evidenced by the phenomenally popular auction site eBay, and Web stores like those operated by Amazon and Yahoo!

Web stores also function as marketing tools, extending your selling presence into the online realm to what may be a new audience. For relatively modest fees there are reputable and reliable companies that can provide you a turnkey merchant presence on the World Wide Web, complete with shopping carts, credit card acceptance, and even drop ship services. At this stage of the Internet's development, online shopping for most companies is a way to expose their brick-and-mortar businesses in another venue, but not yet a replacement for them. Even the most successful of offline merchants still make the lion's share of their sales offline.

But if you can break even online by establishing a Web shopping venue for your products, you may capture the attention of a segment of the market that your offline store is missing. Many Web observers expect that eventually online sales will represent an increasingly larger portion of overall sales. So if you can afford to set up an online store to supplement your offline sales today, you may be able to score a double marketing coup by in effect obtaining not just another sales presence, but also an added promotion for your conventional offline business.

Use E-commerce Evaluation Services

As we discussed earlier, it is extremely valuable to be able to assess customers' satisfaction (or dissatisfaction) in order to gauge how effectively you serve your target market and to adjust to changing attitudes. The Internet can provide this valuable marketing benefit in nearly real time.

If you opt to add an online store to your Web site, you should consider adding services that will measure your customer satisfaction. Why wait for complaints or follow-up telephone calls or even e-mail queries to figure out whether your customers have been pleased or disappointed? Automated services such as BizRate.com (*☞ www.bizrate.com*) and thePublicEye.com (*☞ www.thepubliceye.com*) provide customer feedback at the time of purchase based on customers' experience shopping.

Ratings for You and Your Buyers

Some of these services are available as add-ons to your online store without charge. Moreover, these services provide rating systems not just to you, but also to shoppers so they can judge your company's performance in comparison to competitors. In an increasingly competitive market, with more and more buyers tending to comparison shop before parting with their money, your relative ranking can be a valuable aid in drawing those customers on the fence over to your side. Of course, that means you better provide better service and make happier customers. But that is the whole point, isn't it?

Information of this nature enables merchants to better understand their customers' needs, and as a consequence provide a more satisfying shopping experience.

Promote Online and Off

Whatever the configuration of your online presence, whether it is simply an e-mail connection to the virtual world or an entire Web site replete with shopping services and extensive customer interaction, it is imperative that you promote it not only online, but offline as well.

Direct online visitors to your real world headquarters. On all your offline marketing collateral, promote your online Web site and services. The two should be intimately intertwined, not competitive but serving as supplements to each other.

The more seamless the relationship between your online and offline marketing, the more each can boost the effectiveness of the other.

Load Fast, or Else

Save money on your Web site by sticking to what your customers and visitors want. Among their chief desires is a Web site that loads fast on their computer screen. Overstock your Web site with slow-loading graphics, photos, and multimedia features, and you risk your visitors giving up and leaving before you have had a chance for them to see much, let alone everything. Also be mindful that the chief value of Web sites is informational, particularly in business-oriented sites. While gimmicks, games, and interactive schemes can serve to prolong a visitor's stay, they are counterproductive if they do not ultimately provide what the visitor needs from you—the justification for buying what you sell. Do not lose sight of the purpose of your Web site, which in its essence is the same as all your other marketing efforts.

► Chapter 23

E-mail: The Ubiquitous Communication

PART FIVE   GETTING OUT YOUR MESSAGE

CHAPTER 21 Develop Personal Speaking Skills ■ CHAPTER 22 Do You Need a Web Site? ■ CHAPTER 23 E-mail: The Ubiquitous Communication ■ CHAPTER 24 Internet Networking ■ CHAPTER 25 Online Advertising: Millions of Potential Viewers

The Next Killer App

There is no doubt that computers have revolutionized life for millions of us. But the emergence of the personal computer would have amounted to nothing without the subsequent emergence of "killer applications" that firmly established the device by giving people something to do with the new metal boxes on their desktops. The first killer "app" was spreadsheets, which bestowed immense calculating power previously available only to big corporations with room-sized mainframes. Then came word processors, which almost overnight made typewriters into obsolete relics. And then came the Internet. Although not a software application per se, it did enable computers to be used for instantaneous personal communication and information sharing on a worldwide basis.

The next, and arguably the potentially greatest killer app to evolve in the computer age, is e-mail. Not everyone uses spreadsheets, or even word processors. But virtually everyone who goes online at some point is

Tips for Friendly E-mail

Here are a few ideas to make your e-mail more reader friendly:

1. Use language appropriate to the recipient. If there are sufficiently different types of recipients, create separate mailings that each speak in its target segment's voice.
2. Always find out whether the recipient prefers to receive your e-mail in HTML format or in plain text format. HTML is much more pleasant to read and look at but takes considerably longer to download and view.
3. Never use ALL CAPITAL LETTERS. In online parlance, this is equivalent to shouting.
4. Make the most important and thoughtful line of text in your e-mail the Subject field. Many e-mail readers never even see the body of a message because they decide whether or not to read it based on the Subject field.
5. Configure your e-mail software to distinguish previous messages when replying back and forth with a recipient. In this way, both you and your recipients can backtrack and never lose sight of the original issue or what has already been said.

introduced to e-mail. And for most of these people, e-mail is becoming an incurable addiction. It already is the ubiquitous link between nearly everyone with a computer. And it promises to be an even greater communications solution in the future than it is today.

Let that sink in for a minute. E-mail is used by nearly everyone who goes online, which increasingly is becoming everyone who has a computer. What percentage of your target market is still computer illiterate? Chances are, not many of the people you need to reach. And chances are even better that there will be fewer of them tomorrow than there are today. Imagine the potential. There are few mediums of communication that reach as many people. And there are almost none that reach them as inexpensively.

E-mail, if it has not dawned on you yet, may be the greatest boon to marketing since the handshake.

The First Rule: No Spam

The online marketer's motto might be borrowed from Hippocrates, who admonished physicians to "First, do no harm." Online marketer's should similarly "First, do no spam," which, if not medically harmful, is certainly annoying.

Spam is unwanted, unsolicited e-mail, typically sent en masse much like "junk mail," the derisive term used to describe unwanted, unsolicited offline mail deposited in your curbside mailbox. The difference is that economic realities put limits on how much paper junk mail advertisers and marketers can afford to flood the countryside with. It costs money to create, print, cut, fold, stuff, and send through the U.S. Postal Service every piece of paper mail. A lot of money. But since it costs no more to produce a million e-mails than it does to produce one, and since the cost of "mailing" those electronic missives is infinitesimally less than the paper versions, it is no surprise that we already have reached the glut stage of spam online. We will almost certainly continue to see more and more of the stuff, not less.

Unchecked, this unfortunate trend is likely to have three detrimental effects.

1. It will (further) outrage online users.
2. It will undermine the effectiveness of e-mail.
3. It may prompt government intervention.

So unless you want to have a hand in killing what may be the online marketer's golden goose and inviting government regulation of how you market, it is prudent for you to voluntarily adopt considerate rules of conduct for the use of e-mail, and to make sure that the people you send e-mail to are aware that you take those rules seriously.

Have an E-mail Ethics Policy

Include a concise explanation of your e-mail policy in every electronic message you send, or at least include a hyperlink to a Web site where your policy is explained. Here are some basic starting points for drafting your policy, which of course will be useless if you do not also follow them.

1. Never send e-mail to anyone who has not previously granted you approval to do so.
2. In every e-mail make it clear that recipients can opt out of receiving future communications from you by letting you know they do not want to receive any more.
3. Do not sell or rent your e-mail list to other companies.
4. Never send e-mail with addresses listed in the "CC" (courtesy copies) field because all addresses will be visible to every recipient. Instead, use the "BC" field for blind copies that can be seen by no one.
5. Do not include attachments unless the recipient has expressed a desire to receive them. Attachments are notorious virus carriers, and even if yours is virus-free the added download time for recipients is extremely annoying. Instead, paste supplementary material into the e-mail form itself, or provide an online link.
6. Always reply quickly to any incoming e-mail or any responses to your own e-mail. If e-mail and computers have done anything, they have forever shortened peoples' patience.

These standards are a good baseline for building your e-mail policy, but feel free to be more restrictive and protective. Strive to be an inoffensive e-mailer and take steps not to offend anyone.

Use Auto-Responders and "Sig" Files

One of the inherent powers of the computer is that it can automate many functions. When it comes to e-mail, it is just as easy to send dozens of identical messages to dozens of different people by creating only one original and pressing only one key on the keyboard.

Likewise, there are two other functions that are easily automated with e-mail software. The first is so elementary it is often overlooked. The second is more technical so it is often neglected. The first does not cost you anything, and the second does not cost you much.

"Sig" Files

Adding a "sig" or signature line to your e-mail is often overlooked, even though it is easy to do. Since the process can be automated in most e-mail software, there is no excuse for leaving it out. A sig line may be as simple as:

John Jones
Jones Widgets
jones@widget.com

Or a sig line may be very elaborate, including not just basic contact information, but detailed information, instructions or business hours, mottos or slogans, links to Web sites, or any number of other tidbits that benefit the e-mail recipient and advance your marketing strategy. The sig line may be set off from the rest of the message's text with characters such as: ===== or ++++++ or ***** in this way:

++++++++++++++++
John Jones
Jones Widgets
jones@widget com
++++++++++++++++

Determine Preferences

Some people tend to their e-mail first thing in the morning. Some squirrel it away for later. Some kill it outright if they are busy, but may be more receptive to the identical message at a different time of day. If you have periodic mass or bulk mailings that go out to opt-in subscribers to your e-mail updates, sort them by the preference they have for time of day. Just as you might ask opt-in prospects which of your three updates they prefer—the sale notice, the weekly newsletter, the industry scoops—you also can ask them what time of day they prefer to receive your update. It is a small matter to send the same e-mail at different times of the day to different segments of your market. And arriving at the right time can make the difference between getting read rather than deleted.

Many software packages allow you to create alternate sig lines and choose which ones to attach.

In short, there is no reason to be forced to type your name and address or anything else you want at the end of your message every time you create a new e-mail. Create an automated sig line one time and it will be applied every time to your outgoing mail. It is likely your e-mail software permits you to create more than one version of your sig line, then to choose from a menu which to attach.

Auto-Responders

A more technical function that sometimes is not employed is the auto-responder, which requires either a little programming knowledge or a minor expense to pay someone with that knowledge or to contract with a service, or even buying relatively inexpensive software that can automate the process for you.

Auto-responders are small software routines that automatically generate responses to e-mail that you have received. If you have a Web site and solicit e-mail from visitors, auto-responders can immediately send out a "thank you" or a reminder or instructions to your visitors. Otherwise, they would have to wait until you personally read and reply to their e-mail.

The typical Web surfers have already been spoiled. They expect instant responses and are not content to wait hours or days to hear back when they make an inquiry. Depending on the sophistication of your auto-responding software, your reply not only can be instantaneous, but it can be tailored to the nature of the inquiry. For example, if you want to respond to inquiries about pricing, on your Web site you might place a link or a form that creates an e-mail addressed to "pricing@widgets.com" At another location of your Web site you may be soliciting e-mail from people who want to subscribe to your periodic newsletter by sending you a request at "newsletter@widgets.com." Your auto-responder can be configured to send the appropriate response or instruction, determined by the e-mail address. Some auto-responders can even be configured to tailor the response according to keywords included in the body or Subject field of the e-mail.

Auto-responders are a low-cost way to help you meet the high expectations of your online target market. At the least, auto-responders buy you time. Your immediate automatic response shows that you are not ignoring the inquiry. Use auto-responders to assure your customers that you have received their inquiry and will be addressing it more fully soon. An auto-responder is not a panacea. Much, if not most, of the e-mail you receive ultimately needs to be handled by a human. At least an auto-responder can keep inquiring customers or potential customers appeased until you can give them that more personal attention.

Building E-mail Lists

If you have no one's permission to send them e-mail, how can you use e-mail to promote your business? There are work-around solutions. You can rent e-mail lists of possible customers, or, even better, begin an in-house list based on the customer contacts you already have.

Renting Permission E-mail Lists

In the same way that direct marketing companies rent the use of conventional mailing lists, offline and online marketing companies will provide you with e-mail lists for a fee.

Be cautious, however. Many sellers, resellers, and renters of e-mail lists

The Crucial Subject Line

The subject line of your e-mail is the most important sentence you will write. It is the equivalent of the advertisement's headline, or the opening of your thirty-second elevator speech. It is the grabber. Fail to grab the recipient and you are literally one click from oblivion. The subject line should in no uncertain terms express the benefit of what your e-mail contains. Do not waste this precious space with anything even slightly off-point. Home in on why recipients should bother to open your e-mail. What is in it for them? Employ power words. Be direct. Leave them hungering for more information. One effective technique is to use an interesting or provocative phrase, but do not complete the entire sentence, such as: "To get the most out of your widgets all you do is . . ."

have collected their lists without permission. Web-searching robots scour the Internet plucking e-mail addresses off of Web sites, from discussion groups, and anywhere else they can find them without bothering to ask anyone's permission. Do not pay money for lists acquired in this way unless you want to risk the consequences, which can be severe.

Since most, if not all, of the people whose e-mail addresses you acquire in such a stealthy fashion have not previously requested to be contacted by you, they are most likely going to consider it spam if you send them electronic mail. If you send the e-mail through your own Internet connection via your Internet service provider (ISP), you run the risk of violating the terms of your contractual agreement, which is likely to prohibit spam. In such an event, your ISP can terminate your account. Play it safe—and more importantly, play it properly—and make sure that whoever provides you e-mail addresses has acquired the lists legitimately, which is to say with the owners' permission or at the owners' request.

Create Your Own Opt-In List

As any professional direct marketer will admit, the very best mailing list is the one you compile yourself. While list brokers will insist that

Spell Out Opt-In Rules

When building an e-mail list, be sure to spell out the terms clearly for both potential e-mail recipients and yourself. Here are some possible guidelines:

1. Ask participants to confirm that they are acting on behalf of their own e-mail account only.
2. Make it clear that they are agreeing to receive periodic e-mails from you for specified general purposes.
3. Upon agreeing to accept e-mails from you, recipients also may unsubscribe at any time by following instructions that you provide.
4. You may wish to agree that you will not disclose the recipient's e-mail address or other contact or demographic information to third parties.

they can sell or rent you lists that "perfectly" match your target market profile, the fact is, the only people you can be certain match are the ones who have proven it by buying from you. These people have already traveled the long, arduous road to customer satisfaction, having given you their attention, then expressed their interest in, and later a desire for what you sell, and finally acted upon that desire by making a purchase.

The next best prospects are the folks who have come just short of buying but have indicated a desire, and the next in line are those who may not yet desire what you sell but have expressed interest. In most cases, it is a leap of faith to believe commercial lists can be guaranteed to include folks like these. At best they approximate them. But the lists that you compile, based on your own marketing lures, are much more likely to be chock full of these qualified prospects.

With this principle in mind, you should build an online in-house list in much the way you do offline, by capturing the names of those who express interest or desire, and certainly the names of those who have proven their worth by buying from you.

To build an online in-house list, capture the same data as you do offline—personal identifiers, demographic traits, and psychographic characteristics—but add one critically important piece of information: the person's e-mail address.

Indeed, when done well, online data capture can be more extensive and easier for you and for your prospects. Check-off forms, personalized question-and-answer formats, immediate response, and the ease of entry all can facilitate capturing the information you need. Indeed, the leading Internet browser, Microsoft's Internet Explorer, automates filling out forms for its users who enable that function. For example, people who simply type the first letter of their names will be prompted to select their full names with one click, rather than keying in each letter.

Promise Complete Confidentiality

As always, be sure to promise complete confidentiality, and promise that your Web site visitor's information will not be sold or provided to third parties. And make sure you keep your promise. Reputations online spread

Archive E-mail

There is little cost in archiving the e-mail that flows in and out of your Web site or personal account. You obviously want a record of what you have sent and to whom if for no other reason to know what not to duplicate at a later date. But the responses your e-mail elicits can be even more valuable because they constitute the personally expressed questions, compliments, and complaints of your target market in general, and more importantly, individual prospects and customers in particular. One of the benefits of archiving e-mail is that almost all e-mail software enables the user to search thousands of archived messages at the click of a mouse to retrieve particular names, phrases, or any other text identifiers in any field of the messages. This can be invaluable when resolving disputes, reconstructing conversations, establishing dates or sequences, and countless other customer-service uses.

like wildfire; once you are burned, it is next to impossible to undo the damage.

Besides directly asking visitors to your Web site to fill out forms, you can add to your prospect and customer online list in other ways. For example, whenever you exchange e-mails with anyone, your sig line can include an option for the recipient to click on a hyperlink to a Web page, or to reply to a particular e-mail address if they wish to be added to your mailing list. Likewise, any online sales or online confirmation of offline sales can include similar options for recipients to "opt-in" to your mailing list or subscribe to your periodic product updates.

The online version of mailing list building has one great advantage over its offline counterpart: It can be nearly instantaneous. The process can be almost like impulse shopping because it is so easy to opt-in at such a low cost in time and effort. But the instantaneous nature cuts two ways. It is just as easy for those who opt in to opt out. That is okay. You do not want them to stay on your list if they do not want to hear from you. They will only distort your picture of your target market. So make it as easy for your prospects to opt out as it is to opt in.

Provide Visitors with Update Notifications

Once you have built a list of opt-in prospects and customers, lure them back to your Web site or brick-and-mortar store by providing them something to look forward to. There are as many opportunities for this as there are reasons to talk with them. Here are a few:

- Offer periodic e-mail newsletters with product updates.
- Provide new information geared to their interests and related to your products or services.

- Offer to keep them notified about when your Web site is updated so they can visit to learn the latest scoop on widgets.
- Tip them off about upcoming sales.
- Let them know that you will be giving them advance knowledge of upcoming special offers.
- Promise to keep them abreast on breaking industry news.
- Tell them when you change operating hours, or shut down to go fishing.

In short, use the promise of giving these valued customers and prospects what they want and need to know in order to keep them signed on as bona fide members of your opt-in mailing list.

> **Chapter 24**

Internet Networking

The Personal Touch Online

The Internet has vastly expanded opportunities for low-cost marketing by giving you fast, easy, and nearly unlimited options for communicating with prospects, customers, and all-important gatekeepers.

But just because the process of one-on-one and one-on-many marketing has been hyperaccelerated, it does not mean that you can consign your Internet efforts exclusively to automated responses or mass e-mailings. The best marketing, online or off, retains the genuine, sincere, and personal approach.

To reiterate a frequent theme in these pages, people do business with people they like. Although computers and the Internet have made it possible to reach more people faster and easier, lasting relationships still require genuine commitment and sincere communication. None of the glitz or flash of Internet marketing can overcome reluctance or distaste rooted in personal emotions.

This chapter deals with some ways that you can establish personal relationships in your online marketing, and offers some suggestions for methods that you may employ to capitalize on those relationships.

Host or Appear on Online Chats

A popular online tool that is increasingly being adopted by the business sector is the interactive live chat. Typically these group discussions take place in real time with questions posed by visitors, answers offered by a guest or a host, and the entire procedure sometimes moderated by a third party. The moderator is expendable, but for the conversation to work you must have a guest or host who is the subject of the chat, and visitors who want to interact with the "expert."

Some Internet vendors can create customized online discussion rooms for you, but generally at a rather hefty price for most small businesses. A more cost-conscious solution is to make use of one of the many already established online chat rooms sponsored by community Web sites or even media Web sites.

Book an Appearance

So many of these chat sites need live content that booking such an appearance is certainly not as difficult or competitive as trying to get your face on a television talk show. Others are available free for the asking, such as provided at Yahoo! Groups (*http://groups.yahoo.com/*) or MSN Chat (✑*www.msn.com*). You can even add a chat box to your own Web site, and free versions are available online if you agree to display a small banner ad.

Third-Party Moderators

Some of these Web-based chat rooms operated by third parties will even relieve you of the tedious grunt work of typing your own responses by providing a typist to transcribe your comments. Others require you to punch the keyboard, but in those cases you generally can be at your own computer rather than onsite at the third party's locale.

Moderators might serve merely as conduits, passing on comments to the common screen where everyone can read them, or as quasi-censors, keeping the conversation civil with restrictive editing authority. Some of the instant message software applications such as AOL's Instant Messenger can also accommodate group discussions, but with these there generally is no moderator to keep the ebb and flow moving in an orderly manner, and the

Cheat Sheets Are Okay

When hosting online chats, be sure to prepare a cheat sheet that you can refer to when participants ask you questions. Since these chats are typically conducted live in real time, any delay you have in responding to questions or comments is the equivalent to "dead air" in radio and television parlance. Long pauses that do not advance the conversation can be the death knell for live chats where attention spans are shortened and expectations are heightened. One way to prepare for the conversation ahead of time is to ask yourself the most common questions on the topic you will be discussing, then prepare in Q&A format a frequently asked question form that you can quickly refer to as a reminder.

discussions can get a bit out of hand, falling into a free-for-all style with everyone talking over everyone else.

Engage in a Dialogue

Whichever format you use, the point is to engage interested people in a dialogue about your topic. It is an opportunity to discuss with self-qualifying interested prospects what you have that they may desire. What could be better for a marketer? A captive, already interested target market glued to their computer screens, hanging on your every word.

There are a couple caveats to keep in mind. If you do not think fast on your feet, you may want to pass on this fast-paced interchange. If you must do your own typing and do not type well, or do not spell well enough to avoid embarrassment, also think twice before taking the plunge. And if you have not mastered the subject of your chat, do not bother. It is better to pass on the opportunity than to be documented as a bona fide dunce.

Join and Contribute to E-Zines

For those just a tad uneasy with real time encounters, Internet e-zines provide ample opportunities with less edge-of-your-seat adrenaline. These online publications can range from intermittent e-mail updates to slick, magazine-like electronic publications. There are thousands of e-zines and similarly structured lists, newsgroups, and discussion groups.

Some places to look include:

1. Topica—Bills itself as the leader in e-mail newsletters and publishing solutions. "Topica is the leading independent provider of turnkey solutions for e-mail newsletter publishers, from multinational media companies to individuals publishing news about a hobby or interest."
   http://✐ www.topica.com/

2. Yahoo! Groups—Perhaps the best-known, if not the largest, online publisher of subscription e-zines. "One e-mail address and Web site that allows you to . . . share photos and files, plan

events, send a newsletter, stay in touch with friends and family . . ."
http://groups.yahoo.com/

3. Catalist—A source for seemingly endless lists of Listservs. "Browse any of the 58,605 public LISTSERV lists on the Internet, search for mailing lists of interest, and get information about LISTSERV host sites. This information is generated automatically from LISTSERV's LISTS database and is always up to date."
   ✑ *www.lsoft.com/catalist.html*

These operations and many others offer so many special-interest online publications that you should be able to find several industry or consumer-oriented lists or subscription newsletters germane to your business, product, or services. For example, a search for "marketing" at the Catalist site returned 135 lists that you can subscribe and contribute to.

Once you have narrowed the list of subscription lists or e-zines that match your marketing goals in terms of subject matter and readership, subscribe to the best prospects. Then spend a while, days or weeks or whatever length of time it takes, to become familiar with the nature of the information posted on the publication, the tenure of the talk, and the manner of give and take.

The Straight Poop

Finally, when you are comfortable, begin to contribute comments yourself. The best way to consider your contributions are to think of them as akin to standing around the water cooler sharing stories, tips, insights, and comments with your colleagues. One caution: Do not be overly self-promotional or argumentative. Most subscribers to e-zines and listservs are looking for the straight poop, not hyperbole or sales pitches, and picking fights is certainly counterproductive.

When contributing your own comments to these online

Be a Lurker

The idea of contributing to e-zines and other online subscription dialogues is to market yourself, not shoot yourself in the foot. When first subscribing to online publications like an e-zine, do not be in a great hurry to jump into the conversation. Learn the subtleties of the publication first. Note the length of typical posts. Some publications are like freeway traffic where the speed limit may be posted at sixty-five, but realistically you may be able to do only fifty-five or run the risk of ramming someone from behind. Regardless of what the rules call for, pay attention to see what is the common practice. Note whether posts generally avoid addressing individuals in favor of posts that talk to the generic audience. Note complaints about others who are rubbing subscribers the wrong way. Learn from their mistakes rather than making them yourself.

Use a Signature Line

When posting to online forums or e-zines, include information about yourself in your signature line so that you are identified with what you have written and also to encourage others to contact you, patronize your company, or visit your Web site. Here is an example of a sig line that crams as much useful information into it as possible. (Be sure to check the rules for any publications you contribute to.)

```
!=!=!=!=!=!=!=!=!=!=!=!=!=!=!=!=!=!=!=!=!=!=!=!=!=!=!
Joe Jones
President
Widgets Inc.
"We manufacture widgets that never disappoint"
123 Main Street
Your Town
Your State 12345
E-mail: joejones@widgetsinc.com
Web site: ✐ www.widgetsinc.com
!=!=!=!=!=!=!=!=!=!=!=!=!=!=!=!=!=!=!=!=!=!=!=!=!=!=!
```

A tip: Put the most important stuff at the top and bottom, which is where readers look first, and the next most important item near the middle but in the longest line so it stands out.

publications be sure to include your sig line, which in almost every case is permissible as long as it does not constitute a lengthy, blatant ad. Just in case, check the ground rules with the publication first. If what you have to say is of interest, after a while you will find that other contributors will engage you in conversation by responding on the list and also directly by e-mailing you, or even telephoning, if your phone number is included in your sig. This is networking on steroids. Offline it is nearly impossible to interact directly with as many colleagues or targeted prospects on such a regular basis. Used prudently and persistently, e-zines and listservs can provide great benefits.

Post to Appropriate Discussion Lists

Another version of online communication that can be exploited much like e-zines, listservs, and e-mail are what originally were referred to as computer bulletin boards but have come to be called discussion forums or newsgroups. These online exchanges are international in scope and probably the largest decentralized information utilities in the world. They may be moderated, which means all submissions are routed through a human being who can edit or screen out the posts, or unmoderated, which means anyone can post anything they wish to.

Learn the Ropes of Threads

Some of these forums or newsgroups date back two decades, and most are characterized by ongoing conversations that split off into "threads" of subtopics, and subtopics within subtopics. Join one by following the instructions, which normally amount to sending an e-mail to a designated address. Read threads online and contribute by clicking on appropriate instructions, such as "Post a follow-up to this message," or by sending an e-mail to the designated address.

These discussion lists tend to ramble a bit and obviously split off on tangents, but they also are good for developing a sense of community and conversation among the like-minded.

Offer Online Coaching

If you are verbally inclined, which is to say you communicate well with words, you might consider offering online coaching as another means of networking with prospects, colleagues, and even existing clients.

Coaching, of course, can be something you do for a fee or simply to mentor another. Either way, it can serve as a

Down-Home Talk

As with all written and spoken communication, your tone and vocabulary should be appropriate for your audience. Communication online generally is less formal and more friendly than in many other business venues. You should not assume that everyone is your pal. Nevertheless, if you must err in one direction, opt for folksy, not pompous. Online posts, e-zine contributions, and e-mail in general assume a conversational tone. More formalized verbiage gives the appearance of boilerplate, that-must-be-included stuff like legal disclaimers or copyright notices that nobody reads and no one is encouraged to read, simply because it is written in such stilted language. But you want your posts and e-mails to be read, so be sure to make them readable, which is to say friendly rather than formal, folksy rather than stuffy.

marketing tool for you in establishing yourself as an authority in your field, and if you are not charging for it, a benevolent authority.

The beauty of the online venue for coaching is that it frees you from travel time, face-to-face encounters, and rigid hours. Online coaching can be conducted in real time, or by e-mail correspondence. To "meet" in real time with the people you coach, you might employ one of the instant messaging systems mentioned earlier.

You and your subjects can carry on live conversations, ask and answer questions, and even share graphic files and photos, all live. If schedules do not permit live sessions, coaching by e-mail can work like a correspondence course, only much faster than waiting for the U.S. mail.

A big plus, of course, is the comfort factor. Where else can you coach or mentor admiring protégés barefoot in your bathrobe?

Be Mindful of Online Etiquette

Finally, whatever online option you may choose for Internet networking, there are some basic rules of etiquette, or "netiquette," to keep in mind. Just because the others cannot see you does not give you license to be a jerk.

1. Do not type in ALL CAPITAL letters. It is considered shouting.
2. Do not "flame" or otherwise be disrespectful of others' comments. If you do have occasion to differ strongly with another subscriber or poster, it is best to keep your feuding on a one-to-one basis via e-mail, rather than publishing your brickbats where everyone else must endure them too.
3. Do not use the subscriber base as a captive audience for advancing your personal agenda. Make what you say pertain to the theme of the publication.
4. Similarly, avoid cross-posting your messages to inappropriate publications. One of the great values of e-zines, forums, and all the other online specialized publications is precisely that they are specialized so subscribers and users can expect posts to be on-point.
5. Just because others who contribute to the e-zine, forum, or other online publication reveal their e-mail addresses when they post

their comments, this does not give you carte blanche to lift their addresses for use in online mass mailings or other promotional e-mails. The opt-in rule still applies. While you may feel free to send a one-on-one e-mail to another e-zine contributor, always respect the other person's privacy and do not lump them in with your marketing mailing list without permission.

6. In the age of copy and paste, it is easy to include the work of others in your communications, but always respect copyrights. The Internet has made duplicating others' original work even easier than photocopying. Whenever you copy a segment of anything previously published, be sure to apply the same rules that you would offline. Always attribute the source. Abide by the "fair use" copyright doctrine by being mindful of the amount of copying in relation to the work as a whole. It is better to excerpt a small section set off in quotation marks with proper attribution and to provide a hyperlink to the original piece rather than to copy articles or information wholesale.

7. Be considerate of the amount of bandwidth used and of others' time. Do not repost the entirety of another's comment when responding to it. Although it is helpful to know what prompted your response, it is usually enough to paraphrase or to select a snippet of the previous comment, properly attributed, to put your response in context.

In short, online as offline, do unto others as you would have them do unto you and you will find that networking works on the Net.

Emoticon Shorthand

If you have never participated in online chats before, you may be puzzled by some of the shorthand notations that have come to be universal among veteran online communicators. The following is an abbreviated list of the hieroglyphs and acronyms used to save keystrokes and, in no small part, to have a little fun.

> Whenever you copy a segment of anything previously published, be sure to apply the same rules that you would offline.

:)	Smiley face
:(	Sad face
:-)	Smile with a nose
:-(	Sad with a nose
:-D	Laugh
;-)	Wink
A/S/L	Requesting age/sex/location
ANAWFOS	And Now a Word from Our Sponsor
ASAP	As Soon As Possible
ASCII	American Standard Code for Information Interchange
ATTN	Attention
BAC	Back at Computer
BAK	Back at Keyboard
BBS	Bulletin Board System
BCC	Blind Courtesy Copy
BEG	Big Evil Grin
BOT	Back on Topic
BSF	But Seriously, Folks
BTAICBW	But Then Again, I Could Be Wrong
BTDT	Been There, Done That
BYKT	But You Knew That
CC	Courtesy Copy
CL	Cross Link
CU	See You
CUOP	Catch Up on Posts
CYM	Check Your Mail
DBA	Doing Business As
DIY	Do It Yourself

DL or D/L	Download
DQM	Don't Quote Me
DTP	Desktop Publishing
EG	Evil Grin
EOD	End of Discussion
EOT	End of Thread (do not reply)
ETA	Estimated Time of Arrival
F2F	Face to Face
FAQ	Frequently Asked Questions
FOC	Free of Charge
FOFL	Falling on Floor Laughing
FYI	For Your Information
GIGO	Garbage In, Garbage Out
GMTA	Great Minds Think Alike
IC	I See
IM	Instant Message
IMHO	In My Humble Opinion
IMO	In My Opinion
ISP	Internet Service Provider
LOL	Laughing Out Loud
MYOB	Mind Your Own Business
NP	No Problem
OT	Off Topic
ROI	Return on Investment
ROTFL	Rolling on the Floor Laughing
RTFAQ	Read the FAQ
TGIF	Thank God It's Friday
UL or U/L	Upload

> **Chapter 25**

Online Advertising: Millions of Potential Viewers

Part One

Part Two

Part Three

Part Four

Part Five

Seeking Out Cost-Effective Online Advertising

Every day more and more people go online. Every day more computers are sold, and with them more Internet browsing software and the implicit invitation to connect to the World Wide Web. Every day the growing online community drains a little bit more attention—and money—away from other forms of advertising like newspapers, magazines, radio, and television.

It would seem that the Web is the venue of the future, and consequently that it should make sense for companies that seek growth to advertise in this hot new medium. Perhaps. But here is a little advice to temper the temptation: Cool down. This hot medium is exciting and new all right, but paying to advertise on the World Wide Web can be very costly, and very often not as cost-effective as one might assume.

Are Banner Ads a Good Buy?

Are banner ads a good buy? Generally, no—unless you have a lot of money to throw around and even then only if you can very precisely target your market.

Banner ads are those familiar and ubiquitous rectangular advertisements that appear on millions of Web pages. They can be as plain as simple text, or as elaborate as an animated beckoning message. Click on one and your browser takes you instantly to the advertiser's Web site.

Banner ads were once believed to be the promising new frontier in advertising, expected to bring untold wealth to advertisers whose products would fly (okay, click) off the shelves, as well as to Web sites that sell ad space, theoretically drawing millions of Web surfers, ringing up the cash register with every mouse click.

Alas, one of the strengths of the Internet, its ability to track traffic and online choices, has been generally bad news for banner ads. As the Internet matured it became clear that fewer and fewer Web surfers were clicking on banner ads. As the novelty wore thin and as the number of ads vastly increased, banner ads lost a lot of their glamour. Advertisers were less and less willing to pay big bucks to place their ads online and Web surfers were less and less inclined to bother with them.

Nevertheless, there is no shortage of banner ads all over the World Wide Web. But for the most part, their effectiveness has fallen far short of the hyped expectations of only a few years ago.

Those Annoying Pop-Up Ads

One variation, the pop-up ad, which appears in its own small browser window, has grown in popularity—that is, popularity among advertisers, not necessarily among most Web users, who view them as annoyances. Some research indicates that text links within a Web page are more cost-effective than banner ads, perhaps because they appear less like advertisements and more like information.

It has become fashionable to predict the death of banner ads. But it is likely that they will not die off any time soon. Since advertising and sales are the main sources of online revenue, expect banner ads to persist in some form and perhaps even increase in number, although their effectiveness does not promise to improve. For small businesses and start-up entrepreneurs, the cost of buying these kinds of often-garish appearing ads probably exceeds the return on your investment.

Banner Exchanges Work

Not all is lost, however. Banner exchanges, in which you allow another Web site to place its banner on your site and in turn that site allows your banner to be displayed on its Web pages, can be straight barter arrangements, meaning no direct out-of-pocket cost. If the site you partner with is supplemental to yours (they sell shoes and you sell socks), this is one effective means for reaching a targeted market at little cost.

Some banner exchanges are conducted in what have come to be called "affinity links" or "Web chains." These are

Search Engines Beat Banner Ads

Studies have found that in head-to-head comparisons, search engine listings come out on top compared to banner ads. Moreover, search engines are from two to three times as effective when it comes to generating sales, according to some authoritative sources. Take advantage of this advantage. Spend your limited online advertising budget on maximizing your search engine placement rather than buying much less effective banner ads, which even when highly visible have relatively dismal click-through rates. If you must buy a banner ad, consider banner ads on search engine pages, which may enjoy the best of both worlds. Search engine Internet sites continue to be among the most frequently visited Web destinations, and they are still the principal means that consumers use to shop for sites to shop at.

Hanging on to Visitors

Every hyperlink on your site is an invitation for your visitors to leave. Turn exit doors into revolving doors by inviting other Web sites' visitors to come back your way. When linking to other Web sites, be sure to get them to link back to you. One way to keep visitors around is to create a new window when anyone clicks on a hyperlink on one of your Web pages. Use this HTML code in your hyperlink: *<a href=http.The_URL_of_Your_Target_Site.com target=" _blank" > http:///www. The_URL_of_Your_Target_Site.com</a>*

When visitors click on the link, the open window continues to display your page, with a second window opening to take the visitor to the linked page. Once visitors have finished perusing the second site, they can close the second window and will still see your page on their screen.

similarly themed, or supplementally themed Web sites whose owners have agreed to display one another's banners as a means of sharing similar-minded traffic.

Another variation on this theme is found in operations like Link-Exchange, which permit your banners to be displayed on other sites in return for you displaying others' banners on your own site. You may be required to display two ads on your site for every one of yours appearing elsewhere, but beyond that there is no charge.

Buy Keywords on Specialized Search Engines

If your company has a Web site, you probably want people to be able to find it. In practical terms this means you should submit your Web site to search engines and directories, which function like a combination of the Yellow Pages and that invaluable know-it-all secretary who can find anything you need on a moment's notice.

As the Internet continues to grow, perpetually adding new Web sites, it is unfeasible for every page on every site to expect to appear on the indexes and lists of every search engine and directory. It is already a logistical impossibility.

You Still Need to Rank High

The way indexes and lists work is that the highest ranked Web pages based on keywords, phrases, and other arcane criteria are the ones that are listed first, and consequently the ones most likely to be visited by Web surfers. (When was the last time you clicked through to the last listing on the ninety-fourth page of a search engine result?) In recognition of this increased competition for high placement, many search engines and directories have decided in recent years to sell what they once provided for free—placement in their search results.

Pay for Placement

This new development of selling placement can guarantee that a link to your Web site will be listed prominently among the search results, irrespective of whether a search would normally turn up your site high in its ranking or find it at all.

From the advertiser's perspective, it is sort of the Yellow Pages approach to directory listings. Consider the Internet like the white pages of your telephone book. If you know the precise name of a site, you can find it immediately. Now consider search engines. They are like Yellow Pages, not the white pages. Type in a term like "shoes" and the result page shows you a list of "shoes"-related Web sites. But even better than Yellow Pages, search engines rank their results by how much a site's content matches a query.

Pay for Visibility

Now consider that for a fee, your listing does not have to compete with all similar "shoes" sites to be listed when a search is conducted. Instead, you are guaranteed to be listed on the first page of a search result. Just like in the Yellow

Fine-Tune Your Ranking

Before paying for prominent search engine placement, consider tweaking your Web site to maximize its effectiveness and elevate its ranking. One way to optimize your Web site's search engine ranking is to use software provided by Web Position Gold, a product that promises to "launch your Web site to the top of the search engine results." Also, check out the constantly updated information and how-to tips for maximizing your search engine placement that are located at Search Engine Watch, where Danny Sullivan edits the Web's most authoritative site and newsletter on the subject. Find it at *www.searchengine watch.com.*

Pages, you can pay to get a more prominent placement within the category of "shoes."

It should be noted that from the perspective of Web surfers hunting for "shoes" sites, this is a bit disingenuous, if not misleading. Instead of getting a search result page based on what they want to see, they get results that include what they want to see (unpaid editorial content found by the search engine), but also results that you want them to see (your paid listing).

It may seem unfair, but the same thing happens on the offline Yellow Pages. Just because an ad is prominent does not mean it is more germane to your interests, yet there it is larger than the others in the Yellow Pages, grabbing your attention. Some search engines clearly identify purchased placements as advertisements, while others blur the line between what is a purchased placement and unpurchased content. If you have ethical qualms about search engines that do not clearly label their paid placement, do not use them.

Weigh the Gain

But if you agree with the paid placement policy of a search engine or directory, you can boost the prominence of your Web site by paying what are fairly inexpensive fees to guarantee that your site shows up when particular words or phrases are searched.

You typically can purchase placement based on particular terms, like "shoes." Some search engines and directories allow you to bid against other advertisers for placement on the result pages. The higher your bid, the higher your placement. Others may charge flat fees.

This advertising model is in continual flux, seeking to find what works best for all parties concerned. A few years ago it was virtually unheard of for search engines to charge for placement. Nevertheless, for the low-cost online marketer this is a reasonable option to drive Web traffic to your site.

There's Always a Spoilsport

Search engines use various arcane formulas to determine which Web sites to rank above others when a search is conducted. The exact algorithms are generally kept secret and constantly revised to thwart those seeking to exploit the system. For example, the frequency of a word's occurrence on a Web page was once almost universally recognized by search engines as a significant high-ranking factor. The reasoning was that the more times "shoes" was mentioned in a Web page's content the more likely that the site was to actually have something to do with shoes.

But to exploit this, some Web sites flooded their pages with particular words, and made the words invisible to the naked eye by making them the same color as the page background. Such invisible words like "shoes" could be included hundreds of times on a Web page regardless of how pertinent the site's visible content actually was to the topic of "shoes." This dishonestly bumped that page ahead of other "shoes" Web sites that may have mentioned the word less frequently but in reality had more to do with the topic. Many search engine operators finally figured out what was going on and rewrote their formulas to punish rather than reward Web sites that had excessive occurrences of words and that used words of the same color as the page backgrounds.

The significance of this example is to point out that the rules for what rank a page highly on search engines are in constant flux. Your best bet is to follow the instructions given by each search engine, which typically are more general rather than specific, and to use search engine optimizing software that tweaks your Web pages to conform to the most current known rules.

> The rules for what rank a page highly on search engines are in constant flux.

Boost Your Ranking

Another option is trading hyperlinks with other Web sites. Think of it as a form of cashless advertising. In effect, you are bartering, trading a benefit that you can provide the other Web site (traffic that originates at your site) for a benefit that the other site can provide to you (traffic that originates on the other site).

These mutual links—you to them and them to you—not only boost your search engine ranking, but also result in increased traffic sent to your site from other sites when their visitors click through.

The downside is that whenever you request another site link to yours, you are normally expected to provide reciprocal links back. And every link on your Web site to another Web site is an exit door for your visitors to leave through. This two-edged sword makes it imperative that you weigh carefully which sites you link to. And whenever possible, when linking to other sites negotiate a reciprocal link back to yours.

Affiliate Programs

Affiliate sales programs allow Web sites to sell other companies' products. The seller gets a percentage of the sales price, and the merchants reap sales they normally would not. Consequently, affiliate programs can work for you in two ways—as an affiliate seller or as an original merchant.

Your Web site can bolster its appeal by adding affiliate sales simply by putting a link on your site that connects to the merchant's own Web site, where the sale actually takes place. One of the most popular affiliate programs is offered by Amazon.com, which makes it easy to include book-selling opportunities on your Web pages simply by providing links to the products that Amazon sells. Amazon provides you with all the HTML code, graphics, and even suggested text.

Sources for Affiliates

If you wish to include moneymaking affiliate links on your Web site, or if you want to become an affiliate provider yourself, here are three leaders in the industry to check out:

- be Free, which bills itself as the "ideal host for online marketing programs." *www.befree.com/index.htm*
- Commission Junction, which says it is "the largest pay-for-performance advertising network." *www.commissionjunction.com*
- LinkShare, which says it "pioneered online affiliate marketing, and today runs the largest pay-for-performance affiliate marketing network on the Internet." *www.linkshare.com*

Also check out Associate Programs at *www.associateprograms.com* for a vast directory of affiliate programs and helpful articles with advice in operating as an affiliate.

Easy to Maintain

After you include the hyperlinks and perhaps promotional text or a photo of the books or other products that you offer, affiliate sales require little or no time for you to maintain. All of the responsibility of order taking and fulfillment is handled by Amazon, which provides periodic reports to you on how many of your Web visitors clicked through and how many sales they accounted for, and then mails you periodic checks.

From a low-cost marketer's perspective, adding an affiliate "store," or more modestly just adding affiliate links on your Web site, gives the appearance of substance and variety. There also is a certain amount of reputation boosting to your image that can occur when associating your Web site with known and respected brand names. But even if your affiliate relationships do not earn you a lot of money (typically 5 percent to 15 percent per sale), they cost you nothing except some space on your Web pages and the time you invest in setting them up. And every dime they do earn is a dime you would not have earned without them.

The other way you can benefit from affiliate programs is to offer your products through them as a merchant. Instead of putting links to other companies' products on your site and earning a fraction of the sale price, others put links to your products on their Web sites and you can earn the lion's share of the sales price.

The beauty of this system is that other than the actual product fulfillment, much of online promotion and operation as an affiliate merchant can be handled by intermediaries such as LinkShare or Commission Junction that specialize in connecting affiliates and merchants. As a merchant, it is a means to add hundreds if not thousands of additional outlets for your products. If nothing else, your brand awareness can benefit greatly.

Advertorials

Just as offline, the online world sometimes blurs boundaries between editorial content and advertising. In the offline world these "articles" have come to be known as "advertorials." The principal difference is that most reputable offline publications will not publish an "advertorial" unless it labels it as such. By contrast, much of what passes for straight editorial content on the Internet is in fact thinly disguised advertising.

Advertise in E-zines

E-zines are the electronic news-letters delivered by e-mail to millions of subscribers. Many of them accept ads, generally for a lot less than ads on Web sites. The great benefit of e-zine advertising is that people have requested the e-zines be delivered to them, and e-zines concern very specific subjects in which recipients have already identified themselves as being interested. In other words, you have the potential to reach a self-described, narrow target market for a relatively low cost. Here are a couple of places to start when searching for appropriate e-zines in which to advertise: EzineAd-vertising.com at ✍ *www.ezine advertising.com* and Ezine-Ad. net at ✍ *www.ezinead.net.*

There is nothing wrong with advertising, of course. The problem comes from advertising that poses as something else. Similarly, there is nothing inherently wrong with "advertorials"—as long as they are properly identified as what they are, or what they are not, which would be unbiased editorial content.

There is no shortage of opportunity in the online world for enterprising entrepreneurs to have articles published that can reflect positively on your business, products, or services. And there are many content distribution services online starving for such articles and through which you can offer what you or your employees have written. Because the Internet is an information-driven medium with an insatiable appetite for content, there are plenty of e-zines, Web sites, and other online venues that will gobble up the chance to publish quality material if it cost them nothing.

However, it is incumbent upon you to properly identify your "advertorials" as distinct from your straight editorial content. Some online publishers have no qualms blurring the distinction. You should, for two reasons. The first reason ought to be enough. It is wrong to pass off a self-promotional advertorial as unbiased editorial copy. It is simply dishonest. The second reason is that in the long run it will hurt your reputation and damage your credibility once your target market realizes that what it has assumed to be impartial articles were actually advocacy pieces, or ads in editorial clothing.

Follow the guidelines established by most offline publishers and use advertorials, but label them as "advertorials."

Resources

Keeping Informed

Sound marketing decisions are based on sound information. Unfortunately, gathering and compiling information is a time-intensive, and therefore very expensive, proposition. The good news is that someone has already done much of the work for you. By plugging into the resources listed here, you can benefit from the hard (and costly) work of others at a relatively low cost to you, if not entirely free.

Situations differ among the following resources. Information from some of these is available to members only, but membership is generally not cost-prohibitive for most companies, even solo practitioners. Some of these resources charge a fee to the public, while others provide their data and assistance for free, and some offer a combination.

The one consistent fact is that information drives good decision-making, and these sources are each chock full of good information.

■ Association Web Sites and Industry Portals

American Marketing Association
✑ *www.marketingpower.com*
American Marketing Association
311 S. Wacker Drive
Suite #5800
Chicago, IL 60606
✆ (800) 262-1150

The Web site of the nation's largest marketing group provides "comprehensive and customizable" information for "all things marketing." The site not only provides valuable information on topics running the entire gamut of marketing (advertising, B2B marketing, consumer marketing, direct marketing, Internet marketing, marketing research, promotion, and public relations), but it also provides templates, tools, recommendations, and vast career-enhancing resources. If you have but one Web site to add to your browser's favorites, make it the AMA's home page.

Direct Marketing Association

✎ *www.the-dma.org*
1120 Avenue of the Americas
New York, NY 10036-6700
✆ (212) 768-7277; *fax* (212) 302-6714

The DMA is the oldest and largest trade association "for users and suppliers in the direct, database, and interactive marketing fields." Its Web site is full of helpful information such as news, white papers, and original research. One interesting and helpful low-cost option is the ability to call the DMA toll-free through your computer. The all-everything Web site for the direct marketing industry, the DMA is where to go for breaking news and updates on the state of direct response and information on the basics of direct marketing. Non-DMA members have access to the site's many features, but membership in the organization provides many additional benefits, including access to additional information contained in a 57,000-record database, case histories, white papers, research projects, subscriptions to organization publications, seminars and conferences, networking opportunities, legislative and regulatory advocacy, and discounts to DMA events.

Public Relations Society of America

✎ *www.prsa.org*
The Public Relations Society of America
33 Irving Place
New York, NY 10003-2376
✆ (212) 995-2230

The PRSA is a membership organization of public relations professionals serving about 20,000 members in 117 chapters representing business and industry, government, associations, hospitals, schools, and professional services. Its objective is to advance the standards of the public relations profession and to provide members with professional development through continuing education programs. The person in charge of your public relations should seriously consider membership, which is available on a sliding fee scale beginning as low as $115, based on experience.

■ How-to Web Sites

American Express Small Business Network
✎ *www.americanexpress.com/homepage/smallbusiness.shtml/*

This Web site provides ideas, information, and money-saving tips from American Express. It has practical advice in coordinating your business and marketing plans.

Entreworld
✎ *www.entreworld.org*
4801 Rockhill Road
Kansas City, MO 64110
✆ (816) 932-1000
✎ E-mail: *info@emkf.org*

The Kauffman Center for Entrepreneurial Leadership provides articles, tips, and more for starting and building a successful business. Its online resource for small businesses delivers quality and great quantities of useful information for entrepreneurs.

Service Corps of Retired Executives (SCORE)
✎ *www.score.org*
SCORE Association
409 3rd Street, SW
6th Floor
Washington, DC 20024
✆ (800) 634-0245

This agency of retired experts provides free online and in-person one-on-one business counseling at its numerous local chapters. Many chapters also offer low-cost classes in business marketing.

■ Databases

Information about people and companies is necessary to chart a marketing plan and to carry out tactics such as direct mail. These sources sell such data, although samples of free data are also available in differing quantities.

AccuData

 *www.accudata-america.com*

AccuData America

1625 Cape Coral Parkway

Cape Coral, FL 33904

✆ (800) 732-3440; ✆ (239) 540-5200

✐ E-mail: *info@accudata.com*

AccuData America is a national mailing and telemarketing list provider selling access to "every compiled list available in America." You can obtain data in the format you require in real-time on the Internet. AccuData also offers assistance helping you to achieve your marketing objectives. It serves mailing list resellers, high-volume list users, and first-time mailers alike.

infoUSA

✐ *http://list.infousa.com/*

infoUSA Inc.

5711 S. 86th Circle

P.O. Box 27347

Omaha, NE 68127-0347

✆ (402) 930-3500; *fax* (402) 331-0176

InfoUSA says it is the leading provider of "sales and marketing support for products for all types of businesses, from small Mom & Pop shops to large corporations." The company compiles databases of 14 million businesses and 300 million consumers, and provides products that include sales leads, mailing lists, diskettes, 3-by-5 sales leads cards, business directories, DVD products, and mapping products. The company also operates under trade names including Donnelley Marketing, American Business Information, Walter Karl, idEXEC, and infoCanada.

SRC LLC

✐ *www.extendthereach.com*

✐ *www.freedemographics.com*

SRC Headquarters

131 North Glassell Street, Suite 200

Orange, CA 92866

✆ (714) 516-2400; *fax* (714) 516-2410

This company and its Web sites provide free, unlimited access to U.S. Census Data and much more by offering summary, comparison, and ranking reports for all available geographic locations. FreeDemographics.com offers three distinct data sets for even greater depth and flexibility in analyzing your markets. The company also sells even more sophisticated products to enable you to make business and marketing decisions after analyzing demographic and market potentials.

■ Books and Magazines

AdAge.com

✐ *www.adage.com*

AdAge.com Office

711 Third Avenue

New York, NY 10017-4036

✆ (212) 210-0100

AdAge.com is the Web site of *Advertising Age*, the seventy-one-year-old advertising industry magazine. It offers industry news and provides such esoteric insights as charts that break down how many ad dollars are spent as percent of sales within industries, and such up-to-the-minute marketing news as "Felony Arrests as a Marketing Gimmick: a curious look at celebrity misbehavior and branding." If you do not subscribe to the print magazine, visit the Web site.

AdCritic.com

✑ *www.adcritic.com*
AdAge.com Office
711 Third Avenue
New York, NY 10017-4036
✆ (212) 210-0100

A sister site to AdAge.com, AdCritic.com promises subscribers previews of "the best commercials, the famous archive, news and views—plus a whole lot more!" AdCritic aims to be the best resource for people who love great commercials and want to see and learn about advertising spots that have the industry buzzing. AdCritic.com also offers exclusive breaking news, insight, and commentary.

DEMC's E-Magazine

✑ *www.demc.com*
DEMC
3000 Whitney Avenue, Suite #127
Hamden, CT 06518
✆ (203) 484-5183; *fax* (203) 484-5185
✑ E-mail: *mail@demc2.com*

It is easy to become overloaded with data and sources, but one Web resource that caters to the small office/home office professional for whom time is money is the DEMC E-Magazine, a free weekly e-zine that unlike many others is not merely a promotional vehicle for its publisher's Web site or affiliate programs. The Direct E-Mail Company (DEMC) specializes in publishing useful how-to information to empower small office/home office operators with marketing know-how on what makes e-mail marketing effective, such as how to build an in-house e-mail list, improve your e-mail communication, or gain an insider's view of producing better results from your auto-responder marketing.

Entrepreneur

✎ *www.entrepreneur.com*
Entrepreneur Media Inc.
2445 McCabe Way
Irvine, CA 92614
✆ (949) 261-2325

This magazine caters to entrepreneurs in search of practical information and real-life solutions to grow their companies. Concise, hands-on advice and expert columnists cover the latest developments in technology, money, management, and marketing. Other successful entrepreneurs' stories provide case histories, while the magazine also includes current entrepreneurial news and trends.

Markus Allen's Free Low-Cost Marketing Resource Center

✎ *www.markusallen.org*
MailShop USA
PO Box 1899
West Chester, PA 19380-0143
✆ (215) 893-1716; *fax* (215) 893-4884
✎ E-mail: *info@markusallen.org*

Visit this site to subscribe to Allen's free e-zine, the *$10,000 Marketing Tip of the Day*, which despite its hyperbolic title really is a veritable wealth of tips and insights ranging from Web site promotion, link exchanges, affiliate programs, general marketing, advertising and sales advice, as well as marketing research, media updates, strategies, and articles.

Doctor Ebiz

✑ www.doctorebiz.com
Dr. Ralph F. Wilson
Wilson Internet Services
P.O. Box 308
Rocklin, CA 95677-0308
✆ (916) 652-4659

Advice and tips for online marketing are featured in a free e-newsletter by Ralph F. Wilson, a.k.a. Doctor Ebiz. Wilson answers questions from small businesses and gives brief, no-nonsense answers that help people learn how to succeed in the online world, particularly in the realm of Internet marketing.

■ Trade Indexes

Dunn & Bradstreet Small Business Solutions

http://sbs.dnb.com
One Diamond Hill Road
Murray Hill, NJ 07974-1218
✆ (908) 665-5000; ✆ (908) 665-5803; ✆ (866) 472-7362 (member support)
✑ E-mail: *sbsSupport@dnb.com*

You can look up any U.S. company on the D&B Web site, plus a lot of other useful information, including surveys and answers to business questions. You also can automatically track your existing customers, suppliers, competition, and prospects.

DIALOG

✎ *http://library.dialog.com/bluesheets/html/blo.html*

The Dialogue Corporation

11000 Regency Parkway

Suite 10

Cary, NC 27511

☎ (800) 3-DIALOGUE (North America); ☎ (919) 462-8600

E-mail: *customer@dialog.com*

The Dialogue Corporation has more than 450 databases and millions of documents drawn from what is claimed to be "more sources than any other online service." The topics range from scientific and technical literature to full-text trade journals, newspapers, and newswires. There is information on patents issued worldwide, demographic data, and financial statistics.

The Encyclopedia of Associations

✎ *http://library.dialog.com/bluesheets/html/bl0114.html*

The Gale Group

Search Assistance & Content Support

362 Lakeside Drive

Foster City, CA 94404

☎ (650) 378-5053; ☎ (800) 877-4253; *fax* (650) 378-5442

The Gale Group publishes this comprehensive source of detailed information on more than 81,000 nonprofit membership organizations worldwide. It is an excellent starting place to find organizations in your industry or that represent your target market. It includes related publications such as National Organizations of the United States, covering more than 22,200 American associations of national scope; the International Organizations, covering 10,400 multinational, binational, and non-U.S. national associations; and regional, state, and local organizations of more than 48,000 associations with interstate, state, intrastate, city, or local scope or membership. The database provides contact information and descriptions of groups as esoteric as fan clubs and as mainstream as labor unions and trade associations.

Harris InfoSource
✐ *www.harrisinfo.com*
2057 East Aurora Road
Twinsburg, OH 44087-1999
✆ (800) 888-5900; *fax* (800) 643.5997

The profiles of 750,000 companies from manufacturing, technology, and service sectors are invaluable for business planning research, sales, marketing, and more. This business information can be used to acquire prospecting and marketplace data, which is a necessity for successful sales and marketing.

■ Chambers of Commerce

The chamber of commerce should be one of the fundamental networking and marketing tools at every small business operator's disposal.

U.S. Chamber of Commerce
✐ *www.uschamber.org*
1615 H Street, NW
Washington, DC 20062-2000
✆ (202) 659.6000
✐ E-mail: *custsvc@uschamber.com*

Through this online portal you can access vast business resources, find contact information on hundreds of local chambers of commerce throughout the nation, as well as keep abreast of business and government developments that affect your industry.

■ Government Agencies

FedStats
✍ *www.fedstats.gov*

This is a gateway to statistical data from more than 100 U.S. federal agencies. FedStats is a good place to begin your hunt for statistical information that you may need for market research or industry background. The Internet's links and searching capabilities enable you to track economic and population trends, health care costs, farm production, and other vital information. The site's main strength is that it enables users to access official statistics published by more than seventy federal agencies without knowing in advance which agency produces them.

Small Business Administration
✍ *www.sba.gov*
409 3rd Street, SW
Washington, DC 20416
☎ (800) 827-5722

Here is wonderful nuts-and-bolts help from the government (no kidding) on everything from starting a business to financing a business and, of course, resources and regulations that may affect how you can market your business. One of the SBA's invaluable resources is research statistics that can aid you in compiling market profiles, identifying market segments, and in gleaning the accumulated knowledge contained in an almost endless stream of SBA publications.

U.S. Census Bureau
✍ *www.census.gov*
U.S. Census Bureau
Washington, DC 20233 (mailing address)
✆ (301) 763-4636
✍ E-mail: *webmaster@census.gov*

The Census Bureau provides the familiar tables and maps of Census 2000 data for all geographies, down to the block level, summaries of the most requested data for states and counties, rankings and comparisons, population changes, comparisons with prior censuses, race and ethnic origin, and other topics.

■ Newspaper Databases

Gebbie Inc.
✍ *www.gebbieinc.com*
Gebbie Press
PO Box 1000
New Paltz, NY 12561
✆ (845) 255-7560; *fax* (845) 256-1239

Gebbie Inc. compiles a low-cost convenient and comprehensive media resource directory that includes not just print media, but also broadcast media. You can buy printed or digital directories that include contact information, including fax numbers and e-mail addresses, circulation figures, programming formats, and network affiliation information.

News Directory.com
✍ *www.ecola.com*
A publication of eLibrary, a service of Tucows Inc.

This online resource provides directories for newspapers, magazines, and television outlets worldwide. You can narrow your search by categories such as breaking news, business newspapers, college newspapers, and media industry associations, among others.

NewspaperLinks.com
✍ *www.newspaperlinks.com/home.cfm*
Newspaper Association of America
1921 Gallows Road, Suite 600
Vienna, VA 22182-3900
✆ (703) 902-1600; *fax* (703) 917-0636

NewspaperLinks.com is a comprehensive newspaper portal and a gateway to U.S. daily and weekly newspaper home pages and sections, Canadian and international daily newspapers, newspaper groups, associations, and other media organizations. There also are links to take you to college newspapers and newspaper archives. NewspaperLink.com is a service of the Newspaper Association of America, a nonprofit organization representing the newspaper industry and more than 2,000 U.S. and Canadian newspapers.

A Zippy Zip Code Locator

Here is an online short cut to reduce the time you spend hunting down zip codes: U.S. Postal Service Zip Code+4 Lookup ✍ *www.usps.com*.

➤ **Appendix 2**

Software

APPENDICES

■ APPENDIX 1 Resources ■ APPENDIX 2 **Software** ■ APPENDIX 3 The Twenty Best Low-Cost Marketing Tips

Stay Legal

The first thing to consider when shopping for software to outfit your office or your business is not to even consider using pirated or bootlegged software.

Beyond the threshold fact (which should be reason enough) that using unlicensed, illegally obtained software is theft, the penalties and fines for being caught with such illicit programs on your computers can cripple a small business. Another real life consequence of using illegal software is that you cannot register it, so you will not qualify for tech support (which can be invaluable) or for discounted upgrades (which keeps your capabilities current at minimal cost).

If all this is not enough to dissuade you and you still believe you can get away with bootlegged software on your company's machines, just remember that all it takes is one disgruntled employee—or former employee—to pick up the telephone and make an anonymous call for the hammer to fall. The civil penalties alone can be substantial.

Stay Standard

The next bias we will inflict upon you is to recommend buying and using whenever possible only software that is accepted as the standard in its niche. You may be able to shave a few dollars off in price by buying off-brands, and you may have an affinity for a different, less universal operating system, but in the long run using what most of the rest of the world uses will save you heaps of time, effort, and money. Nonstandard file formats, nonstandard procedures, and nonstandard questions when something goes wrong all kill productivity and eat up profits. Our bias, which has served well so far, is to use Windows-based software on computers running Windows operating systems, and to use only widely accepted software brands, preferably the leaders in their fields. To do otherwise is to risk being pennywise and pound foolish.

Now that we have all decided that honesty is the best policy and standards are the best choices, here are some recommendations, which do not in every case include the least expensive software, but do include what are likely to be good, long-term, low-cost options.

■ Planning Software

It is foolish to embark on your business and marketing journey without first plotting the course. Many entrepreneurs avoid creating a business plan and a marketing plan simply because the task seems too daunting, or they are eager to plunge right in.

Delay your plunge at least long enough to plan ahead. Two low-cost software packages can step you through the procedures painlessly, inexpensively, and relatively quickly.

Business Plan Software—Automate Your Business Plan

Out of Your Mind and Into the Marketplace
✍ *www.business-plan.com*

There are several good software packages on the market that can help you create a basic business plan. This one, Automate Your Business Plan, is used in every U.S. Small Business Administration information center from coast to coast and in Women's Business Development Centers. The companion book, *Anatomy of a Business Plan*, also is condensed into the SBA's Publication MP-32, *How to Write a Business Plan*. The book and software walk you through, in clear and easy-to-understand stages, the creation of basic elements to get your business off on the right foot. The cost is about $95 for both.

Marketing Plan Software—Marketing Plan Pro

Palo Alto Software Inc.
✍ *www.paloalto.com/ps/mp/*

There are fewer off-the-shelf software choices for creating a marketing plan, but this one is as good as it gets. It comes with more than thirty sample plans to quickly and easily create your marketing plan, aided by wizards that walk you through the entire process. It is suitable for product, service, or even nonprofit organizations. This software also is available for under $100.

While the template approach of these software packages is extremely helpful in getting started and even in crafting complete and comprehensive plans, one caveat should be raised: Do not rely exclusively on the fill-in-the-blank method. Do not be afraid to go outside the box and bring innovative solutions to bear on creating your business and marketing plans.

■ Graphic Design and Page Layout Software

There are two ways to go with these graphic-oriented software options: the high end, and not-so-high end. Unless your budget protests too loudly, it is probably worth the money to get the best software you can afford.

Graphic Design (Top of the Line)—PhotoShop

Adobe Inc.
www.adobe.com

This is not what most people would consider a low-cost option, and certainly PhotoShop, available for Windows and the Mac, is anything but a quick study. You will spend close to the list price of $609 at most places that sell PhotoShop, but just keep reminding yourself that every penny is an investment in the best and most widely accepted solution for your graphic design needs. The learning curve to completely master this powerful software extends well beyond the patience level of most novices. But if you stick to it, the capabilities are vast, and once you master its extensive power, you will be capable of overcoming just about any graphic challenge that your small business will face. However, for the software-phobic, a less intimidating option might be more appropriate.

Low-Cost Alternative—Paint Shop Pro

Jasc Software
✎ *www.jasc.com*

For those scared off by the steeper learning curve and stiffer price of PhotoShop, Paint Shop Pro offers a very low-cost alternative. You can do many of the same sophisticated things you can with PhotoShop, and unless you are a push-the-envelope creative type, you probably can do without what you will miss by settling on this low-end option. Edit photos, add special effects, create graphics, and do it all for a fraction of PhotoShop's price, usually in the $100 range. Paint Shop Pro is touted as the "easiest, most affordable way to achieve professional results," yet not a "slow, cookie-cutter" program that relies on templates. It is a realistic option.

Page Layout Standards—QuarkXpress and Adobe PageMaker

Quark Inc.
✎ *www.quark.com*
Adobe Inc.
✎ *www.adobe.com*

Do not let the list prices for these two packages scare you off. QuarkXpress and Adobe PageMaker at $899 and $499, respectively, are the de facto standards for document creation. Tinker-Toy alternatives will create more problems than they will solve for you, particularly if you need to take your creations to commercial service bureaus for film creation and to commercial printers for printing. These are not open-the-box-ready-to-use kinds of software, but if you spend a day with the manual and the tutorial you will be familiar enough with the basics to create brochures, advertisements, and just about any other hard marketing collateral necessary. Tech support is superb, should you need it.

The main benefits of using the industry standards are that despite steep learning curves, once you have mastered the programs you will not be satisfied with lesser software, and you will be compatible with virtually any commercial printer when you are ready to have your creations printed. This is one area in which it pays to pay a bit more upfront because the savings down the line will be recouped in time and quality.

Getting Online—Microsoft FrontPage

Microsoft
✎ *www.microsoft.com*

FrontPage has its critics, most of whom are far more skilled than you probably are when it comes to creating HTML code for the Internet. They will complain that FrontPage is a simplistic, menu-driven software that creates bloated code, not as elegantly or powerfully as higher-end software. But if you are creating your own Web site, FrontPage will serve you as well as any other off-the-shelf alternative, and is a much easier-to-learn (and less costly) option than the more sophisticated alternatives. Sure, there are more powerful options, but leave those to the professional Web makers. When you hire others to create your Web site, it is likely they will be using the higher-end software, the luxury cars of the fleet, so to speak. But if you are going to create your own Web site, you can get by nicely with this sedan version. There is no need for the luxury model.

■ Writing Software

Microsoft Word

You can look long and hard and find nothing better in a word processor than you will find with Microsoft Word. It has clearly established itself as the preeminent and universal standard in business and industry. Sharing Word files is as commonplace as sharing any kind of computer software file. The capabilities of Word are so vast as to be well beyond the needs of the vast majority of its users and at the same time as easy to use for the most rudimentary purposes as you will find. For compatibility and value for your dollar, you cannot do better. Word comes in the Microsoft Office Suite of business software, which in its smallest configuration also includes Excel for spreadsheet uses, Outlook for e-mail and scheduling, and PowerPoint for presentation graphics, all for about $239. License one office package for each employee and you are on your way to seamless communications within and outside your company, which is definitely the low-cost way to go.

Brainstorming Software—IdeaFisher Pro

IdeaFisher Systems Inc.
✑ *www.ideafisher.com/salemarch.htm*

This tool unleashes your creative juices with its patented word-linking database that leads you on a word association odyssey to realms you probably would never have imagined without it. It is a great tool for brainstorming ideas for advertising, marketing strategies, and strategic planning. Writers, scientists, marketers, and every kind of creative professional will find that IdeaFisher squeezes days of work into mere minutes. If you can click a mouse, you can use it.

Its ability to retrieve and cross-reference millions of words, phrases, and concepts has resulted in IdeaFisher being widely acknowledged as a leading creativity tool. It is available for about $208.

The Twenty Best Low-Cost Marketing Tips

Twenty Gems

Here they are. The twenty best low-cost marketing tips. Okay, that may be a tad hyperbolic, since marketing is such a subjective field. Instead, make it twenty *of the best* low-cost marketing tips. Either way, these twenty tips will serve you well, and nearly all of them are likely to fit in your marketing plan.

#1—Know Thy Target

The most cost-effective and lowest low-cost tactic, the absolutely indispensable marketing fact of life, is that you must know your buyers and your prospective buyers. If you do not, nothing else you will do will matter. Unless you know what it is that they want from you—the answer to the "What's in it for me?" question—you risk trying to sell steaks to vegetarians. Make all of your other marketing tactics more effective by knowing your target market as intimately as you can so that you can give them what they want.

#2—Keep Current

Never assume your market is the same today as it was yesterday. Working from an outdated customer profile can be as disastrous as working without any customer profile. Your market research must be an ongoing effort in order to keep your eye on your customers' behavior, because when they begin to change, you need to change with them.

#3—Be Consistent and Persistent

One of the fatal flaws of marketing is that when business is brisk, many marketers tend to slow down their efforts. Then when business slows down, these same marketers feel the urgency to redouble their efforts. This is a bit like applying the brakes as you climb a hill, then accelerating on the way back down.

The preferable—and ultimately low-cost—technique is to market consistently and persistently at an even keel. Be the tortoise, not the hare. The marketing seeds that you sow in the times of brisk business will come to flower when economic downturns tend to slow down business generally. And you will not waste marketing dollars in times of economic downturn by overmarketing at a time the return on those investments is much less. Spread it out evenly. Be consistent and persistent.

#4—Create a Web Site

Whether it is a comprehensive corporate presence with e-commerce capabilities, chat rooms, free downloads, and a companion e-zine or simply an online version of your brochure, a Web site is expected of any business these days. Create a Web site at least as a means of permitting your customer and prospects to find you online, and then to communicate with you. If you cannot justify all the bells and whistles, do not fret. You can always upgrade the site later.

#5—Develop an Opt-In E-mail List

Begin with the customers and prospects whose e-mail addresses you already possess. You probably already have accumulated dozens if not hundreds of e-mail addresses, but it is also likely that you did not get their permission to send them periodic electronic missives later on. Sure, they probably will not mind if you do. But make certain. Send them notifications that you would like to include them in your periodic e-mail updates, and ask them to formally opt in. Unless you hear back from them in the affirmative, do not add these to your marketing e-mail list.

From this point on, however, accumulate additional new e-mail addresses for your opt-in list only by requesting that people first confirm their desire to be added. This can be done by asking them to confirm their subscription by "replying" to your e-mail message, something they can do with one click in their own e-mail software. And of course, always give everyone on your opt-in list the opportunity to opt out at any time.

#6—Load Fast

The temptation is to load up your Web site with a lot of flashing, noisy, gimmicky graphics and multimedia. But too much of this stuff simply makes it difficult for Web visitors to get inside your online front door.

Make sure that every page—but especially the entry page—of your Web site loads quickly. That means keeping the graphics and gadgets to a minimum. One way to have the best of both worlds is to provide a hyperlink that says, "Skip introduction" or "Skip graphics." Check your Web logs if you do this. You probably will find that very few visitors prefer to sit through elaborate graphical presentations or time-consuming Java animations. And if that is the case, why would you want to pay to put that stuff on your Web site in the first place?

#7—Maximize Your Site for Search Engines

Now that you are online, you need to help Web surfers click a path to your door. You should already have your site's URL (Uniform Resource Locator) printed on all your offline marketing collateral, ads, products, etc. You also need to have your site submitted to the major search engines and directories so the vast majority of Web users who are not exposed to your offline marketing collateral have a chance of finding you.

For the best up-to-date advice on all of this, including how to maximize the effectiveness of your submissions in light of the ever-changing rules and regulations of these search engines and directories, check out Search Engine Watch at *www.searchenginewatch.com*, the Web's foremost authority on the subject.

#8—Press the Flesh

Offline you have opportunities to leverage your marketing in ways that are simply impossible to do on the World Wide Web. The most personal of these is face-to-face encounters. Armed with your thirty-second elevator speech and other tools of engagement, get out there and press the flesh.

People do business with people they know. And people are more likely to do more business with people they know and like. The best way to be known and liked is to be knowable and likable. Introduce yourself at every occasion. Wear a smile. Be sincere. Have your USP (unique selling proposition) committed to memory. Go to where your target market congregates and congregate with them.

No matter how glib or smooth-talking you become, face-to-face marketing works best when you are listening, not talking. Pay attention, be interested, and hear what they have to say, and you will find that they will tell you what they want, making it unbelievably easier to deliver it to them.

#9—Ask for Referrals, and Make Some Yourself

If you are doing your marketing right, and if you are running your business well, you ought to have a lot of satisfied customers. Every one of them is a potential sales rep for you. Take advantage of the good will that you have created. Ask them if they know of other potential customers. Ask them to refer you to other potential customers. Ask them if you can use them as references even if they do not make overt referrals.

A slight twist on this practice is to make referrals yourself. If you have customers or clients in need of something that you cannot provide, but you know of a quality provider, do not let the customers fall through the gap. Let your customers and clients know where they can get what they seek. By fulfilling the needs of your happy customers, you have provided a value-added benefit at no cost to you.

#10—Have Clear and Attainable Goals

Your marketing plan is supposed to be a road map to success. But if your goals are so vague that you cannot tell when you have reached them, there is no way to measure whether you have succeeded. When establishing the goals and objectives, make certain they can be measured. Determine what is a reasonable goal, then set up standards to measure it in order to know whether and when you have crossed the finish line. Build these into every marketing tool, technique, and campaign.

#11—Never Leave Home (or Anywhere Else) Without Them

Business cards are nearly as essential to marketing as products are to a business. As a newly gregarious marketer, you should be prepared to market in any venue. That includes standing in line at the grocery store, buying a ticket to a movie, or visiting your doctor for your annual physical. At the very least you should be able to leave behind your business card.

#12—Make Sure Your Mailings Get Opened

The first obstacle you must overcome when you mail to prospective customers or even existing customers is to get them to open your mail.

Odd-sized envelopes are one way. Interesting paper textures can even be provocative. Unusual colors work too. Here is a way to combine all three and create a mailer that is all but certain to be opened.

Mail your material in a brown paper bag. Make sure the bag's thickness is sufficient to withstand the rigors of the U.S. mail. Do not open the bag fully, but keep it flat and slide in your letter, flyer, brochure or other collateral. Use an address label to seal the bottom of the bag to the side so that it lays flat. Seal the open end with a sticker.

Of course the plain brown paper bag will work better—and make more sense—if you can tie in the bag theme to the theme of your mailer. But that is easy to do. If you are mailing coupons for shopping at your store, for example, simply print a sticker for the outside of the bag explaining, "Your coupons are in the bag!"

#13—Use Spel (uh, Spell) Check

How much does it cost you to look ignorant or amateurish? How much does it cost you to spell check your marketing collateral? Spell checkers are such an easy tool to learn how to use, even the most computer-phobic among us can master them in a few minutes.

However, do not relegate the final approval of a document to your computer-driven spell checker. Use human eyes and gray matter. Your spell checker will find "Come sea us" to be perfect because it has no way of telling that you meant to say, "Come see us."

#14—Follow the "One or Most" Rule

When you amble into a potential networking gathering, whether it is a chamber of commerce mixer or a grand opening for one of your clients' businesses, you have essentially two options: Try to make contact with everyone, or get to know one person very well. Anything in between is a compromise, and by definition falls short.

Vow to yourself that the next networking opportunity you face—and everyone after that—you will either make a genuine attempt to shake the hand of every person at the function (leaving behind your business card) or if that is unrealistic, buttonhole one very good prospect and get to know that person extremely well by the time you leave.

#15—Celebrate Groundhog Day—and Everything Else

Chances are your competitors who are a little aggressive when it comes to marketing probably already use all the major holidays as excuses to contact their customers.

Go them one better. Celebrate the oddball holidays that are certain to be recognized by virtually no one but yourself, and do it in such a way that you come to be associated with the event. Institute an annual celebration every Sept. 7 for the invention of television by commemorating the Philo Farnsworth Day, after the fellow who invented the tube. Or how about a "Hug an Australian Day?"

Once you have settled on a holiday to commemorate, get extra mileage out of it by counting down periodically during the year as a reminder and as another excuse to contact your customers, "Only 292 shopping days until . . ."

#16—Include E-mail Links Galore

Always have a hyperlink that Web visitors can click that automatically either creates an e-mail message in their e-mail program, or that links to another page in your site where they can fill out a form that is sent via e-mail to you. One click should be all that's required. You may wish to also code those hyperlinks so that you can tell which pages your visitors were looking at when they got the urge to contact you. In that way you can turn their questions into market research at virtually no extra cost.

#17—Fix Those Hyperlinks

The last thing a marketer wants is an aggravated customer or prospect. And on the World Wide Web there is nothing more aggravating than hyperlinks that lead to nowhere. Hyperlinks become broken for a variety of reasons, some of which are known only to Internet goblins, but also because the pages they link to have been moved, modified, or deleted. Periodically check out the links on your page to make sure they still function properly and send your visitors to where they expect to go. When you are checking out the reliability of your own links, it is a good time to check those reciprocal links, too, the ones that other Web sites have included on their pages to send people back to you.

Web surfers associate broken links with sloppiness and inattentiveness. Keep your links live and keep your visitors happy and your traffic flowing.

#18—Summarize Your Web Site in Your E-mail

Just as you include a standard signature line in all your outgoing e-mail, you should also create a current synopsis of your site that is routinely included but set off from the bulk of your message. For example, if your site has three segments called "On Sale," "Free Information," and "What's New?" include hyperlinks to each within the e-mail, set off with accents and with teaser headlines for each link. Like this:

> =*=*=*=*=*=*=*=*=*=*=*=*=*=*=*=
> On Sale—This month's specials
> ✍ *www.widgets.com/on.sale.htm*
> Free Information—Get our latest free widget white paper
> ✍ *www.widgets.com/free.info.htm*
> What's New?—See our new flexible multicolored widgets
> ✍ *www.widgets.com/whats.new.htm*
> =*=*=*=*=*=*=*=*=*=*=*=*=*=*=*=

#19—Make Winners by Bundling Losers

Most companies have something in their product line or service offering that just does not seem to capture the imagination of their target market. These are the dogs. Before you get rid of your old dogs, try a new trick. Bundle them with popular products or services and greatly discount their price. If your widgets sell like hotcakes, but your widget fasteners are dogs, offer them together for just a tad more than the price of the widgets themselves.

At the least you will recoup some of the investment you have in widget fasteners, and you just may succeed in introducing their benefit to buyers who had never tried the fasteners before but suddenly discover they are just great for fastening the widgets they love so much.

#20—Show Your Customers Appreciation, and Mean It

The fastest way to lose customers is to take them for granted. And worse yet, it is their perception that counts, not whether you really take them for granted or not.

Ultimately there is only one way you can control what they think of you and your competitors. That is to treat them better than your competitors do, and to continually remind them that the reason you treat them that way is because you appreciate their business so much.

Here are just a few of the little (and extremely low-cost) ways that you can say and demonstrate just how much you appreciate your customers:

- Tell them
- Always say "thank you"
- Tell them again
- Give them more than they expect
- Charge them less than they expect
- Offer them something they do not expect
- Tell them again
- Include handwritten thank-you notes in deliveries
- Ask them if you can help with _____ (fill in the blank)
- Tell them again

The low-cost marketer knows that what works costs less than what does not work. The low-cost marketer also knows that knowing customers and keeping them satisfied is the most efficient and therefore lowest low-cost marketing.

Index

STREETWISE® BOOKS

New for Fall 2003!

Low-Cost Marketing
$19.95 (CAN $31.95)
ISBN 1-58062-858-3

Business Valuation
$19.95 (CAN $31.95)
ISBN 1-58062-952-0

Also Available in the *Streetwise®* Series:

24 Hour MBA
$19.95 (CAN $29.95)
ISBN 1-58062-256-9

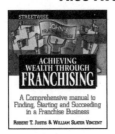

Achieving Wealth Through Franchising
$19.95 (CAN $29.95)
ISBN 1-58062-503-7

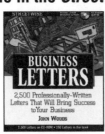

Business Letters with CD-ROM
$24.95 (CAN $37.95)
ISBN 1-58062-133-3

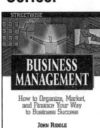

Business Management
$19.95 (CAN $29.95)
ISBN 1-58062-540-1

Complete Business Plan
$19.95 (CAN $29.95)
ISBN 1-55850-845-7

Complete Business Plan with Software
$29.95 (CAN $47.95)
ISBN 1-58062-798-6

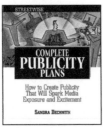

Complete Publicity Plans
$19.95 (CAN $29.95)
ISBN 1-58062-771-4

Customer-Focused Selling
$19.95 (CAN $29.95)
ISBN 1-55850-725-6

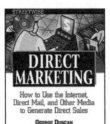

Direct Marketing
$19.95 (CAN $29.95)
ISBN 1-58062-439-1

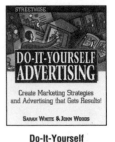

Do-It-Yourself Advertising
$19.95 (CAN $29.95)
ISBN 1-55850-727-2

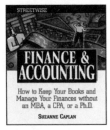

Finance & Accounting
$17.95 (CAN $27.95)
ISBN 1-58062-196-1

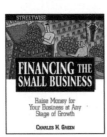

Financing the Small Business
$19.95 (CAN $29.95)
ISBN 1-58062-765-X

Get Your Business Online
$19.95 (CAN $28.95)
ISBN 1-58062-368-9

Hiring Top Performers
$17.95 (CAN $27.95)
ISBN 1-55850-684-5

Human Resources Management
$19.95 (CAN $29.95)
ISBN 1-58062-699-8

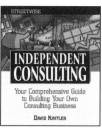

Independent Consulting
$19.95 (CAN $29.95)
ISBN 1-55850-728-0

Internet Business Plan
$19.95 (CAN $29.95)
ISBN 1-58062-502-9

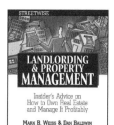

Landlording & Property Management
$19.95 (CAN $29.95)
ISBN 1-58062-766-8

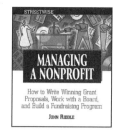

Low-Cost Web Site Promotion
$19.95 (CAN $29.95)
ISBN 1-58062-501-0

Managing a Nonprofit
$19.95 (CAN $29.95)
ISBN 1-58062-698-X

Managing People
$19.95 (CAN $29.95)
ISBN 1-55850-726-4

Marketing Plan
$19.95 (CAN $29.95)
ISBN 1-58062-268-2

Maximize Web Site Traffic
$19.95 (CAN $28.95)
ISBN 1-58062-369-7

Motivating & Rewarding Employees
$19.95 (CAN $29.95)
ISBN 1-58062-130-9

Project Management
$19.95 (CAN $29.95)
ISBN 1-58062-770-6

Relationship Marketing on the Internet
$17.95 (CAN $27.95)
ISBN 1-58062-255-0

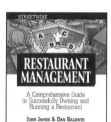

Restaurant Management
$19.95 (CAN $29.95)
ISBN 1-58062-781-1

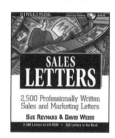

Retirement Planning
$19.95 (CAN $29.95)
ISBN 1-58062-772-2

Sales Letters with CD-ROM
$24.95 (CAN $37.95)
ISBN 1-58062-440-5

Selling Your Business
$19.95 (CAN $29.95)
ISBN 1-58062-602-5

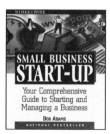

Small Business Start-Up
$17.95 (CAN $27.95)
ISBN 1-55850-581-4

Small Business Success Kit with CD-ROM
$24.95 (CAN $35.95)
ISBN 1-58062-367-0

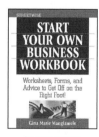

Time Management
$17.95 (CAN $27.95)
ISBN 1-58062-131-7

Start Your Own Business Workbook
$9.95 (CAN $15.95)
ISBN 1-58062-506-1

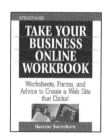

Take Your Business Online Workbook
$9.95 (CAN $15.95)
ISBN 1-58062-507-X

Available wherever books are sold.
For more information, or to order, call 800-872-5627 or visit www.*adamsmedia.com*
Adams Media, an F+W Publications Company, 57 Littlefield Street, Avon, MA 02322